Successful Writing for Qualitative Researchers

Second Edition

Peter Woods

Routledge
Taylor & Francis Group

LONDON AND NEW YORK

First published 1999
by RoutledgeFalmer

Second edition published 2006
by Routledge
2 Park Square, Milton Park, Abingdon Oxon OX14 4RN

Simultaneously published in the USA and Canada
by Routledge
270 Madison Ave, New York, NY 10016

Routledge is an imprint of the Taylor & Francis Group

© 1999, 2006 Peter Woods

Typeset in Bembo by Graphicraft Limited, Hong Kong
Printed and bound in Great Britain by TJ International, Padstow, Cornwall

British Library Cataloguing in Publication Data
A catalogue record for this book is available from the British Library

Library of Congress Cataloging in Publication Data
A catalog record for this book has been applied for.

ISBN 0-415-35538-9 (hbk)
ISBN 0-415-35539-7 (pbk)

For Kath

Contents

Acknowledgements

I would like to record my thanks to all those who have contributed to my own writing abilities, such as they are, over the years. My earliest recollection is of writing 'compositions' at junior school, which I much enjoyed. We were given subjects that inspired us to write, were encouraged to be creative, and to share our efforts with others. Through this freedom and regular opportunity to express thoughts and feelings on matters close to my concerns and interests, I discovered the excitement and joy of writing, and the gratification that comes from the positive response of others. At secondary school, I learnt more about the mechanics and techniques of writing; different forms, such as free-writing articles, more formal essays, literary criticism and journalistic pieces. I was introduced to great writers and to the world of books. I remember little of 'clause analysis' – which featured strongly in my experiences as a young teacher in the 1960s – but I have reason to be grateful for the prolonged and detailed attention given in English lessons to comprehension, paraphrasing, reported speech and summarising. I learnt much, too, from my study of French, and particularly Latin – a beautifully constructed language. My thanks to the teachers of my childhood and youth. I did not fully appreciate your contribution at the time, but I have grown to be more aware of it as time has passed.

Since those days, the main influences on my writing have been other authors, colleagues and editors. I like to think that the largest part of my writing is 'me', and that I have my own distinctive style – as I encourage in the book – but writing is an act of communication. It has to be understood by, and impact on, others. At the very least you need feedback from others on to what extent you are doing this. For the best results, you need advice and examples from other practitioners and experts in the field. I have been lucky in my contacts in these respects over the years, particularly at the Open University. As a distance teaching institution, the main medium for its products is the written text, and it dedicates major resources to producing work of the highest quality. The main ones are: the course team – all commenting on each other's work through a number of drafts; external assessors, checking for comparable standards with other universities; in-house editors, scrupulously studying every word and sentence; and proxy students who take part in the 'developmental testing' of draft material. At times, an author might feel quite beleaguered, but that is how it should be. As the product becomes worthier, the pressure eases, appreciation ensues, and you see the point of it all. My thanks to the Open University, and all who work there. It is no coincidence, perhaps, that everything I have had published to date has been written while I have been employed at this institution.

A number of colleagues have helped with this particular book. Among these, I am particularly grateful to Bob Jeffrey, Geoff Troman, Andrew Hannan, Pat Sikes, Denise Carlyle, Mari Boyle, Nick Hubbard, Barry Cocklin, Bruce Mason, Denis Hayes, Sue Waite, Peter J. Woods and Martyn Hammersley. My thanks to Martyn for providing the interview on which Example 4 in Chapter 3 is based. I have appreciated the expert secretarial assistance of Aileen Cousins and June Evison.

Chapter 2 is an updated version of Chapter 6, 'Writing Up', from *Inside Schools* (Woods 1986). Chapter 7 draws on two journal articles: Woods, P., Jeffrey, R., Troman, G., Boyle, M. and Cocklin, B. (1998) Team and technology in writing up research, *British Educational Research Journal*, 24(5): 573–92; and Woods, P. Jeffrey, R., Troman, G. and Boyle, M. (2000) A research team in ethnography, *International Journal of Qualitative Studies in Education*, 13(1): 85–98. I am grateful to my co-authors and to the publishers for permission to reuse some of this work here.

The following material has been reproduced with the kind permission of the publishers: Figure 3.1, An evaluation scheme for teachers, from Stubbs, M. and Delamont, S. (eds) (1976) *Explorations in Classroom Observation*. Reproduced by permission of David Fulton Publishers (www.fultonpublishers.co.uk). Example 2 in Chapter 5 from *Angela's Ashes* by Frank McCourt (1996). Reproduced by permission of HarperCollins Publishers Ltd. Figure 9.1, Advice to referees for *BERJ*, reproduced by permission of the editors of *The British Educational Research Journal* (*BERJ*), published by Carfax Publishing. Figure 9.2, The *JIME* open peer review lifecycle, reproduced by permission of the editors and publishers of the *Journal of Interactive Media in Education*. Figure 9.3, Guidelines to authors on submitting a proposal, reproduced by permission of Routledge. Figure 9.4, Guide to referees of a synopsis, reproduced by permission of Open University Press.

Note on second edition

This second edition includes a new chapter on writing implements (Chapter 8), co-authored with Andrew Hannan. Chapters 3–5 have been considerably revised; and the rest have been reviewed and updated.

1

Introduction

The only end of writing is to enable the readers better to enjoy life or better to endure it.

(Samuel Johnson 1757)

Good writing comes from complex sources: intense motivation and sensibility, passion and cultural curiosity, from energy and craft.

(Malcolm Bradbury 1998)

True ease in writing comes from art, not chance, As those move easiest who have learned to dance.

(Alexander Pope 1854)

The writing of this book was not at all straightforward, quite the opposite in fact, since chapters were written in reverse order, and I did get stuck on occasions. I wondered at times what authority I had to write a book on 'successful writing'. But then I persuaded myself that these were not uncommon experiences among writers. What mattered was not whether they suffered writer's block or tackled several chapters at once in reverse order, but whether and how they got going again, how they put the final product together, and whether they managed to finish it.

As well as 'getting it written', however, there is the question of quality. How can one write a successful book as well as succeed in writing it? This kind of success depends on one's aims. There are many forms of writing, and writers have a number of different purposes. I am mainly concerned in this book with academic writing such as appears in books, learned journals, theses and dissertations, conference papers, research reports, commissioned articles and the professional media. A successful product, therefore, involves work being judged of sufficient quality to be accepted for such things as publication – and receiving reasonable reviews from your peers, the award of a postgraduate degree, lodging in the British Library by a research agency, or a conference presentation.

There has been much lively debate about quality recently, with educational research under particular scrutiny. There are those who argue that much of it is 'second rate', or partisan and poorly executed and presented (e.g. Hargreaves 1996; Tooley 1998). Educational researchers have mounted a robust response (e.g. Gray *et al.* 1997). However, to a certain extent the contributors to this debate talk past each other, since what quality constitutes is determined, to some extent, by the particular epistemology you work within and the concomitant discourse of presentation that you adopt. Sparkes (1995: 185, quoted in Hodkinson 1998: 17), for example, argues:

> Given that different epistemological and ontological assumptions inform qualitative and post-positivistic (quantitative) inquiry, it makes little sense to impose the criteria used to pass judgement on one upon the other. Attempts to do so are at best, misguided and at worst arrogant and nonsensical, a form of intellectual imperialism that builds failure in from the start so that the legitimacy of other research forms is systematically denied.

I need to make clear, therefore, the approach taken in this book.

QUALITATIVE RESEARCH

A number of approaches come under the general heading of 'qualitative research'. These include case study, life history, biography, documentary analysis and community studies. They may be influenced by different disciplines (mainly sociology and anthropology) and by different theoretical approaches. Some might have an applied orientation, for example in the field of educational evaluation. The most prominent approach, and the one with the most general influence, is 'ethnography', and indeed this term is sometimes used interchangeably (and rather misleadingly) with 'qualitative research'. You can use qualitative methods (e.g. simply by using unstructured or semi-structured interviews) without doing an ethnography (which involves field research on a way of life).

My concern is qualitative research that derives particularly from symbolic interactionism in its application to education. This approach has had the most general influence in social scientific research in recent years among qualitative methods, and many of its principles and techniques are shared with other forms of qualitative work. In all of them, writing is particularly important, because their warrant rests on description, narrative, argument and persuasion, unlike quantitative research with its reliance on statistical and technical instruments.

Main features of qualitative research

Most forms of qualitative research have the following main features:

- a focus on natural settings
- an interest in meanings, perspectives and understandings
- an emphasis on process
- inductive analysis and grounded theory.

A focus on natural settings

Qualitative research is concerned with life as it is lived, things as they happen, situations as they are constructed in the day-to-day, moment-to-moment course of events. Qualitative researchers seek lived experiences in real situations. In general, they try not to disturb the scene and to be unobtrusive in their methods. This is in an attempt to ensure that data and analysis will closely reflect what is happening.

The researcher tries to make as few assumptions as possible in advance on what problems and issues will be found. It helps if the researcher 'makes the familiar strange', not taking things for granted, questioning the bases of action (Becker 1971); though, at other times, 'deep familiarity' with the scene and the people in it can aid insights (Goffman 1989; Strauss and Corbin 1990).

Qualitative researchers prefer fairly lengthy and deep involvement in the natural setting. Social life is complex in its range and variability. It also operates at different levels and has many layers of meaning (Berger 1966). A long stay is necessary to gain access to these.

There has been some dispute as to whether there are such 'real situations', let alone whether they can ever be represented in research accounts. However, few qualitative researchers these days would subscribe to the view that there is one objective reality that is totally knowable. More common is the modified view of 'critical', 'analytical' or 'subtle' realism (Hammersley 1992), or, as Snow and Morrill (1993: 10) put it, 'securing a close *approximation* of the empirical world'. This holds to the view of knowledge as a representation of reality, but one that can only ever be known partially, not totally. The more we refine our methods, the more rigorously we apply them, and the more skilled we become in the art of writing, the closer we approximate to that reality. But as knowledge is never total or certain, it can only be provisional, and subject to alteration or refinement by later research. There is no fixed, immutable truth in social science, no design (that we can know at any rate) by which things all fit together: 'The social world is an interpreted world . . . [analytic realism] is based on the value of trying to represent faithfully and accurately the social worlds or phenomena studied' (Altheide and Johnson 1994: 489).

An interest in meanings, perspectives and understandings

The qualitative researcher therefore seeks to discover the meanings that participants attach to their behaviour, how they interpret situations and what their perspectives are on particular issues. Just as situations can influence perspectives, so people can redefine and construct situations. Research methods have to be sensitive to the perspectives of all participants, and must sample across place and over time, as perspectives may vary accordingly. Researchers have to be close to groups, live with them, look out at the world through their eyes, empathise with them, appreciate the inconsistencies, ambiguities and contradictions in their behaviour, explore the nature of their interests and understand their relationships.

The researcher tries to appreciate the culture of these groups, to capture the meanings that permeate the culture as understood by the participants, to learn their particular use of language, and to understand their in-group behaviour. The association of these cultures with social structures might then be traced.

An emphasis on process

Qualitative researchers are interested in how understandings are formed, how meanings are negotiated, how roles are developed, how a curriculum works out, how a policy is formulated and implemented, how a pupil becomes deviant. These are processual matters, not products. Social life is ongoing, developing, fluctuating, becoming. It never arrives or ends. Some forms of behaviour may be fairly stable, others variable, others emergent. Some forms of interaction proceed in stages or phases. This again emphasises for the researcher the need for long and sustained immersion in the field in order to cover whole processes and produce 'thick description' (Geertz 1973) that will encompass this richness.

Inductive analysis and grounded theory

Qualitative researchers do not, on the whole, start with a theory which they aim to test and prove or disprove, though there is no reason why they should not do that if they wish. They mainly work the other way round, seeking to generate theory from data. The theory is then said to be grounded in the social activity it purports to explain (Glaser and Strauss 1967).

Validity

The validity of interactionist qualitative research commonly rests upon three main features:

- *Unobtrusive, sustained methods.* These are methods that leave the situation undisturbed as far as possible, hence the emphasis on long-term participant or non-participant observation, unstructured interviews or conversations, the use of key informants and the study of documents.
- *Respondent validation.* If our aim is to understand the meanings and perspectives of others, how else to test how faithfully we have represented them than with the people concerned themselves? This is not appropriate, however, in all situations, for example where the researcher unavoidably gets caught up in the internal politics of the institution under study, or in some instances where criticisms are being advanced.
- *Triangulation.* The use of different researchers or methods, at different moments of time, in different places, among different people and so on, strengthens the account. For example, information learned at interview is reinforced, and perhaps modified, by observation, and by study of documents – or by more interviews. Eisner (1991: 110) uses the term 'structural corroboration' – 'a means through which multiple types of data are related to each other to support or contradict the interpretation and evaluation of a state of affairs'.

There are a number of variations on these. Writing up within this framework, therefore, consists essentially of stating the results of the research and the evidence on which they are based, and demonstrating the adequacy of that evidence by the above criteria. This has been the standard model in qualitative research for many years.

THE POSTMODERNIST CHALLENGE

Some claim a 'crisis of representation' occurred during the 1970s and 1980s when 'postmodernists, poststructuralists, and feminists challenged us to contemplate how social science may be closer to literature than to physics' (Bochner and Ellis 1996: 18). Postmodernists argue that the traditional approach as outlined above sits within a realist frame wherein the researcher/author is paramount. The traditionalist author presents a kind of objective reality that they have perceived as some kind of omniscient onlooker. In the written account, it is the writer who is describing, analysing, interpreting, representing. Even where transcript is liberally used, selections are made and they are organised within the author's framework. With the 'literary' or 'postmodernist' turn (Tyler 1986) have come new forms of writing, more relativist than realist, that stem from the belief that the knowledge in the text is not independent of the author, and what we know can only be partial anyway. There is not one truth, not one single explanation of anything, but many overlapping truths operating at different levels and constantly subject to change. Richardson (2000: 934) consequently feels that 'crystallisation' is a more useful validating concept than triangulation. The latter assumes a fixed point, a single truth; it is too rigid and two-dimensional for the many-sided complexity of social life. The crystal, by contrast, 'combines symmetry and substance with an infinite variety of shapes, substances, transmutations, multidimensionalities, and angles of approach' (*ibid.*). Some find formal writing in consequence – the traditional kind for research texts – not only misplaced, but boring and outdated (Bolton 1994; Richardson 2000). They advocate experimenting with new modes that offer deeper understandings of the phenomena they describe.

Van Maanen (1988) has summarised the main genres that have emerged as:

1 '*Realist tales*' – the traditional approach with the emphasis on realism and objectivism, with the writer adopting a detached stance, and employing 'scientific' criteria to validate the research.
2 '*Confessional tales*', where writers actually see themselves as part of the research act and make 'confessions' about the problems and limitations of their research methods and their own actions as researchers. However, these tales largely remain within the paradigm of realist tales.
3 '*Impressionist (postmodernist) tales*', which are much more concerned about giving voice to others in the research, those who might be regarded as 'subjects' of the research in realist tales. Writers of impressionist tales use a range of literary devices to evoke situations and experiences, arouse feelings

as well as stimulate thought, and to celebrate differences, numerous and changing realities, incompleteness and partiality. Hitchcock and Hughes (1995: 338) conclude that, 'This results in a very different story, a very different way of reporting field research, but one which is striking, exciting, vibrant, richly descriptive and imaginative'.

Some argue that these different approaches are products of different epistemologies. They claim that there has been a paradigmatic shift, and that we have arrived at a new, clearly identifiable 'moment' in qualitative research (Denzin and Lincoln 2000). As seen in sharply delineated realist or relativist terms, there is clearly a huge difference. My own view is that these approaches are not mutually exclusive; that the new approaches extend the possibilities for ethnographic representation largely within the traditional frame; and that these are promoting exciting new developments rather than a 'crisis' in representation. I shall discuss this in more detail in Chapter 4.

There are different kinds and levels of social life with which the researcher deals. Some are more objective, such as items involving some kind of quantification or hard description; some are more subjective, like individuals' emotions, values, beliefs and opinions; and some are impressionistic, as in one's representation of the 'climate' of a situation, or of the 'mood' of a group of people. Certainly, some of these areas have not featured strongly in traditional qualitative research as yet, but there is no epistemological reason why they should not. Thus it is possible to tell an impressionistic tale within a realist context. It is in this respect that we need to seize the postmodernist moment to extend our research, and to develop and refine our methods.

At the same time, we have to recognise that experimentation is risky. It can yield high gains, but equally abysmal failures. For students, Hoadley-Maidment and Mercer (1996: 291) feel that 'the plain truth remains that academic success usually depends on following the conventions for academic English in the relevant field of study'. Weiner (1998: 21) concludes her review of academic journals by opining, 'In an era such as this – of "paradigm proliferation" – it would seem that articles which represent more traditional forms of research and discourse in the dominant paradigm are likely to remain predominant in academic journals'. One does get the feeling, however, that the scope for experimentation is gradually widening, and that we should go in search of those 'high gains'. Creativity should not be restricted to data collection and analysis, but applied also to modes of writing in the continuing quest to improve all aspects of research: 'If academic writing in general is not to become a sterile, formula-oriented activity, we have to encourage individual creativity in writing. It is the tension between received conventions and the innovative spirit of the individual that produces good writing in academic disciplines as well as in creative literature' (Kachru 1996: 311).

STRUCTURE OF THE BOOK

Many of the issues discussed in this book are common to most forms of writing. For example, as I discuss in Chapter 2, authors need to be in the right frame of mind for writing. In my early career, I tried sitting back and waiting for the muse to descend upon me, as I understood it did with famous poets and writers. This was not the best use of my time. I had to find other ways of cultivating mood, of pushing myself to get down to it and of keeping at it, especially when all seemed hopeless. This is more a matter of psychology than technique. I consider, therefore, the psychological disposition of the writer, and the pains and perils of writing. It helps to know that many writers in many different fields have wrestled with these problems.

Qualitative researchers traditionally do data collection, analysis and writing up simultaneously in a kind of spiralling process (see e.g. Lacey 1976), engaging in 'progressive focusing' as they go. These stages of research blend into each other so that it becomes impossible at times to see the join. Analysing an interview, for example, might yield a potential structure for writing up while simultaneously indicating where more data is needed. Analysis is the first major step in the work of writing, for it will provide us with our framework. After that the task is not so daunting, for we can tackle the account piece by piece in more manageable portions. In Chapter 3, therefore, I present the most common mode of organising accounts in qualitative research, that is by category and/or by theme, or concept, before considering the whole structure of a typical journal article.

This is a solid and secure approach. However, it is not suitable for all purposes. Indeed you can organise and write your account in any way that you like. The 'literary', 'performative' and 'hypermedia' 'turns' are opening up fascinating new opportunities here. I review some of these in Chapter 4. These styles appear to make a sharp contrast with that of the previous chapter. Whereas Chapter 3 might imply a one-method approach to organisation, and a standard academic discourse, Chapter 4 carries a message of any approach being suitable that serves the purposes of the writer and meets certain, more diverse, criteria of adequacy. I consider some alternative forms of writing, most of which, in my opinion, can be accommodated within the methodological framework of this book. I then go on in Chapter 5 to look at expressive modes of writing, which can characterise modernist and postmodernist frames alike. In both, authors are concerned at times to evoke atmospheres and moods, represent feelings, paint word pictures and establish empathetic communication with the reader.

However you proceed, the work is going to require firm editing. Indeed some writers, myself included, spend far more time editing than creating text from scratch. Jean Hegland (in Moggach 1998) says that 99 per cent of her writing is rewriting. I find that PhD students might take six months to a year applying the finishing touches to their final draft, reordering, rephrasing, rewriting, correcting, deleting, adding, modifying, and so on. Much of this is a matter of mastering the basic rules of English. Editing, however, can itself be a creative process. It is not simply a technical exercise of correcting grammar, punctuation and spelling, though that is involved. I rehearse some of the considerations in Chapter 6.

The ethnographic brand of qualitative research has been typically a lone pursuit. But qualitative and ethnographic teamwork is becoming more common. In Chapter 7 I illustrate how electronic mail (email) aided the collaborative work between members of a research team who were composing a multi-authored document. We felt that team and technology were a potent force here in getting the job done speedily and to a standard above that any of the individual members could have reached in the time available. The team opened up new research horizons, facilitated the 'muddling-through' process typical of qualitative research, provided extended bases of comparison, helped in the refinement of arguments, enhanced validity, enriched the text, provided a support base for members and helped to sustain impetus. The conjunction of team and technology is not a recipe for all occasions and can have its dangers, but we found it helpful in tackling some of the problems raised in earlier chapters here.

With what do we write? There are technical considerations here, but also psychological ones. The link between choice of writing implements and the researcher's self and identity has been little explored, yet it is crucial to this most difficult stage of the research process. In Chapter 8, Andrew Hannan and I examine the links between writing tools and writer self, and the respective benefits of computers, pens and other instruments. It is not a question of one device being better than another; but rather of writers finding the mix that best matches their personal self and writing style, and methods of working.

The final mark of success for many is whether their work gets published. Chapter 9 looks at some of the issues involved here. This is not just a matter of quality of product, though that obviously is important. It also involves adopting the right strategies, of directing your writing toward the right audience and the right publishing outlet, of approaching and negotiating with the latter in appropriate ways. Again, also, there is the question of psychology, of having the right kind of mental set; not, for example, becoming too easily dispirited. Indeed, one should not be writing at all if that is a tendency!

This book combines consideration of techniques of writing within an educational and social scientific framework, with some attention to aspects of the personal struggles involved. Books on qualitative research writing have something in common, but they are also different because they derive from their authors' unique experiences. They are products of the reflexivity that is an essential part of the ethnographic process. This reflexivity continues with the readers, for they will be making their own constructions based on their own particular stock of resources – books they have read, experiences they have had, studies they have made, personal predispositions. These will feed into their own unique styles of writing.

2

Getting started and keeping going

I think all writers of prose live in a state of induced insanity.
(J.G. Ballard, in Moggach 1998)

I think I'm either frighteningly sane or incorrigibly mad.
(Iain Banks, *ibid.*)

I can't think of any great writers who are sane.
(Phyllis Nagy, *ibid.*)

If we are to be successful writers, it seems we must be prepared to become a little insane. We must be somewhat mad to take on the activity in the first place, but we also have to destabilise our minds in order to shake up the commonplace, play with ideas, look for new insights. It is easy to see how this can become a way of life for professional writers. What we researchers might aim for, I would suggest, is a kind of controlled madness. In this way, we might gain the benefits without suffering the consequences. So what is involved? And how can we become mad without becoming certifiable?

THE 'PAIN' THRESHOLD

Ideas can be fleeting, hazy, ill-formed, fanciful, irrelevant, inconsequential. Often, it is only when we apply the iron discipline of writing to them that we come to realise this. Sometimes, writing can pin them down. Bolton (1994: 63) finds writing 'a way of grasping experiences that are otherwise lost in the depths of the mind. Things that are almost impossible to say can often be expressed in writing'. Sometimes it is a task approached with some trepidation, as with the budding author in Piers Paul Read's *Polonaise* (1977: 131): 'The difficulty he faced with the white sheet of paper was not that he had no ideas, but that he no longer trusted his ideas to keep their shape as he gave them expression'.

Thus we might find what we thought a particularly useful concept rather difficult to grasp; or a seemingly beautiful, but light and airy idea only wafted further away as we try to seize it; or an apparently imposing edifice, encapsulating our research and all others in a totally original way, knocked over, like a castle of matchsticks, by a touch of the keyboard or stroke of the pen. As the parody of the poet's lines has it:

> Pope springs eternal in the human breast
> What oft was thought, but ne'er so well expressed.

With other ideas we find, as we put on them the best constructions we can, a certain emptiness, banality, impossibility, inappropriateness, unoriginality. We may be forced back to a reconsideration of our data, perhaps to more data collection and re-categorising, certainly to re-conceptualising.

Failure at this point of data analysis can be a disheartening experience. Perhaps this is why so many promising PhD studies founder, why some research studies never get reported, and why some spend so long in data collection. It is not, however, an insurmountable problem, and the potential gains are considerable. Charles Morgan has said of the artist 'no one can be effectively an artist without taking pains . . . This technical part of an artist's life may be learned, and the learning may be carried so far that it ceases to be narrowly technical and becomes a study of the grand strategy of artistic practice' (1960: 119). Thus there is a certain amount of craftwork in the creative enterprise. Additionally, it may be helpful to conceive of the problem not so much in terms of what you do to the data, but what you do to yourself.

Pain is an indispensable accompaniment of the process. How often do we hear somebody admitting they 'sweated blood' in writing a certain piece; or that 'getting the words out is like pulling teeth' (Andrew Miller, in Moggach 1998); or stating that they know a certain stage in the research is near, and must be faced, but that they are 'dreading' and 'hating it'? Moreover it does not get any easier. For Barry Hines (*ibid.*), for example, though his 'prose is very simple' and must seem 'easy to write', 'writing is actually getting harder the older I get'. Bernice Rubens also thinks that writers do not improve with age (*ibid.*). This aspect of the research is best conceived as a rite of passage, a ritual that is as much a test of self as anything else, that has to be gone through if the research project is to reach full maturity. If we do not feel pain at this point, there is almost certainly something wrong. Perhaps we are not progressing and simply marking time, being satisfied with analysis at an elementary level that plays safe and avoids the risk of burning in the ring of fire, as well as the burden of hard work. While such reports may not be entirely without value, they may not be making the best use of their material. Researchers must be masochists. We must confront the pain barrier till it hurts. Dea Birkett likens writing to sex – 'agony, agony, agony and then release as the words finally come' (in Moggach 1998). Judy Blume finds writing 'hard. The first draft of a book is terrible. With my last, it took me a few years just to find the right tone' (*ibid.*). Jennifer Nias (1991: 160) writes:

Producing a manuscript which I feel is fit for publication is hard and tiresome work, inducing broken nights, bad temper and the kind of pre-occupation which is often difficult to distinguish from utter egocentricity. I can truthfully say that whereas data collection is generally enjoyable and analysis is intellectually rewarding, writing is painful drudgery.

We share this experience with all kinds of creative people. I recall hearing Philip Gardiner (a Norfolk artist) describing his experience of painting as 'tense and draining – but it has to be, I wouldn't have it any other way. It's very precarious, but it adds a certain lustre to life'. The biographical annals of composers, writers, poets and artists are strewn with similar accounts of self-imposed suffering.

MORAL IMPERATIVES AND MENTAL CONDITIONERS

How then might we break out of this psychological state and render our chief research instrument – ourselves – more effective at this critical juncture? There is, first, a baseline of physical, mental and situational fitness without which it would be difficult to do this sort of work. I cannot write if I am tired, worried or ill, or if I am distracted. Nor does the creative urge in research and art necessarily go well with teaching. Research may benefit teaching, but the converse does not apply. As Hugh MacDiarmid has noted of art (in the general sense, and in the same sense that Nisbet 1962 saw it as applying to sociology):

> To halt or turn back in order to try to help others is to abandon artistic progress, and exchange education for art. There is no altruism in art. It is every man for himself. In so far as he advances, the progress of others may be facilitated, but in so far as he is conscious of according any such facilitation, his concentration on purely artistic objectives is diminished.
>
> (MacDiarmid 1969: 45)

If peace is essential, so too is pressure. I have heard some writers (novelists) say that their best work is done in situations where time hangs heavy on their hands, but for myself I have not found that always so. Perhaps their pressure derives from a self-generating muse, whereas I am very much a product of the Protestant Ethic. I need external motivators. In fact the danger is that, given time, I sink into even greater torpor. Certainly you must have time for analysis and writing, and research sponsors rightly stress the need to make due allowance for it. But nothing concentrates the mind more wonderfully than schedules. We might bemoan them, but where a research report is due, a publisher's deadline to be met or a paper to be prepared for a certain seminar or conference date, then there is necessity whipping the flaccid mind into activity. For this reason it pays to contrive to have inserted in the research programme at strategic points dates for the production of papers on some aspect of the research.

They must of course involve some investment of status, and this might mean addressing a public. Thus status will be lost if the schedule is not met. At the same time, it needs to be recognised that there is a fine dividing line between a nicely crowded agenda and overwork, the latter possibly having grave consequences for the quality of product and personal well-being.

Schedules can be awesome and counter-productive if they ask for too much in too short a time. The most serviceable, possibly, are those that are staggered, that do not require a finished article at a stroke, but permit degrees of sophistication. The leap from data to presentation then need not seem too vast, and the perfectionist instincts that many researchers have can be requited and exploited in a legitimate way instead of adding to the difficulties of the task. For there is a need to take risks in the early stages of analysis, to 'play' with the data, to 'try out' certain configurations and explanations. It helps to bounce these ideas off other people. Not only might colleagues provide some useful input, but the mere fact of having to articulate your ideas might bring you to see them in a new way.

Having internalised the moral imperative to write, I feel the need for some mental stimulants and conditioners. These are of two kinds, techniques and aspirations. Techniques are to do with the mechanics of communication. Here I might recall certain aspects of my training: 'Where to begin, how to end, how to orchestrate, how to be simple and direct . . . these things are the armoury of writers' (Morgan 1960: 132). And Morgan recalls his indebtedness to his own former studies, for example Greek and Latin: 'For case, mood, tense, voice and a thousand refinements different from his own . . . and while he fights his own battle for an elusive meaning, he may be fortified against the accursed blight of "It couldn't matter less" by the sound and memory of battles long ago' (*ibid.*).

The stimulation of mental agility no doubt varies greatly from person to person. Quite a bit of help comes from reading what other people have written. David Lodge (1996: 172), for example, learnt:

> From [Graham] Greene, how to use a few selected details, heightened by metaphor and simile, to evoke character or the sense of place; from [Evelyn] Waugh, how to generate comedy by a combination of logic and surprise, of the familiar and the incongruous; from [James] Joyce, how to make a modern story re-enact, echo or parody a mythical or literary precursor-narrative. I learned many other things from these writers as well – above all, I would like to think, a craftsmanlike approach to the business of writing, a willingness to take pains, a commitment to making the work as good as you can possibly make it.

I prefer at these times to read material other than sociology or education. To be sure, you cannot research in a vacuum, and a thorough knowledge of the relevant literature is essential. However, academic research has a curious tendency to be all-consuming. There is so much of relevance to read that we feel we should know about. Thus if there is any time at all to spare we probably invest it in that further academic article or book that sits on the top of the large pile in our reading in-tray. But while a certain amount of such reading is essential for research context, it may not serve us very well for models of presentation. For some, of course, it might inspire. Others might find forcing themselves to embrace a wider field of literature and art product-ive in terms of mental stimulation and models for writing.

For power and economy of words, for mental leaps, comparisons and metaphors, I would recommend poetry. Whereas for strength of description, powers of observation, and the ability to bring off a point, give shape to an episode and form to a story; for sustained development and integration, for social commentary, human insight and sheer inventiveness, I would go to a novel or to drama.

A critic made this comment about Virginia Woolf's *To the Lighthouse*:

> It is a book that has deeply influenced me. I might be walking down the street involved in a series of thoughts which probably don't seem to have any connection – the brilliance of Virginia Woolf is that she dis-covered there were connections and, more important, she could make sense of them and write them down.

This is essentially the same kind of creativity involved in research.

Music and art are also helpful in this respect: they can calm the frenzied mind and reduce pain. Edward Blishen played a recording of Schubert's octet obsessively whilst engaged in his *Adaptations*. Schubert 'can't have imagined that, 130 years after it was written, this enchanting music for the chamber would be used as a lenitive by a literary oddjobman' (1980: 38).

What all these forms of art have in common is:

- in their timeless, eternal beauty, a kind of absolute validity
- a perfection of form – their various parts all hang together and follow one another almost inevitably
- a sense of growth – as point follows point, it is not simply a matter of addition, but greater depth to the message
- human creativity – they are among humankind's highest achievements.

All this is neatly illustrated in the play *Amadeus* by Peter Shaffer. Salieri, in wonderment at some new Mozart compositions, exclaims, 'Displace one note, and there will be diminishment; displace one phrase, and the structure will fall'. As he looked at the manuscripts he realised that he 'was staring through those ink-notes at an absolute beauty'. Mozart himself realised his worth. 'Too many notes!' complained the emperor. Replied the composer, with absolute certainty: 'There are just as many notes, your majesty, no more, nor less than are required'. In all these respects, works of art serve as worthy models, in their mental processes, for our qualitative work. All forms of art have the same properties. William Trevor, for example, himself a former sculptor, likens his storytelling to moulding and chipping away at a sculpture. It is what the writer David Lodge is alluding to when he says, 'Every word must make an identifiable contribution to the whole'. Structuralists argue that there are basic common properties to these different artistic areas. Though 'transfer of training' theory was not popular some years ago in the debate over the usefulness of Latin as a school subject, Levi-Strauss, for example, believes that the receipt by the brain of musical messages can serve as a model for the receipt of all other kinds of cultural message. For example, he argues that melody and harmony illustrate the structural linguist's distinction between sequence and content. Interestingly, Levi-Strauss himself is often described as an artist as well as a scholar, and 'his style remains a baroque combination of order and fantasy' (Sperber 1979: 24).

There is a further point – that whatever we select to consider in the area of art will reflect our own personal concerns and makeup, and encourage reflexivity. Thus it not only helps put our research on a broader plane of people's affairs, but also to give it depth. Qualitative work can be extremely personal. To a greater extent than other forms of research, it allows a working out of one's own destiny within the context of 'public issues'. In other words, it offers insight into problems and anomalies you might have experienced in the past in a structured way aligned to general human experience, and thus avoids the excesses of self-indulgence.

CRANKING UP

And so, from hour to hour, we ripe and ripe,
And then, from hour to hour, we rot and rot,
And thereby hangs a tale.

(William Shakespeare, *As You Like It*)

The models cited above are the Rolls-Royces of the artistic world. When I address myself to writing up research, I am reminded of my first car, an ancient Morris 1000, which had to be cranked up before it would start. It was rather erratic in its running; its tappets had a tendency to seize up and it occasionally boiled over, but it usually got there in the end, though not very quickly.

The 'cranking up' is a necessary preliminary. Analysis is multi-layered – it does not all take place on the same mental plane. Writing is such a different activity from other responsibilities of teaching and academic life that we are not usually in the right frame of mind. Nor do we fall into it naturally; it has to be artificially induced. We might regard it as another one of those 'challenges' and as potentially very rewarding intellectually. We might persuade ourselves that we actually enjoy writing, though any intellectual reward or enjoyment usually comes long afterwards, certainly not at the beginning. 'Writing up' research is nothing like the delightful essays we used to do at junior school, or the cathartic bits of biography, diary or magazine articles we may compose from time to time, which have a stronger measure of journalese about them. Academic writing is a strongly disciplined activity, and we have to gear ourselves up for it.

I might have to set aside anything from a day to a week for 'cranking up'. I might find that I have two or three clear days that I can give over to making a start on writing, to generate a bit of impetus that may then be carried on over the next two to three weeks. This is an average time for getting to grips with a writing project, and in general I find I have to devote all my attention to it during that period if I am to master it. I am very unsociable and rather ill-tempered during this time. Some of us may actually have to appear to undergo profound personality changes in order to do the work. Unlike Dr Jekyll, however, we have no magic potion.

I find it is done almost by default. That is, I always delude myself into thinking that I am actually going to commence writing on those first days. I rarely do, for what happens is confrontation and engagement with the pain barrier. Part of this is to do with forcing yourself into psychological over-drive. What these initial two to three days consist of, then, might be a reconsideration of all the research material, a continuous sifting and re-sifting, clearing out the debris and identifying the strengths, aligning the material towards them, checking on key associated work, reclassifying, having one or two attempts at an introduction, and, if that fails, putting together one of the more complete, coherent and interesting sections. If the latter works, it can snowball and provide a comparatively easy passage. More typically, it is only the beginning of the struggle.

What you are doing, then, in these early stages is, first, undergoing a process of 'psyching up' to writing pitch (a process attended by some disorder and discomfort) and second, going through the initial stages of preparing your material for presentation. The cranking-up process is partly systematic and consolidating, partly disorderly and adventurous, as you search for new configurations. This latter indicates a third activity therefore, one of trying to develop new insights. It comes from reading and rereading field notes, transcripts, summaries, categories; examining comments made along the way, perhaps in a research diary made at the time 'for future reference'. You test out a few more ideas, seeing what they look like on paper. Diagrams are useful in trying to show interrelationships. The wastepaper basket fills up rapidly. Robert Graves was told by an early mentor that his 'best friend was the wastepaper basket', and this, he later discovered, was 'good advice'.

At the end of the first day, therefore, all that may have been produced is a side of A4, which will probably be at once discarded the following day, but a great deal of mental preparation and ground clearing of data will have been done. I have a standard 'production rate' of five written pages, or a thousand words, a day. This seems to be about right for me when I am working properly. But writers vary considerably. Joseph Connolly used to write 5000 words a day, now 'half that' (Moggach 1998). Penny Vincenzi writes '4000 words on a good day, 1500–2000 on a bad one' (*ibid.*). R.M. Eversz writes 'a great deal each day because I often disregard everything I've written' (*ibid.*). Charles Frazier is happy with 'a page a day' (*ibid.*). Flaubert is reported to have said, 'A good sentence can be a good day's work'. The quality of my first efforts may be variable, but I do not worry about that at this stage, as long as the brain is being oiled into gear and some ideas are beginning to come. The 'quota' stands as some tangible and identifiable product of the work of the day. While this is a stage for throwing ideas around in the mind and testing out alternative constructions, the acid test for them is whether they retain their potential value in communication. The quota is a reasonable amount to provide for such a test – long enough to require sustained and coherent thought and to reflect fairly large-scale organisation, and short enough to tackle in a day without exhausting front-line concentration.

A Protestant Ethic (PE) person also internalises time regulation. The ritual of sitting down to work at 9 a.m. and working through to 12 or 12.30 p.m., and then a further two hours in the afternoon, is a good mental discipline. Without this moral impulsion behind the ritual I doubt whether I would ever get round to writing at all. However, it is a curious thing that, while I keep to the ritual, 'off duty' hours can be vastly more productive. Thus winter evenings, weekends, late at night and occasionally early in the morning are all comparatively high productivity times. PE standards dictate that these are 'free times', and the psychology of it is that I cannot make a mess of them, or it does not matter if I do. I am consequently more relaxed, and often more productive. There is a feeling that this is all surplus and that you are 'getting ahead'. Periods before holidays are also useful. Holidays must be earned and, if a project is unfinished, will not be enjoyed. There is, too, a strong practical impulsion, for a partially finished project means that 'cranking up' has to commence again on the same piece, after the 'limbering down' of the holiday – hardly the best use of scarce resources.

Having got cranked up, successfully engaged a gear and begun moving, I will at various points meet a roadblock. I take comfort, however, from the fact that this happens to the best of authors. In one of his novels, Tchekhov agonised for days over how he was going to get one of his heroines across the threshold of a house. Hemingway rewrote the ending of *A Farewell to Arms* 39 times before he was satisfied. Conrad had terrible torments. He sometimes wished to be a stone breaker, because, 'There's no doubt about breaking a stone. But there's doubt, fear – a black horror, in every page one writes' (Karl and Davies 1983). Edward Blishen speaks of a highly capable novelist of his acquaintance who, after writing 'a hundred splendid pages would be overtaken by literary dread at its worst' – fear of reviewers, and fear that 'the narrative had come to a halt' (1980: 118–19). He would beg Blishen to tell him frankly 'if I thought his skills were in decline . . . And at the end, always, as I made the noises necessary to keep him writing, he'd ask, "Does it move? It does move, doesn't it?"'. The moral here is that we need friends, mentors, trusted colleagues whom we can rely on for good advice and support. This kind of therapy does not rule out the equally valuable constructive criticism you look for from colleagues, which at times might be quite trenchant – though that is addressed to a different problem.

Writers develop their own psychological boosters. John Mortimer (1983: 9) has his study plastered with his own playbills: 'I've never been strong on confidence. When the page is blank and you fear, as I regularly do, that it may never be filled again it does help to look up and think at least I wrote *that!*'. Bernice Rubens has 'a row of my books opposite the desk and I look at them and think that even if I can't write, I can still publish' (Moggach 1998). For those of us who have not got that far, we must have recourse to basic elements of character – confidence in your ability to pass the threshold; patience, in not expecting too rapid a return and in tolerating difficulties and hold-ups; stamina and determination to keep at the task, exploring all avenues and employing all your resources in countless configurations to find a way ahead.

There are strategies you can bring to bear on blockages. The first one perhaps is not to recognise blockages. Samuel Johnson observed, 'A man may write at any time, if he will set himself doggedly to it'. Bernice Rubens finds that 'the only thing that shakes up my head is to sit down and stay sitting – that's the important thing. I don't believe in writer's block – it's just a convenient phrase' (*ibid.*). Philip Larkin, similarly, rejected the notion of 'writer's block'. If he only produced four poems in a year, 'that's all there is' (Motion 1993). However, call it what you like, most of us do get stuck from time to time. We need to analyse the problem. Is it because of tiredness (even though perhaps you have not reached your quota)? The answer, clearly, is rest, or a change of activity. Do you have the right materials? Muriel Spark will only use Edinburgh's finest lined exercise books sent out to her in Italy by James Thin of Chambers Street, and pencils she will not use if someone else happens to touch them (*The Times*, 13 June 1998: 22; see also Chapter 8). Is it the situation you are in? Ronan Bennett (in Moggach 1998) needs 'total silence' while he is working. R.M. Eversz is also very anti-social when writing: 'My fiction is like a giant bubble I'm blowing, and I'm inside it and I want to stay in the little world I've created' (*ibid.*). Dea Birkett (*ibid.*) needs solitude, and writes in a caravan in a field in Kent. Charles Frazier retires to a 'cabin in the mountains' (*ibid.*). Have you allowed enough time? Nias (1991: 162) argues the need for time to think, and for taking time out for other things, since 'not all cerebral activity takes place at a conscious level and ideas can form while left to "compost" slowly'. Is it because of a lack of preparation or inadequate groundwork, so that you really do not know what you want to say? This would require a reconsideration of data, more reading perhaps, and certainly more preliminary thought. Or perhaps you have an uneasy feeling that the account is going up a blind alley, or that what seemed like the right direction in planning now in writing turns out to be a mirage. There is no alternative but to return to the beginning of the faulty line. The important thing is not to get consumed by the blockage, but to master it.

Otherwise, there are numerous little ploys that I am sure we all use to avoid such blockages. Gazing out of the window at the panoramic vista ('I will lift up mine eyes unto the hills from whence cometh my help'), drinking numerous cups of coffee (as much for the breaks as for the caffeine), pacing the room, listening to a cheerful thrush, examining distant activity on the allotments through binoculars (Damn! The coalman is getting ahead of me again!), conversing with the dog, holding a conversation in your head, taking a walk around the garden, playing the violin . . . and so on. C. Wright Mills (1959) recommended explaining a point or making a speech to an imaginary audience; Nicholas Royle gets most of his ideas 'walking to the tube or sitting on a bus' (Moggach 1998). Terry Pratchett (*ibid.*) plays a computer game. Ronan Bennett (*ibid.*) goes on a long run ('Because running is so hard and painful, my mind will focus on the story rather than think about it'). Christopher Fowler (*ibid.*) listens to music, especially Mozart ('Apparently research in America showed that Mozart helped you to concentrate'). Thomas Keneally (*ibid.*) has a snooker table in his study for such moments. Some recommend a bout of strenuous exercise, almost as if thrashing the ennui out of your system – squash, swimming, gardening. One headmaster I knew used to keep a punchbag in his office for 'insoluble problem' times. Joseph Connolly (*ibid.*) 'goes out' because he feels 'You've got to have contact with the outside world or you can end up as a drivelling loony in the attic strumming your lips'.

However, you need to distinguish genuine blockages from self-induced ones. Work-avoidance strategies are particularly subtle in writing activities. In a study of student methods, Bernstein (1978: 30) describes the 'creativity fritter':

> It is best to wait until you are bursting with ideas or are sufficiently motivated, even if the motivation is guilt due to unsuccessful previous application of fritter techniques. This is therefore the let-it-brew-for-a-while fritter (closely related to this is the I'll-lie-down-and-think-about-it fritter; the possible danger in this tactic is, of course, very clear; listing all things people are designed to do horizontally, studying is one of the lowest on the list).

We might take heart again from the fact that even the best writers 'fritter'; indeed they excel at it. Coleridge wrote to a friend, 'To-morrow morning, I doubt not, I shall be of clear and collected spirits; but tonight I feel that I should do nothing to any purpose, but and excepting Thinking, Planning and Resolving to resolve – and praying to be able to execute' (letter to John H. Morgan, 1814). William Cowper similarly:

> Difficult (I say) for me to find opportunities for writing. My morning is engrossed by the garden; and in the afternoon, till I have drunk tea, I am fit for nothing. At five o'clock we walk; and when the walk is over, lassitude recommends rest, and again I become fit for nothing. The current hour therefore which (I need not tell you) is comprised in the interval between four and five, is devoted to your service, as the only one in the twenty-four which is not otherwise engaged.
>
> (Letter to the Rev. William Unwin, 1781)

Christopher Isherwood, an extremely prolific writer, nonetheless records:

A morning of pathological sloth. What brings on this disgraceful, para-
lytic laziness? It is always dangerous, of course, not to dress before
breakfast. I spent nearly two and a half hours reading *Life* magazine.
Then I got shaved, collapsed again into a chair. Then I washed.
Another relapse. Then, at last, I dressed. It was now two o'clock. The
beautiful, intact morning, which might have been used for all kinds
of valuable purposes, was wasted – as vulgarly, as meaninglessly as a
millionaire wastes ten dollars on a flower which he will immediately
throw away.

(Bucknell 1996: 63)

Emily Perkins makes:

a really slow start – I'll do anything to put off starting work. I have tea,
toast, read the papers – I have to do the crossword every morning – and
deal with my post. I usually get to my word processor about 10 a.m.
Then I sit there, slopping tea over the keyboard and looking out of the
window, thinking about my book.

(*The Times*, 30 May 1998: 21)

Bernice Rubens will 'even rather do the ironing than start (writing). When
there's finally nothing left to do, I'll go upstairs' (Moggach 1998).

Work-avoidance strategies may indicate a genuine need for relief, or an
only too-human reaction to steer clear of pain. We might at least recognise
them for what they are. As for blockages, you might try to head them off by
ensuring a stream of options. Pen and paper should be carried at all times, and,
if possible, a recording machine. Ideas may be sparked off by autosuggestion
when watching television, listening to the radio, cooking a meal, digging the
garden, walking the dog, and should be noted down before forgotten. When
writing at my desk, I often find the mind playing with future possibilities
at the same time as concentrating on the point in hand. Even as I write, I
scribble down a key word at the bottom of the paper to remind me of them,
lest they be lost.

If a blockage is unavoidable and immovable, I go elsewhere to some other
part of the analysis where the going is easier. This helps recovery of fluency
and confidence and helps salve the PE conscience as it fills out more of the
quota. Or I may go back over what I have done, filling out a point here and
there and further rationalising my plan. I shall then return to the blockage
later, with newfound impetus. The whole report, paper, article or book is
then put together later like a film at cutting and editing stage. I rarely write
an article or book sequentially. The introduction is usually written last, for
only then will I be sure of what the account is about.

If all else fails, the blockage may lead to discarding that particular element,
or at least pigeonholing it for future reference. However, it is as well to bear
in mind that these are likely to be the most gratifying, worthwhile and

celebrated aspects of the work if the problems are overcome. They should not be set aside lightly. It all adds to the excitement of doing research. It must also be noted that sometimes good can come from apparent misfortune. Nias (1991: 162–3) observes that 'chaos' is a good 'seedbed for creativity', and has 'repeatedly found that an acutely uncomfortable period of ambiguity and confusion seems to be a necessary condition for the birth of a new idea'. She discovered, 'in seeking not to drown in the data . . . unexpected reefs under my feet'. Fine and Deegan (1996: 435) discuss the value in research of serendipity – making fortunate discoveries by accident. The chance occurrence can of course help or impede. What makes the difference, according to them, 'Lies in being prepared to turn what seems like the ashen remains of a project into a creative opportunity for scientific discovery. In this way, courting serendipity involves planned insight married to unplanned events'.

Capitalising on chance, therefore, requires a quality of recognition in the researcher – the ability to see and grasp the opportunity. The moral is to try to cultivate conditions in which creative thoughts might happen; and, in circumstances where exactly the opposite is prefigured, to develop and maintain a state of mind which will enable you to turn apparent adversity to good account.

The opposite of a blockage is a 'run', which typically follows a stoppage. Things suddenly begin to move. You see the solution to a problem and, as in crosswords, this leads to solutions of other problems. You see connections and patterns that you did not see before. Your writing begins to flow. You get excited as more brilliant ideas begin to emerge. You have a great compulsion to get them down on paper while they last. You resent having to stop for other things – teaching, meetings, family engagements, sleeping, weekends, holidays. It depends, of course, on your priorities, but there are things to be said for deferring or postponing what you can of other events while the inspiration lasts. Interrupted 'runs' have a habit of coming to an end with the interruption. Writing, a supremely sociable activity in aim, is an extremely unsociable activity in execution.

In between blockages and runs are other variations in mood and disposition. I might feel too tired or heavy-headed to do any original or creative writing, but fit enough to do some editing or fine tuning of existing material. Reading what others have written makes for a pleasant change; while looking up and making up references is the sort of purely technical exercise which is often all that I can do at the end of a busy day. It helps to play the variations depending on mood and state of mind, rather than wasting time, mental ability and nervous energy on an ill-matched activity.

PLANNING

I recall in my school days the requirement to 'plan' an essay in rough. It was a one-off activity. You did your plan – you 'thought' – and then you followed it and 'wrote'. Planning in writing up research is immensely more complicated. The former is secondary work, and not particularly creative. The latter is a search for new formulations, and almost by definition cannot be planned in advance, for the creative process continues into writing up. In fact it may be *the* most creative part of qualitative work, and at times it is difficult to distinguish between planning and writing.

However, like patios and paint, as I have found over the years, you cannot apply the finish successfully without a good foundation. Your whole research, of course, involves planning, but in qualitative work, data collection ranges in a free and relatively uncommitted way. Plans for the final product usually begin to take shape during initial analysis. This phase will involve the writing of memos, fieldnote annotations, diary entries, short accounts, summaries of data, and presentations to colleagues or at seminars (see Delamont 2001 for an illustrated account of this kind of build-up). Beyond this phase I find four main planning stages. Actual schemes of organisation around which this planning might focus I shall consider in Chapter 3. The four stages are:

1 A preliminary, partly systematic, partly randomised, speculative scheme.
2 A provisional working plan.
3 A reworked plan at first draft stage, which may be repeated in subsequent drafts.
4 A final tidying-up plan.

Their nature is as follows.

Speculative scheme

The initial scheme attempts to combine the solidity of the work already done with more speculative attempts to theorise and conceptualise. You must be heavily selective, reducing the data to a manageable size for the presentation vehicle in mind. Ideally, the plan should present an all-inclusive, see-at-a-glance picture of all the most important features of the research. This facilitates seeing what relates to what and how various elements might hang together. Weak, unsupported elements are discarded. Data are marshalled to support others, and examples chosen. At the same time this fairly mechanical work is accompanied by 'brainwaves' – attempts to see the data in a new light. I will make plenty of notes at this stage, scribbling down these brainwaves as and when they come to me. I shall end up with a file of these, which I duly go through on an appointed 'planning' day. They will be annotated and classified, added to as further thoughts occur, and reduced as I find similar points repeated. The preliminary plan may be fairly detailed, and certainly the more thoroughly it is done, the easier the passage into writing, even though that particular plan may soon be radically altered. For it is performing another function – preparing the mind. It is not only giving it a grasp of the whole enterprise but also forcing it to concentrate on the mechanics of construction. In the next stage, 'writing' will combine with this to produce the more lasting plan.

Provisional working plan

The provisional working plan is abstracted from this. It consists, in essence, of a number of major headings, with subheadings where appropriate, and an indication of the content (and where it is to be found) to be included under them. I may have a special chart for points I wish to emphasise in the conclusion. The latter is not easily written, yet is one of the most important sections. One solution, therefore, is to carry forward an ongoing plan of the conclusion, to which notes are added as writing proceeds. All the notes and data headings are systematically reconsidered to check for omissions or misrepresentations. Then the working plan is re-examined for order and for connecting links. These are not too strong at this stage, for the working plan will inevitably be changed once writing commences. In qualitative work especially, it is important to carry this divergent cast of mind through almost to the end product.

Reworked plan

A reworked, 'realised' plan emerges in writing the first draft. The preliminary plan will not be slavishly followed, for improved ideas will emerge as you begin to write. Some sections may prove very productive, others less so. In fact, any overall plan may be suspended temporarily while promising lines of thought, themselves with several branches, are investigated. If they prove productive, they may be afforded greater prominence within the scheme, and others relegated. The first draft may thus have a kaleidoscopic quality about it which is stitched together to provide an element of coherence and continuity, and which may bear little resemblance to the preliminary plan. This coherence, however implicit, should be real, and available for strengthening in subsequent drafts. However, what you may find yourself doing at this stage is indulging the development of the separate sections. You have a notion of the finished product, but its eventual quality depends on the quality and strength of its component parts as well as the way they are put together. You cannot make a Rolls-Royce out of Morris 1000 parts.

Final plan

It follows that there must be a further plan, where the linkages, development and explanation are strengthened, and the material, possibly, again reordered. It sometimes pays to set the first draft aside for a while to 'mature'. Returning to it with a fresh mind, it is easier to spot strengths and weaknesses. Also new resources are brought to bear, in the form of new thoughts, more 'focused' research and reading, and, most importantly, the reactions of others. Also, by this stage, the pain barrier has been overcome, and the tidying up can be done with greater confidence and equanimity. You have successfully externalised the product, and can now relax and 'chip away' at its improvement, deleting here, adding a further word of explanation there, finding a more mellifluous and accurate phrase perhaps, reordering, tightening up, fitting it into the general framework of research to which it relates, adding references, drawing conclusions.

At this stage the severest tests are applied. What is missing here? What is wrong with this argument? What does it need to strengthen it? How else could this material be interpreted? How could this be criticised? What prejudices am I indulging? What do I really mean by this? Here is a nice quote – but is it really needed? Here are some impressive-sounding sentences – but what are they saying? There are some good points in this paragraph – but do they really relate to what goes before and after? Though in some ways easier to do than initial composing, in some ways it is still quite hard to summon up the resolve to rewrite sections once they have been typed. Nonetheless, it has to be done.

The twin principles here, I think, are that you must plan at each stage, but also maintain flexibility. It is not only important to have some sense of the overall scheme – we cannot just sit down and start writing – but equally important to realise that as the intensity of mental involvement with the data increases at each stage, so the previous plan may be amended or discarded. William Walton said he had not wanted to do *Facade* at the time he composed it. His comment later was, 'One sometimes happens to do something very good by mistake'. This is equally true of writing. You must aim for a productive tension between constructive planning and anarchic, but potentially highly productive, freedom.

With all these stages of writing and levels of thought, it is helpful to the psychological management of your output to have several projects, or aspects of a project, underway at the same time, all at different stages. Malcolm Bradbury, for example, used to have various exercises in different typewriters around his house. It is comforting to be in the final stages in one, and to have the option of 'chipping away' at a second draft for another, when you are working up inspiration for assaulting the pain barrier with a third. If they are related, they might feed off each other; and certainly allow for ease of switching between psychological states, thus maximising the use of your time and energies. This, however, calls for careful scheduling – overproduction can lead to underachievement.

CONCLUSION

The point where rich data, careful analysis and lofty ideas meet the iron discipline of writing is one of the great problem areas in qualitative research. While true to some extent of all kinds of research, it is more of a difficulty in qualitative approaches because of:

- the emphasis in them on the investigator as the chief research instrument, which tends to make such problems appear more personal than they really are

- the nature of the research as process – an open-ended ongoing dialogue between data collection and theory, where the search for ideas militates against early foreclosure
- the necessity, in view of this, to regard the writing-up process as an important inducement to the production of ideas, as well as to their communication
- writing, analysis and data collection being coterminous.

The disjuncture produces pain, which I have argued is the inevitable corollary of the rites of passage we must go through in our quest for a fully matured product. Regarding it like this externalises and demystifies the problem, making it less personal. Further analysis then reveals the patterned nature of the complexities involved, which renders them susceptible to treatment. I have made suggestions, from my own experience, of the form that this 'craft-work' might take – the cultivation of amenable situations; pandering to the PE (if a 'PE person') one minute with schedules and quotas, and out-flanking it the next with productive use of 'free' time; calculated risk-taking; giving special attention to models of excellence in areas which may be outside that of the research, such as literary or other artistic work; 'cranking up' to the appropriate mental state, and undergoing apparent personality changes; meeting 'blockages' in similar analytical style and applying to them a range of techniques; and maintaining flexibility in the complicated planning procedures without loss of rigour or impetus.

Using such techniques, we might eventually come to believe, like Graham Greene, that it is the rest of the world that is mad, and not us: 'Writing is a form of therapy; sometimes I wonder how all those who do not write, compose or paint can manage to escape the madness, the melancholia, the panic fear which is inherent in the human situation' (quoted in Lodge 1996: 79).

3

A standard approach
to organisation

First the book must be threshed out.

(Lichtenberg 1789)

Let us consider another miracle – the mutation of a mouthful
of air into a penful of ink.

(Anthony Burgess 1992: 71)

An early problem is how to organise your article, report, thesis or book. There are many ways of doing this according to what you wish to convey and to whom. As Stake (1995: 122) notes, 'A write-up can be organised any way that contributes to the reader's understanding of the case'. In effect, however, journal articles, academic books and theses largely follow a traditional model, at least in relation to the presentation of empirical material – the main concern of qualitative research. I shall consider some examples of this in this chapter. Nonetheless it needs to be borne in mind that this is a matter of convention. As noted in the Introduction, modes of presentation are under debate at present – and conventions can change. I shall consider some alternative forms of writing in Chapter 4.

I shall begin by looking at the organisation of data – the central part of qualitative writing – through categories, themes and concepts; I shall then consider how these items are generated, suggesting some strategies for working at organisation. I go on to examine the structure of an article as a whole, before concluding with some examples of variations on the standard approach.

ORGANISING THE DATA

Common modes of organising qualitative data are by category, by theme and by concept. These terms are sometimes used interchangeably, but they do convey different levels of generality and/or abstraction. Categories are to do with basic properties, themes are unifying links running through wider spans of data and concepts are ideas which elevate the data or parts of the data to a more theoretical level.

Organising by category

What categories you decide on will depend on the aims of the study and your interests. They may be to do with perspectives on a particular issue, certain activities or events, relationships between people, situations and contexts, or behaviours. There is no one master framework. But there are tests of adequacy. Categories need to be:

- generated from the data, not superimposed on the data from some other study
- exhaustive (all the data fit somewhere into the categories)
- mutually exclusive (cases go into one category and one alone)
- on the same level of analysis (in any one set), and relating to the same criteria.

These criteria need to be relevant to the topic of research. You usually have to have several shots at this before coming to the most appropriate arrangement. Such distillation helps you to encapsulate more of the material in a glance, as it were, and to gain an overview. Even so, you will probably need to revise first attempts. You may find that:

- two categories are really two sides of the same one
- one category is really a subcategory of another
- the categories are generated from a frame that you feel uncomfortable with
- similar material appears under more than one category.

The following are some typical examples of categorisation.

Example 1: Paul Willis (1977) 'Elements of a culture' from Learning to Labour

Willis chose to divide his book into two parts: 'Ethnography' and 'Analysis'. These were the main features of the lads' culture, which formed the 'Ethnography' section:

- opposition to authority and rejection of the conformist
- the informal group
- dossing, blagging and wagging
- having a 'laff'
- boredom and excitement
- sexism
- racism.

Under these headings, Willis reconstructed the lads' outlook on life, using liberal portions of transcript to build up a graphic and evocative picture. Note that the categories include a mixture of the lads' own terms, which alerted the researcher to major areas of activity, and Willis' own summarising features.

Example 2: John Beynon (1985) ' "Sussing out" teachers: pupils as data-gatherers'

Beynon observed a class of boys during all their lessons in the first half term of their first year at a comprehensive school. His focus was on 'initial encounters' between boys and teachers. He became interested in 'the strategies the boys employed to find out about classrooms and type teachers; the specific nature of the knowledge they required; and the means they employed to (in their words) "suss out" teachers' (p. 121). He found there was a main group of boys who used a wide variety of strategies. One of his first tasks, therefore, was to organise his data and identify the kinds of strategy. He found six major categories:

- group formation and communication
- joking
- challenging actions (verbal)
- challenging actions (non-verbal)
- interventions
- play.

Within these, he put forward subcategories of activities. For example, the category of 'joking' included the subcategories of:

- open joking
- jokes based on pupils' names
- risqué joking
- lavatorial humour
- repartee and wit
- set pieces
- covert joking
- 'backchat' and 'lip'
- closed joking
- Michelle: a private joke.

This, then, shows an organisation of a mass of data using categories and subcategories, each being graphically described by classroom observations, notes and recorded dialogue and interaction. The effect is to re-create 'what it was like' for these pupils and their teachers and to show the considerable depth and range of their activities of this particular kind.

Example 3: Howard Gannaway (1976) 'Making sense of school'

One of the questions raised in the construction of categories is the interconnections between them. Gannaway was concerned to identify priorities and interrelationships among his categories. He summarised his conclusions as shown in Figure 3.1. Gannaway's research threw up certain categories, but also revealed different values attaching to them in pupils' minds. Thus, without the ability to keep order, a teacher would be sunk, whatever his or her other qualities. But a number of deficiencies could be redeemed if the subject the teacher taught was seen by pupils to be useful to them.

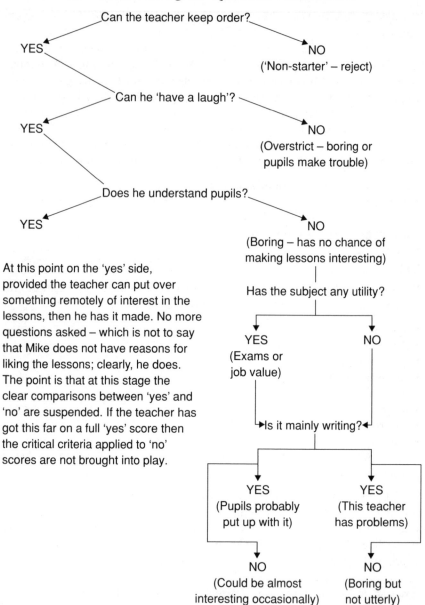

Figure 3.1 An evaluation scheme for teachers
Source: Gannaway (1976)

Example 4: 'Features of a boy's perspective on school'
There might be interconnected categories at different levels of generality or abstraction. The following is my analysis of one interview with a 15-year-old boy in the last year of his schooling in the early 1970s. My aim was to try to convey the main features of his perspective on school, the effects on his

attitude and behaviour, and possible explanations (see Table 3.1). The analysis illustrates how categories often include polar *dimensions*. The contrasts in the latter alert you to the category.

This is by no means the only way to analyse this particular material, but it is one way. It illustrates these features of qualitative analysis:

- It divides the analysis into four interconnecting levels:

  a) Attempts to establish the major categories in the boy's perspective; they are presented, as they appear in the interview, as antitheses, good and bad.

Table 3.1   Features of a perspective

A FEATURES

1 Freedom
The boy referred to 'making up your own minds', 'you can take lessons you want to take', 'it's up to you to learn', 'go in what clothes you want', 'more choice', need 'more trips' and 'to get out more', 'need to be allowed to finish'; 'don't force you to learn'

Control
They were 'chained together', 'made to work', 'cooped up', 'teachers would get the law in', you had to 'do what you were told, go to lessons, wear uniform'

2 Personal
Preferred junior school where you were with one teacher all the time

Depersonal
References to bureaucracy, divisions of time and labour, rules and regulations; doesn't like doing questions and writing out of books, copying off the blackboard at the teacher's pace

3 Manual or utilitarian, vocational
'I started making stuff and really, asking them if I could stay off history and go into the metalwork room'; 'When we have theory I don't usually like that, so I ask him if I can do practical'

Mental or academic
'Well, geography is no good to you is it, stuff like that'

4 Masculine
References to leisure pursuits like motor bikes, football, war films

Feminine
Doesn't like 'love stories and things like that'

Table 3.1 (*Cont'd*)

B EFFECT

Interest
Active, ownership, learning

Boredom
'Not doing anything, waste of time';
'everything's to a routine and you just get
bored with it'; 'it seems about five hours
longer than the lesson really is'; 'it seems to
drag on a bit', 'any chance you get, you
laze about; all you do is loll about';
'teacher's droning on'

C BEHAVIOUR

Work

Messing about
Many strategies mentioned, for example,
absence, running off, knocking off, dossing,
work as therapy (i.e. it becomes so boring
'you start doing stuff to occupy your
mind'), escapism, disruption, playing up,
rebellion, negotiation, 'getting the rest of
the kids not to like it', making noises

D EXPLANATION

Possibly relate to social class, community (cf. Dubberley); school organisation
(Lacey); peer culture

---

b) The 'good' line leads to interest in school and work, the 'bad' to
boredom.
c) Interest produces work, boredom a number of messing-about strategies.
d) The explanation merely suggests at this stage some theories that might
be relevant.

- The spiralling relationship between data collection, analysis and writing up.
Writing is part of the analysis − and also part of the data collection. Some

of the categories above are more strongly supported by the data than others. So I would want to re-interview the boy to test and fill out this formulation. In the course of this, new categories might emerge, and old ones disappear. Or priorities might emerge among them. If, of course, I were interested in a group of pupils, I would want to interview more of them, for the same purpose. The analysis procedure would be the same as for this one.

- Some parts of the analysis are still hypothetical. Part D, for example, points the way toward possibly relevant theory and literature, which might be explored in any future data-gathering. Further data, and more rereading then feeds back into the developing organisation.

Organising by theme

Another common mode of organising data derives from the identification of a common theme or themes throughout the material. Ely *et al.* (1997) refer to the search for themes as 'one of the most frequently mentioned analytic approaches used by qualitative researchers'. By 'theme' they mean 'a statement of meaning that 1. runs through all or most of the pertinent data, or 2. one in the minority that carries heavy emotional or factual impact' (Ely *et al.* 1991: 150). Categorising can then follow on the basis of aspects of the theme. This might be said to be theoretically, rather than empirically, led. The latter, as represented by the examples above, could develop into the former.

This procedure is well illustrated in the work of Pollard and Filer in their series of books on '*The social world of the pupil*'. For example, Filer (2000) identifies key themes in their research which led them towards an 'emergent sociology of assessment' (Filer and Pollard 2000: 7). These themes are set out in the introduction to the latter book, together with a model of key questions that guided their research, as a framework for the whole work. The four main themes (p. 8) are:

- the sociocultural and historical contexts of policy
- the technologies and testing used in assessment processes
- classroom contexts of assessment
- assessment as lived experience.

The interrelating guiding questions were:

- Who is being assessed?
- Who is assessing?
- What is being assessed?
- How does assessment function in classrooms?
- How are assessments interpreted and mediated?

Also considered was where and when the assessment was taking place.

Two chapters are devoted to each of these five questions, one theoretical and one empirical, with the result that 'a model of greater sophistication thus gradually emerges and is elaborated as the book progresses' (p. 9). The basic structure as presented in the introduction can be seen to be succinct yet comprehensive, integrated, with pointers towards an 'emergent' theory, and provides a very clear framework for analysing a mass of complicated data.

Organising by concept

Accounts of qualitative data might be of interest in their own right, as with those of Willis, Beynon and Gannaway as reported above. But most researchers would go on to ask 'why' questions following the 'how', and thus to consider how their research might relate to other similar sets of circumstances. Thus Willis went on to conceptualise from his data and develop theory in the second part of his book, seeing the 'lads' behaviour as the production of a culture which had affinities with the shopfloor culture of their fathers in the factories. 'Penetrations' (of the conditions of existence of a culture's members) and 'limitations' (effects which impede the development of penetrations), were major concepts, as was 'partial penetrations'. Beynon wanted to know what all those categories and subcategories from his data analysis meant. Why did the boys behave in that way? He concluded that they were 'sussing' strategies directed toward finding out just how far they could go with their teachers, and what were to be the parameters of control in the classroom – necessary knowledge for all concerned. So 'sussing' became his central concept. Concepts, thus, are often generated from the data via categories and themes, as I discuss next.

THE GENERATION OF CATEGORIES, THEMES AND CONCEPTS

Categories are identified by scrutinising the data, over and over, making comparisons and contrasts, noting items which have common properties and then testing and refining them through more study of the data (Glaser and Strauss 1967). It might then be seen that the categories can be put together in separate groups around a common theme. In seeking to explain the data as presented in the descriptive themes and categories, the researcher might then try to conceptualise the material and to raise it to a higher level of understanding, so that it might inform our general understanding of such issues.

Hallam *et al.* (2004: 122) illustrate how themes and categories combine, and how they might be generated. They draw on a process developed by Cooper and McIntyre (1993), which has affinities with Glaser and Strauss (1967), involving:

1 Reading a random sample of scripts.
2 Identifying points of similarity and difference among these transcripts in relation to the research questions.
3 Generating theories (on the basis of 2) describing emergent answers to the research questions.
4 Testing theories against a new set of transcripts.
5 Testing new theories against transcripts already dealt with.

6 Carrying all existing theories forward to new transcripts.
7 Repeating the above process until all data have been examined and all theories tested against all data.

Initial analysis using the above process revealed some 28 subcategorisations. These seemed to fall into groups, so were ordered into higher-level categories. These in turn seemed to relate to five major themes. The five themes, with their constituent categories where relevant, are:

1 Learning (includes issues relating to differentiation, raising attainment, developing pupil skills, flexibility).
2 Teaching and curriculum (includes benefits to teaching; academic subject considerations).
3 Introduction of the National Literacy Strategy.
4 Practical issues (includes school or cohort size, resource issues).
5 School self-evaluation.

The resultant article was organised on this basis.

An excellent example of how a similar process worked in a book containing a mass of detail organised around categories, themes and concepts is given in Barton and Hamilton (1998: 68–72). In summary, they identified these practical strategies for analysing their data:

1 Reading and rereading the transcripts and notes and making notes on them ('memoing'). They were guided at first by existing themes in their 'orienting theory', some being developed, some changed, some modified. Constant reading and rereading led to new themes and concepts.
2 A constant process of selecting some parts of the data as more significant, each selection involving 'interpretation and . . . a reduction of the data'. Summarising parts of the data was useful in identifying significant themes.
3 Coding and categorising, saying that 'different instances are all examples of similar phenomena'.
4 Constant 'cycling back and forth between theory and data in order to identify patterns and regularities'.
5 Alternating between focusing on individual people and focusing on themes common to the entire sample.
6 Using three distinct forms of analysis on texts: (a) words and phrases; (b) theme analysis; (c) the broader discourse.
7 Using the computer to aid reading, memoing, coding and developing themes (see Chapter 8).
8 Constantly evaluating reliability and validity, through, for example, various kinds of triangulation.
9 Moving to different stages of analysis over time, from, for example, initial themes to discovered themes.
10 Selecting at all stages, especially at the writing-up stage.

An example of concept generation from my own research on exceptional events in schools followed this line of development:

The genesis stage

I noticed that all the exceptional events had a number of things in common. One of these was the use of experts other than teachers from outside the school – a children's writer, a group of architects, a drama expert, archaeologists. I felt that this merited an article. I could have written an article simply cataloguing their various contributions. I had begun to do that, simply to order the data so that I could 'see' it better, and had constructed two, apparently separate, unconnected sections. But I felt that something more was needed. I needed to conceptualise their contributions, to raise the discussion to another level that might have more general applicability.

The exploration stage

To help towards this end I asked myself a number of questions. What exactly were these outside experts contributing, and how? What was special about it? What did they do that teachers were unable to do? How did their contributions fit within the educational framework of the school and within teacher plans? What role were they performing, and how did this compare with the roles of the teachers? What was distinctive about the effect they had on teachers and pupils?

The discovery stage

Clearly they were introducing special first-hand skills and knowledge. Comments from teachers and pupils showed that they were held in high esteem. There was something exciting in their participation, and a special quality in the relationships they fostered with the children, involving trust, inspiration and admiration. They were consequently highly motivating. How could I depict this effect?

The ideas stage

I experimented with the notion of 'charisma'. This was not just pulled out of the air. I have always been intrigued by the nature of charisma and its effects, ever since hearing my old mentor, Frank Musgrove, lecture on the topic in my student days. I can still recall him concluding with the opinion that, 'We need more charisma in teaching'. I agree, and perhaps that is why I was studying exceptional events anyway, though that is not how I saw it in the first instance. Here, possibly, was an opportunity to explore the idea a little further.

The confirmatory stage

At this point I consulted the literature. I went back to my old lecture notes, reread Weber, Freund and others on charisma; and for contrast and to highlight its characteristics, effects and significance, some commentaries on the prevailing condition in schools, the obverse of charisma, one of bureaucratic rationality (Rizvi 1989). This confirmed the appropriateness of 'charisma' as a centralising concept, and suggested some aspects that could appear in the organisation of the article. Further, looking again at my data, I could see that the two apparently unconnected sections were indeed connected within the concept of charisma.

The getting it right stage

'Getting it right' is not meant to imply that there is only one correct outcome; but rather that there is a stage in writing where things come together and work as well as you judge they can. You are making a point you feel is worth making and doing it in a way you feel satisfied with. You do get a feeling that this is 'about right', 'as good as it gets' or 'my best shot'. This stage 'means more than mere accuracy. It means portraying something significant of human experience' (Charmaz and Mitchell 1997: 206). A number of drafts and one conference presentation followed the confirmatory stage. At this stage I was teasing out the properties, or categories, of the charisma and its effects – and testing out my tentative analysis at the conference. Looking again at the data from the viewpoint of charisma, I saw that there were in fact three main categories, not two. The subcategories also now seemed to fall into place – a good test of the overall schema. The charisma of the 'critical others' derived from:

• The fact of being 'other'. They challenged the taken-for-granted, introduced novelty into schools, and presented new role models for students.
• Personal qualities that induced trust, faith and inspiration, contributed to the generation of 'togetherness' among those involved, and were motivating.
• Professional qualities which contributed to the authenticity of teachers' work. The work they did was real, not simulated. They integrated knowledge, fostered information and communication skills, and validated teachers' and pupils' work within their professional fields.

This may look rather neat in the end, and you might wonder, 'Why didn't I think of that in the first place?' I very rarely do, however, without going through this sort of process. And if the process looks straightforward, it did involve a great deal of work, especially 'getting it right'.

What strategies can we deploy in trying to 'get it right'?

SOME ORGANISING STRATEGIES

Each time I confront a body of data I have no idea where the eventual plan is going to come from. I have found that if the data are of any value, a breakthrough usually comes. It is a relief when it happens, for it seems a huge impenetrable barrier at the time. Then one insight, one realisation that sees connections, can unlock a whole chain of thought. I find the following strategies helpful in these circumstances (in addition to those discussed in Chapter 2):

- *Persistence*. Don't give up. Keep looking, keep thinking, but in combination with the following strategies.
- *Variability*. Study the data at different times of the day or week, in different situations, when you are in different moods, so that you come at the problem from different angles.
- *Search*. Seek to reinforce your own knowledge and creativity base by reading or rereading notes, transcripts and relevant literature, and by talking to others. A sentence, a remark, might stimulate a new line of thought.
- *Look for contrasts, inconsistencies, contradictions.*
- *Play, experiment*. Construct sketches, figures, diagrams, flowcharts. Summarise data and tabulate them on a chart. Rehearse a number of possible modes of organisation. Be flexible. Keep chipping away at it. Move text around, add bits here, delete bits there. Some schemes look as if they might work – save these to compare and/or to build on, jettison the rest.
- *Appreciate the value of imperfection*. Recognise that the first draft is probably only one of many. It might not be very good at all, not one that you would want to show to others, but it is a basis on which to build.
- *Write*. Often the solution to blockage lies in the activity itself. Resolve that 'tomorrow morning I will really start to write'. Providing that all the necessary resources are to hand, such as good data, adequate preparation on your part, and a conducive situation, forcing yourself in this way may yield a few possibly excruciatingly painful sentences which nonetheless gradually free up the mind. This was true of this particular chapter. In two weeks I had only written one sentence, and that was a quote from some-body else (which I later deleted). Eventually I made greater and more concentrated and realistic efforts, and summoned up the necessary resolve to get started. Once moving, the construction of the chapter proceeded reasonably well.
- *Make the task manageable*. It may be that you see a way to organise part of your data but not all. If you do not improve on the plan after due reflec-tion, start writing out the part that works. Again, the act of writing brings a kind of closer concentration and might lead to your seeing a way to incorporating the whole.
- *Keep a file*. This will include the data of course, but also notes on and photocopies of the relevant literature; and some thoughts and ideas that you might have had at different times during data collection. Some of these might have been fleeting thoughts with only possible relevance at the time. If not recorded, they might well vanish. Keeping them in a file and then reviewing the file at the time of analysis is another aid to thinking.
- *When you do start to write, keep a 'table of contents'*. In other words, a summary list of headings and subheadings reproduced at the beginning of the text. This enables you to see the whole construction easily, and to

make amendments if necessary. The overall organisation can get lost in the richness of the data of the text. Or, you might proceed on a good organisational basis for a while, then 'lose it', the words coming out in a format that not even you can understand. The summary list can help clarify.

A TRADITIONAL STRUCTURE OF THE WHOLE

Organising the data is the most difficult part of qualitative analysis, but there are other aspects that need to be taken into account. A traditional structure of a whole piece of work, in this case a journal article, follows the format of:

- title page, with title of the piece and author(s)
- abstract
- introduction to the research issue
- review of relevant literature and how the issue relates
- research methods used (these last two might be incorporated in the introduction)
- theory, through which the data is going to be interpreted
- data
- discussion
- conclusion (these last two are often amalgamated)
- notes (if any)
- references
- appendices (if any).

It might be useful to see how this was done in an actual journal article. I selected an article fairly randomly, noting only that in large part it followed the standard structure. It is from the *British Journal of Sociology of Education*, and was written by Stephen Ball and Carol Vincent (Ball and Vincent 1998). Its features are as follows.

Title

The title of the article is '"I heard it on the grapevine": "hot" knowledge and school choice'. The title is very important and worth considerable thought. This will be the main signal to others that you have constructed something worthy of their attention, and will identify the product for posterity. It should be:

- *Informative*. It should tell the reader what the article is about.
- *Accurate*. It should not mislead or overclaim.
- *Succinct and clear*. I once examined a PhD thesis whose title ran to four lines. Even then, and after reading the title several times, it was not entirely clear what the thesis was about. Some are tautologous as well as verbose – 'Towards a tentative outline of a provisional model . . .'.
- Designed to awaken interest.

I would say the title of our chosen article meets all these criteria. It manages to incorporate three major components of the article: school choice (the general area), the 'grapevine' (the organising concept for the data) and 'hot' knowledge (a theoretical product). It does this clearly, briefly, and the quotation in the first part adds extra interest.

Authors

How you wish to be known also requires some attention. You might be 'Lizzy Dripping' to your friends, and that might be the name that appears on drafts, but you might prefer your authorial name that actually appears in print to be 'Elizabeth F. Dripping'. Then again, you might not. It does need thought and a principled decision, as this will be the name that for writing purposes you will be known as, and your writings referenced and filed under.

Abstract

All journal articles require an abstract – a summary of about 200 words of the content. This gives readers a little more idea of the content before they commit themselves to reading the whole article. It is also used in collections of abstracts, where readers can readily find articles on particular topics. It is a useful thing to do anyway, as it reveals the basic structure and argument and forces you to try to be absolutely clear about what you are saying. In a book, I like to do abstracts of each chapter in a section of the introduction called 'Structure of the book', as in this volume. This is so that both reader and writer can see the whole book in outline. The exercise might bring about some reorganising, yielding a more effective structure.

Introduction

Ball and Vincent begin with a quotation. The idea is to spark a little interest with an apposite comment, designate a key point in a particularly telling way, and form a link with the person making the comment. But it is not absolutely necessary. The introduction contextualises. It will establish the relevance of the subject matter, in terms of things like theoretical development, new understanding of a key issue and policy implications. In this case, the uncertainties for parents of choosing a school for their children in the educational market is a big current issue not only for parents, but for sociologists and educationists seeking to make theoretical sense of what is currently happening in education.

The authors go on to discuss previous studies of parental choice of school, identify limitations and omissions, and indicate how they are going to try to help fill a gap. Alternative approaches would be to develop previous literature, to test it, or to take up suggestions others have made. It is important that the literature review is organic to the text, and not just summated and added in. The latter can be a problem in theses, where the literature review may consist of a list of summaries of what is considered to be the relevant literature. In effect, the same process has to be applied here as in analysing the data – common properties, categories and themes have to be identified, their interrelationship to the writer's research examined and their strengths and deficiencies noted.

Next, Ball and Vincent introduce the dominant concept of 'grapevining', and point out that while previous papers of theirs have examined its content, they will be more concerned in this article with its structure and functions. They indicate how they will be analysing their data, which will be in relation to social class differences.

There is a very brief reference to research methods; too brief, some might think. Normally this might merit a section to itself following the introduction, but there should certainly be an extended paragraph. The authors here might be relying on the exposition of their methods that is readily available to the readers of the journal in their previous articles on the same research.

At the end of the Introduction is a brief summary of what they are going to do, making the aims and objectives of the paper very clear. Such summaries discreetly placed around an article are very 'reader-friendly' devices. They also help the writer in the same way, as does compiling the abstract.

Defining the grapevine

In effect this is a section on theory. In qualitative research, it has often been generated from the data in the section that follows, but in the written-up article the theoretical lines through which the data will be analysed are presented in advance – necessarily so as this is not a research methods paper on how the research was done, but one using theory and data to explicate an issue. Sometimes this theoretical discussion is included in an extended introduction, sometimes in a section under the heading of 'theory', or, as here, the particular theory highlighted in the text. As the 'grapevine' is the major concept in the article, it is headlined. The concept is explained and linked to related literature on informal social networks, gossip and rumour. The ideas of 'local structures of feeling' from Raymond Williams, and 'local class structures' are introduced; and then distinctions between 'hot' and 'cold' knowledge are explained and illustrated. We are now set up for the presentation of the data.

Analysing the grapevine

This is the data section, and it is by far the lengthiest. There are three broad categories of parental responses to the grapevine – suspicion, doubt and acceptance. The first has three subcategories of 'filling out', 'rejecting' and 'exclusion'. These are illustrated with lengthy quotations from transcribed interviews. The authors draw attention to factors influencing each group, such as social class, but also 'a kaleidoscope of other factors'.

Conclusion

Following the data section there is often a 'discussion of results', but some-times, as here, this is incorporated in an extended Conclusion. The authors conclude that the substance of the grapevine is conditioned by where you are and who you know. They pick up some of the points from the literature made in the introduction, and argue that access to particular grapevines is socially structured and patterned, though not straightforwardly. They then broaden the discussion to relate to more general theory and higher levels of abstraction, such as responses to 'authoritative knowledge' in late modern society, and indications of a 'crisis of representation'. They refer to the political-economic context, where 'choice of school is being subsumed within general class-related strategies of consumption'. They end by emphasising the necessity of seeing choice as a socially constructed activity.

Notes

Ball and Vincent have several notes here that have been indicated by a number (1–7) in the text. These contain information that is thought relevant, but would get in the way of the developing narrative or argument if placed in the body of the text. It is a legitimate device, and indeed the notes of some texts make for good reading (the footnotes in Gibbon's *Decline and Fall of the Roman Empire* have the reputation of being better than the text). On the whole, however, I find them a distraction – if a footnote is indicated I want to look it up there and then. If they contain essential information they can often be worked into the text. Where this is not possible, I would advise they be kept to a minimum.

References

There follows a list of references of every work cited in the text. They secure the account within the literature, indicating the particular selection made, and provide the sources in case readers wish to check up, follow up or develop the research. It is essential that these be complete, both as a list and within themselves, accurate, and correctly formatted, otherwise the accept-ance of a paper might be jeopardised. Sherman, a journal editor, notes that 'in all frankness, writers are extraordinarily careless when referencing their work. Some references are missing altogether, some are incomplete, and others are inaccurate – not to mention inconsistencies in citing references' (Sherman 1993: 237).

Appendix

The authors present two tables that summarise the social class data for the families quoted in the text. This is in terms of mothers' and fathers' occupation and education, ethnicity and housing. This information is useful and appropriately situated as its specificity would have been out of place within the body of the text. Research instruments, such as a questionnaire or a sample interview, are other items often included in an appendix.

VARIATIONS ON THE STANDARD APPROACH

There are many variations on the basic model of a journal article. Some articles might have no data, for example discussions of the literature, or purely theoretical expositions, or philosophical or methodological debates. Non-empirical articles in fact constitute the majority in some journals, such as the *British Journal of Educational Studies*. However, many reflective pieces follow the same traditional principles as outlined earlier, except that the data are given, and critical reflection follows on them. They would not, therefore, need sections on methods and data, and the organisation of the rest would be determined by the particular argument being made. Hargreaves' (1988) article, for example, on 'Teaching quality: a sociological analysis' is a review of the literature pointing to sociological factors that affect teaching quality in contrast to the government's 'common sense' view, with markedly different implications for policy. Its construction follows a simple formula:

- *Introduction*. Identification of the important issue of 'teaching quality', government action being taken and the apparent 'theories' on which it is based. Introduction of the argument of the paper – an alternative explanation of 'poor' teaching quality based on sociological factors.
- *Discussion* of the official view on teaching quality and its deficits, based on analysis of official documents.
- *Presentation of an alternative view* based on a review of sociological literature. This section is divided into subsections, such as 'situational constraints', 'examinations' and 'subject specialism', rather as data is categorised in empirical papers.
- *Conclusion*. Summary of the main points of this alternative view contrasted with the official view. Finally, the punch-line – the implications for policy, which are markedly different from those being taken as stated at the beginning of the paper.

Empirical articles can vary considerably. Those based on life histories, biographies, events or histories, for example, might follow more of a narrative structure, interweaving theory and data as they progress. Frank Musgrove's (1975) article on 'Dervishes in Dorsetshire: an English commune', is based around day-by-day extracts from a diary the author made when he stayed there for a week. Wolcott's (2002) account of his experiences with 'Brad', a drop-out who took up residence on Wolcott's land with dramatic consequences, takes the form of a story, with the analysis interwoven with the tale. It begins in classic story style: '"I guess if you're going to be here, I need to know something about you, where you're from, and what kind of trouble you are in", I said to the lad, trying not to reveal my uncertainty, surprise and dismay at his uninvited presence until I could learn more about his circumstances' (p. 68). There is detailed description of character and behaviour, but basically it is a story about cultural acquisition.

The illustrations in this chapter represent a largely conventional approach to the writing up of qualitative research. I shall consider some alternatives in Chapter 4.

4

Alternative forms of representation

I write because I want to find something out.
(Richardson 2000: 924)

If I could have said it, I would have.
(Blumenfeld-Jones 2002)

The examples in Chapter 3, while varied, are still all coming from the same direction, that is, the voice of the author. In early realist tales this was a disembodied voice. Indeed, at times it was as if there were no human author there, but some supernormal being. Charmaz and Mitchell (1997: 193) talk of the 'myth of silent authorship'. Thomas (1992: 10) refers to the 'frozen text', where all the dynamism between researcher and others in the course of data collection is lost in the written account. It is the 'style of no style, windowpane prose' (Golden-Biddle and Locke 1997: 75). However, after the first wave of ethnographic studies in the UK in the 1970s, it was perhaps a natural development for researchers to become more reflexive about their work and tell 'confessional' in contrast to 'realist' tales (as, for example, in the collection by Burgess 1984). Soon, ethnographic authors began to write themselves into the text. An early example of this is Davies (1982: 5). She writes: 'My reasons for presenting myself as "I" rather than as "the author" stem not just from a stylistic preference, but from a recognition of the fact that the pragmatic nature of this study necessarily involves me as a person. To present the data as if I had not been involved would be to tell only part of the story'.

It has now become the custom rather than the exception for qualitative researchers to include some autobiographical details, in recognition that their 'selves' – their personal histories, beliefs and values – are all bound up in the study in some way and that the account is a construction by a particular author. Readers, therefore, need to know something about the author to aid them in their own construction of the text. It is also now much more the custom in qualitative work to use the active rather than the passive voice in recognition of the author's close engagement with, rather than detachment from, the research. Sherman (1993: 236) further argues that 'received views' are usually framed in an 'official style' based on the passive voice, so that the active voice, as indeed qualitative research in general, acts as a defence against such views.

It is a small step from recognition of one's self to recognition of others in the text; and to move from 'confessional' to 'impressionist' tales, wherein other voices are recognised and given expression in the research. One obvious voice, always present but not always acknowledged, is that of the reader. Wilson (1998: 173), following Barthes ([1970] 1990), comments on the distinction between 'readerly' and 'writerly' texts. The former

> Lead the reader logically, predictably, often in a linear fashion, through the research process, leaving little space for the reader to make his or her own textual connections between the stories and images presented . . . The writerly text is less predictable. It calls on the reader to engage with the text to more deliberately bring to the reading his or her experiences as a way of filling . . . the gaps in the text.

As the writer constructs a text, so the reader constructs a reading. Wilson invites readers of her article to do just that, providing a linear development, but interspersing it with other data, and with responses to the article by a partner in the research who does not always agree with what she is saying. Similarly, Winter (1989), talking about 'action research', which is designed to inform practice, says that 'readers will expect a report to be sufficiently organised to be accessible to a conventional act of reading, as well as sufficiently open to allow for readers' various interpretations' (p. 64). Elsewhere he talks of the 'creative reader', whose 'critical response is more than an imaginative play with the text; it is, as it were, also a reformulation of the self' (p. 238). In some respects, the 'authority of the text [shifts] from the writer toward a co-authoring of the reader with the writer' (Peterat and Smith 1996: 17).

Much has been missed in the use of conventional methods, particularly in the area of emotions and feelings, atmospheres, climates, moods and tones. Customary academic writing is unable to reach these areas. Richardson (2000: 924) argues that traditional texts have been guided by a 'static writing model [which] coheres with mechanistic scientism and quantitative research'. She complains of the countless number of boring qualitative texts she has tried to read. For 30 years, she has 'yawned her way through numerous supposedly exemplary qualitative studies' (*ibid.*). She asserts that now, 'We have an historical opportunity to create a space for different kinds of science practice' (Richardson 1993: 706). Rose (1990: 46) urges us to 'break frames, disciplinary rules, received notions, and the conventions of fieldwork with its repetitious intellectual labours' and Hargreaves (1995: 32) to 'diversify what are to count as legitimate forms of knowledge about teaching and education' and 'broaden the forms of discourse through which research knowledge is presented'.

These considerations have induced a range of experimental writing in qualitative research. They might be seen in terms of literary texts, performance texts and hypermedia texts. These are all closely related and in practice there is considerable overlap among them. But each emphasises a different and important focus. I will discuss some examples of each, and then consider criteria of adequacy for this kind of writing.

LITERARY TEXTS

Voices in the text

Here as elsewhere, different terms abound. In the area of personal narratives alone, there are first-person accounts, narrative ethnographies, personal narratives, personal ethnographies, autoethnographies, 'new biographies', autobiology, autobiographies, critical autobiographies, fictional autobiographical ethnographies, mystories, self stories, narratives of the self, memoirs, personal essays, stream of consciousness novels, reflexive and recursive life stories, sociological introspection, social autobiographies . . . However, they all follow certain principles:

- They make the writer part of the text. In so doing they establish the authority of the writer by demonstrating that they were actually there. They also show the human qualities of the fieldworker, however fragile these might be.
- There is a move from description, from simply telling a story of a life, to communication, with a focus on the actual means of construction. Such texts establish intimacy with readers. They aim to interest, engage, involve, move the reader. It is in this conjunction, the meeting between author and reader, that meaning is produced. Ronai (1995), for example, by giving readers insights into intimate details of her own experiences of sexual abuse, encourages them to 'project more of themselves into it and take more away from it' (p. 396).
- They prefer to use literary forms of language rather than social scientific. Rather than categories, theories and concepts they employ devices like metaphor, irony, parody, humour, imagery, immediacy, scene setting, unusual phrasings, cadence, plot, innuendo, dramatic tension and constructions, fleshed-out characters, puns, subtexts, allusions, flashbacks and flashforwards, tone shifts, synecdoche, dialogue and interior monologue (Richardson 2000: 931). I give some examples in Chapter 5.
- Their own emotions and inner experience are prime data. The aim is not only to know but to feel truth, and to become fully immersed in both intellectual and emotional forms of knowledge. 'The head and heart go hand in hand' (Bochner and Ellis 1999).
- Evocation is a prime aim. They want readers to see, think, feel 'what it was really like', as if they were there, or as if they were actually undergoing the experience themselves.

- Despite the high level of subjectivity, these authors consider themselves social scientists in the first instance, and relate their work to their social scientific knowledge and experience. They fracture the boundaries between literature and social science using the self as a source. They draw on their own emotions and experiences to gain ethnographic insights into other cultures and issues. Thus Tillman-Healy (2001) uses her own marriage to illustrate crossing boundaries between straight and gay cultures; Ronai (1995) uses a 'layered' method moving to and fro between a narrative account of her own experiences of child sexual abuse and a theoretical analysis of abuse; Bochner (1997) presents his very emotional reaction to the death of his father, within the context of structures of power and academic socialisation. Anderson's (2003) 'ethnographic memoir' combines his experiences with a group of men in a bar with human group interaction in general.
- Many use mixed genres and/or mixed techniques. Once you are free of the standard approach, there is nothing to stop you using whatever method or combination of methods suits your aims. Hence the bewildering array of approaches which do their best to defy classification. To Plummer (2002: 398), Ellis' (1995) book reads like a 'hybrid between a novel, a fiction, an autobiography and a research tract'. All sorts of 'fragments and shards of events may dance in and out of a narrative' (Manning 1995: 249–50), depicted in all sorts of different ways.

Personal narratives use the author's experiences and emotions as the main source of data. They tell stories, relate events, conduct dialogues, and postpone analysis and interpretation. They may be narratives about where and how the writing was produced, and how they relate to other parts of the author's life. They can be reflexive items on previous writings, moral and ethical musings. They might even be fiction, 'using the imagination to discover and embody truth' (Richardson 2000: 933).

Carolyn Ellis and Art Bochner's (2000) definitive article on autoethnography in Denzin and Lincoln's *Handbook of Qualitative Research*, is interesting not only for its content but for its autoethnographic construction. It contains several features of the genre and follows this format:

1 A telephone conversation between Art and Carolyn introducing the issues.
2 Art reading over the phone a section he has written for the article in conventional social scientific prose about the constraints of writing for a 'handbook'. This is presented in italics.
3 More conversation about 2, interrupted by a knock on Carolyn's door.
4 It is a PhD student, Sylvia. She wants to do research on breast cancer. A conversation ensues between her and Carolyn on the implications, and rehearsing some of the basic features of autoethnography. Carolyn's personal, reflective self is very evident. She recommends some key texts.
5 A fax from Sylvia to Carolyn expressing excitement and asking for more reading.

6 Carolyn sends some prominent articles, and also the draft she is writing for the *Handbook* on 'what is autoethnography' – a formal section, reproduced here, in italics, containing many references and very social scientific. She 'smiles' at the social scientific prose (p. 743).

7 More conversation between Carolyn and Sylvia when Sylvia returns having read what Carolyn sent her. 'Wow, these personal narratives just blew me away!' (p. 743). But Carolyn only has five minutes as she is about to attend a colloquium where Art is speaking.

8 Art's formal presentation at the colloquium on 'Why personal narratives matter'.

9 The question and answer session afterwards, featuring some of the basic criticisms.

10 More description of the scene at the end of the colloquium, Carolyn pointing out some interesting people. Sylvia finds it very exciting, but where would she start?

11 They go for a cup of coffee and talk about 'doing autoethnography'. They are joined by Art.

12 Two weeks later, Sylvia appears in Carolyn's office. They chat about how she is progressing. She has more questions – but first, what has she learned?

13 A year later, Carolyn phones Art. First she has to quieten the dogs, then she tells Art about Sylvia's PhD committee. Her thesis was attacked from a traditional standpoint, but Carolyn won over the oncologist, reaching him 'where he lived, at the site of his subjectivity and deep feelings . . . both of us had let down our guards and were communicating with each other as human beings' (p. 760). 'Wow,' says Art, 'that must have been some moment.' They talk about the future and their hopes for autoethnography. They feel its credentials are established, and are now keen to show its usefulness in the public realm.

Here we see a mixture of the personal, the literary and the social scientific; a number of voices, though there is clearly one main authorial voice – that of Ellis; the writer featuring in the text; use of a number of literary devices – phone conversations, actual conversations, formal discussions, presentations, humanising asides, overall narrative format situating all within one master story; the inclusion of feelings and emotions; personal reflectivity; possible use of fiction (Were these conversations real? Does Sylvia exist? Did these things really happen? Does it matter? If Sylvia does not exist, there are many postgraduate students like her, and it is with these especially perhaps the author seeks to engage). Also, Ellis and Bochner cleverly handle the formal requirements of writing a definitive article for a 'handbook' by (a) discussing that very issue at the beginning of their article, and (b) including some formal pieces, but distancing themselves from that style of writing, by, for example, the discussion about 'handbooks', by putting the formal pieces in italics, by subsuming them within the story, and by the 'smile'.

In many multi- or polyvocal texts, there is an empowering as well as an enlightening motive in the use of other voices. Thus Fox (1996) has three voices in her presentation of child sexual abuse – her own, as a survivor and researcher of such abuse, that of another survivor and also that of the latter's offender. She feels this makes more space for marginal experiences to be expressed and thus enables a fuller, more complicated view of abuse. She points out that the account has to be read, not as a 'master narrative', but 'subversively', challenging the view of child as victim and seeking to understand the child's sexuality and agency.

Robertson's (2003) article on the aftermath of 9/11, evocatively entitled 'Listening to the heartbeat of New York: writings on the wall', contains a number of voices: the authorial voice, collating, tying together the different items presented in different ways; the voices of her graduate students as they 'negotiate and scribe their understandings about the changing landscapes of their lives through dialogue, reflection, artwork, and writing' (p. 129); and the voices of New Yorkers, poignantly expressed through the 'writings on the wall' that were desperately posted in Lower Manhattan. These are presented in bold at points throughout the text to give them prominence and to illustrate the 'multiple modes of representation' that people use to express themselves in such circumstances. Photographs throughout, of writings, and students reading writings, help further to bring home to the reader the emotions of the aftermath. There are also newspaper extracts and internet messages. Here is a city in grief, but the article is also a celebration of the human spirit, and its creativity in trying to make sense of the most appalling events. The devices used draw readers into a maelstrom of emotions, but leave them with hope. The multidimensionality, arguably, makes the message more powerful and meaningful than a traditional article could ever hope to do.

Lather (1991) is critical of the way in which, in conventional research, quotes are presented in the final product possibly out of context and their original frame of meaning to suit the author's own framework. Theory should fit the data, not vice versa. The validating device of respondent validation is not entirely adequate since this is only a correctional voice, not a proactive one. It can only comment on the constructions the author has made; it cannot make constructions of its own. Lather (1997) gives an example of how you might maximise the voice of the other with the book produced from her work with women living with HIV/AIDS. She and her co-author had produced an earlier desktop version in order to 'get feedback from the 25 women we had interviewed and to solicit publishers toward what the women call a "K-Mart book", widely available to women like themselves, their families and friends as well as a more general audience' (p. 286). The later book, *Troubling the Angels*, follows this structure:

• The book begins with two prefaces, the first introducing the book and the second the women, many of whom have written their own introductions.

- The heart of the book consists of a series of short chapters that narrate the interview data around topics on the day-to-day realities of living with the disease, relationships, efforts to make sense of the disease in their lives, death and dying issues, and the role of support groups. The titles were chosen from the words of the women themselves.
- In sidebars, references are made to such things as further resources for dealing with HIV/AIDS in the deaf community, information on gynaecological signs of HIV infection in women, and the demographics of AIDS as a global crisis, with references for those who want further information.
- Interspersed with these short data chapters are . . . texts and illustrations . . . [that] function both as 'breathers' between the themes and emotions of the women's stories and as shifts from the women's testimony to short engagements with history, poetry and sociology around AIDS issues.
- Running across the bottom is a subtext commentary where [the authors], as co-researchers, spin out [their] tales of doing the research. This subtext provides the background for the study and researcher efforts to make sense of the 'data' and the study and the larger context in which the AIDS crisis is such a cultural marker.
- Scattered throughout the book are some of the women's own writings in the form of poems, letters, speeches and emails.
- Finally, the book concludes with an epilogue that updates the reader on each of the women and the support groups and includes their reactions to the desktop published version of the book (pp. 287–8: my bullet points).

This is a kind of so-called 'messy text', fragmented and polyphonic, designed to counter the 'comfort text' producing the 'romance of knowledge as cure', the authors hoping that 'the very fragmentation of the book, its detours and delays, will unsettle readers into a sort of stammering knowing about the work of living with HIV/AIDS, a knowing not so sure of itself' (p. 288). Foley (2002: 480) thinks this technique is not unlike the 'impressionist painter or poet who intuitively arranges light and colour and shapes or words in disjunctive, unexpected ways'.

There have been criticisms that many of these approaches have been too self-interested, biased, subjective, emotional; therapy instead of research; and that the self can dominate to such an extent that the work becomes 'narcissistic and egotistical' (Bruner 1993: 6). Plummer (2002: 399) notes 'almost an extreme preoccupation with novelty and self-analysis. What seems to have gone missing is the straightforward sense of a person's life as they tell it'. Note, too, that in multi-voiced texts there still has to be a collator, a researcher-presenter who has to put it all together. Further, it is not always clear that the voices in the text are coming from the same standpoint. For example, those in the Fox text mentioned above include adults recollecting their childhood. How accurately have these been perceived? How have they been affected by time and new experiences? Foley (2002) finds it hard to conceive of entirely authorless texts, and finds many experimental texts strewn with modernist elements, such as the use of theoretical constructs, or making knowledge claims based on data. Readers might also find some of these texts lacking in clarity and succinctness. I find many of these accounts fascinating and enlightening, but I yearn at times for more directness.

Poetry

Given the aims of the new approaches, it is not surprising that poetry has come to feature as one of the modes of expression. Poetry says a great deal in a short space, and by its choice and juxtaposition of words, phrases, imagery, metre, rhythm, rhyme and layout, conjures thoughts and feelings in a particularly vibrant form. Poetry serves as 'more than words in a short line on a page . . . this . . . may be more heartfelt, more concentrated, more distilled' (Piirto 2002: 435). Smith (2002: 461) found that poetry captured the 'passion factor' of middle-class reality which his more traditional writing failed to convey. For Richardson (1994a: 9), poetry is one answer to the boredom factor she identified with many traditional texts. She argues that 'lyric poems concretize emotions, feelings and moods – the most private kind of feelings – so as to re-create experience itself to another person. A lyric poem "shows" another person how it is to feel something'. Hewitt (1994: 202) notes that poets have 'strategies' for arranging familiar elements in an unfamiliar way. Thus, 'by disrupting readers' usual views of the elements under scrutiny, poets make it possible for readers to develop an alternative understanding of them' (p. 202). Moreover, they lead them to participate in the experience in an interactive way (p. 204).

Just as with narratives, however, these writers are first and foremost social scientists. Richardson (1993: 696) explains how she combines the literary and the sociological in her approach to the writing of her poem on 'Louisa May':

> Louisa May is the speaker in the poem, but I crafted it, using both scientific and poetic criteria. I used only her words, repetitions, phrases . . . and narrative strategies, such as multi-syllabic words, embedded dialogues, and conversational asides. My intent was for the poem to stand aesthetically and emotionally, for it to be, as Robert Frost would define a poem, 'the shortest emotional distance between two points' – the speaker and the listener/reader, but I also wanted it to be faithful to my sociological understanding of Louisa May's story of her life.

Her aim was to create a 'vivid, immediate, emotional experience for the reader/listener' using the person's own words, and 'to integrate the sociological and the poetic at the professional, political and personal levels'. The purpose of the poem is to evoke, to startle, to stimulate thought, to move, to give expression to the essence of the person's experience, to help the reader understand how the person feels, to induce fellow-feeling.

In commenting on nine short poems she presents elsewhere, Richardson (1994a) notes that the overall narrative is implied, but spaces between the poems invite greater reader participation than do traditional forms of presentation. The principle, well known in poetry circles, is to 'show not tell'. This stands in sharp contrast to the traditional approach, which requires the exposition to be as full and as explicit as possible. The message in the poems does not have to be spelled out, but exemplified through the use of images, actions or narrative. This has for long been the case for some in qualitative research. Kerr (1975: 3–4) notes, 'The less complete the canvas, the more there is for the viewer to contribute. He (or she) must work with hints, and the more he (or she) must do for himself (or herself), the more deeply engaged he (or she) becomes in the work'. Thus each poem in Richardson's selection is a 'mini-narrative', an episode, representing 'an emotionally and morally charged experience' (p. 8). The poems could be reordered, focusing on different plots or story lines. They retell 'lived experience', each poem being a 'candid photo', or 'critical moment'. One could argue that lives are structured on such moments.

We do not know the origin of the poems, or who wrote them, or if they all refer to one and the same life. Richardson asks, 'Does it matter?' The important point is that the distance between author and reader is minimal, and the 'reader is not simply "told" but *feels* the experience'. The lyric poem's task is 'to represent actual experience – episodes, epiphanies (Denzin 1989), misfortunes, pleasures – to capture those experiences in such a way that others can experience and *feel* them. Lyric poems, therefore, have the possibility of doing for ethnographic understanding what normative ethnographic writing cannot' (p. 12).

Richardson claims this is a more interesting way of representing research findings. However, it has to be noted that some readers might be bored (or worse!) by attempts at 'poetic texts'! The things that make for interest are intellectual coherence, originality, quality of argument and insight, appropriateness of presentation and organisation. Any one manifestation of these might interest one person, and bore another, depending as much on the reader's predilections, knowledge and understanding as on the text, whether poetry or prose.

Many of us may have difficulty, too, in constructing a quality product in this form. Writing poetry is a hard-earned, rule-governed discipline in its own right, as well as requiring a considerable amount of creative artistry. As Schwalbe (1995: 411) points out, rule-breaking and boundary-crossing are fun, and the 'turn to poetry and other forms of experimental writing may be a way to keep ourselves awake and amused before retirement'. This, perhaps, is too cynical a view, but the point about the need for caution is well made. 'Showing not telling' carries dangers as well as possible benefits. A poem needs a shared frame of reference for it to be understood and appreciated. Yet it operates by terseness and suggestion. A reader has a great deal of indexing to do – that is the point – if the index is provided by the author, the point is lost. A traditional, analytical text, by contrast, provides a wealth of data and explanation, together with commentary on how it was acquired and derived.

As Schwalbe (1995: 406) notes, 'whereas poetry is coy, prose is exhibitionist'. Even where a poem, or collection of poems, 'works', is it sufficient within itself to stand as sociological analysis? Will it answer all the questions one will want to ask about the material, or about the issues that it raises? More likely it will be a sensitising device, tuning the reader in to a particular aspect of the research, or aiming to spark a particular response, to evoke, to startle or to stimulate. For these reasons, I prefer to see it as one of a whole armoury of techniques that one may use, depending on the point one wishes to make, or reaction to stimulate.

In this vein, I adapted an interview with a primary school teacher, concerning her reactions to a school inspection. The first Ofsted (Office for Standards in Education) inspections in the early 1990s were highly traumatic affairs for teachers. Several well-established and able teachers broke down in tears recounting their experiences to us, which they did at considerable length. In such a case, it is the strength of the emotion that is remarkable and that cries out for explanation. My problem was how to get this across in the limited space and/or time available in an authentic way that connected with the lines of analysis. First attempts to do so included quoting selected excerpts and/or playing parts of the actual tape on a tape recorder, neither of which were very satisfactory. Rereading the transcript, I noticed a number of highly distinctive comments and put them together in the following poem:

Ofsted Blues

> Anti-climax, non-event.
> Whoopee! It's over,
> But no sense of joy
> Or of achievement.
> Who did we do this for,
> All this hard work?
> It's about them validating
> What they have done to a particular system,
> But I don't subscribe to this one we had . . .
> Are we going to get any extra money?
> An unreal week
> Like a surrealist painting.
> How do I hold on to it?
> When will I *feel* something?
> The event turned everything upside down
> That you'd ever done before.
> No one asked to look at a sodding record,
> So how do they know what we do?
> They haven't told me anything I didn't know.
> They didn't need to take a week.
> It's frightening that you go along,
> Instead of saying 'Stuff you and your bloody timetable!'

I want to get back to *feeling*.
Look! We're all going early today.
Bye, Selina! Are you coming in tomorrow?

The poem uses the teacher's own words, but aims to present the essence of her response, picking out the startling expressions, cutting out all the rest, and through the stark contrasts and juxtapositions, to highlight the cruel ironies in the situation. It tries to do this with a mind to content, feeling, cadence, rhythm, contrast and context. Each line contains a subject that could give rise to considerable discussion. Like Richardson (1993: 696), my aim was to create a 'vivid, immediate, emotional experience for the reader' and to 'integrate the sociological and the poetic at the professional, political and personal levels'. In the monograph that was eventually produced, the interview on which the poem is based was analysed with other interviews for common themes and categories, as recommended in Chapter 3. Some of these appear in the poem, for example:

- The feeling of anomie and a curious 'no feeling' induced by the dehumanisation and sense of uselessness.
- Power and control – who for, and how accomplished?
- The question of values – those of the inspectors are not the only ones and the speaker does not subscribe to them.
- 'Strategic compliance', and how the speaker feels about it ('frightening' – another commentary on power).
- And, at the end, an attempt to draw a line under the week with an early departure, and perhaps a note of recovering the old routines on the morrow.

'Ofsted Blues' will not win any poetry prizes, but I found it a useful way of getting these points over during presentations at conferences and seminars, and both content and method gave rise to some interesting discussion.

PERFORMANCE TEXTS

Some feel that they have to move beyond the written word to achieve the effect they seek, and performance is a natural extension. Much of the poetry that is produced is meant to be spoken out loud for full effect. Then, if voices are going to be heard, why not real voices spoken out loud? If we wish to explore every nuance, every shade of meaning, every emotion, what better than to present the full context of its spoken, embodied and acted situation? 'Actions speak louder than words' as the adage goes. Stanislavski, (in Hodgson 1972: 94) argues that one kind of performance, drama, provides opportunities for a range and depth of emotional expression that has a relevance for real life. It also provides experience in searching for truth, and for what is real, for the discovery of genuine, rather than theatrical, emotion. The same idea is expressed in social science thus: 'Building upon what has been described and inscribed, interpretation creates the conditions for authentic, or deep, emotional understanding. Authentic understanding is created when readers are able to live their way into an experience that has been described and interpreted' (Denzin 1994: 506).

The performer is partly exploring, partly conveying. By exploring and discovering emotions within his or her self, and by permitting the audience to witness the discovery, audiences are enabled to make a similar discovery about themselves. Audiences are thus caught up in the play, or in the research, in a full-bodied way, not just reading it as script.

Performance texts thus seek to give the text back to informants and readers in a kind of co-production. They are dynamic, alive, fluid and open to audience discussion at the end and through other means. It is research *with* people rather than *on* them. Pifer (1999: 542) believes that 'through perform-ance the lives, voices and events presented will have a life and power not possible through other forms of presentation'. Performances are immediate, but are ongoing, constantly being updated depending on feedback. They are particularly suited to material that is 'intractable, unruly, multisited, and emotionally laden' (Richardson 2000: 934). Unsurprisingly, illness and trauma feature strongly as subjects.

There are several kinds of performance text, including plays or drama of various kinds, spoken poetry or prose, ethnodramas, natural texts and impro-vised texts. They all involve action of some kind, and they are all embedded in language. A typical example of an evocative, multi-dimensional, highly personalised, revealing performance text is that of Ellis and Bochner (1992: 80). In their personal story of abortion, using themselves as subjects, they aimed to re-create an 'experiential sense' for their audience of what it was like to live through it, using 'systematic introspection'. Too engaged at the time of the abortion to write anything, they each separately wrote up an account two months later, 'including the emotional dimensions of our decision making, turning points, coping strategies, the symbolic environment of the clinic, and the abortion procedure as each of us experienced it' (*ibid.*). They then trans-formed these accounts into a dialogic mode of narration. Other people involved contributed their own experiences, creating a multi-voiced narrative. They finally wrote up the text with the express purpose that it would be performed as a 'staged reading', so that

> nuances of feeling, expression, and interpretation could be communicated more clearly . . . An audience that witnesses a performance of this text thus is subjected to much more than words: they see facial expressions, move-ments and gestures; they hear the tones, intonations, and inflections of the actors' voices; and they can feel the passion of the performers.
>
> (p. 80)

Their aim was to add an important missing ingredient to the understanding of abortion, a subject 'steeped in political ideology and moral indignation' (p. 97); and to cause others to 'feel and think about themselves in new and important ways and to grasp and feel the ambivalence, confusion and pain associated with experiences of abortion . . .' (p. 99).

Paget (1990: 150–1) emphasises the link for her between experience and analysis: 'The multiple interpretive acts of performance enhance, rather than diminish, the intelligibility of the text as a scientific account, because [they] enhance our understanding of the complexity of the reality to which the text and the science of the text alludes' (p. 152). Becker *et al.* (1988) also make this connection, through what they term 'performance science'. Acting out situations studied by ethnographers, they believe, encourages viewing from multiple perspectives, which in turn can enhance the researcher's understanding of those situations. McCall (2000: 424) describes their method thus:

> We carried and read from scripts, did not wear costumes or use props, sat in chairs or stood behind podiums, and moved only to exchange seats or to get from chairs to podiums and back. We played multiple characters: ourselves, as sociologists, and various people one of us had interviewed . . . We shifted body positions and visual focus, and occasionally stood, to mark character and scene changes and to guide audience attention.

Performance texts such as this downplay the more dramatic elements of conventional forms which create on stage a particular kind of reality, in order to focus on presentational forms of theatre in which the 'audience becomes an active participant in the making of meaning' (Donmoyer and Yennie-Donmoyer 1998: 400). 'Readers' theatre' is another example of this kind. Here, actors reading selected excerpts from data that are thematically linked 'act' in a highly stylised way. They read from scripts on a simple stage with minimal scenery (Donmoyer and Yennie-Donmoyer 1991, 1998). This has the effect of highlighting voices. Adams *et al.* (1998) chose this method to represent the complex ways in which women teachers construct their life and work histories. They say, 'Although the life histories have been collected individually, they have been orchestrated into a chorus of voices that express multiple ways of knowing and being, the whole becoming greater than the sum of its parts' (p. 383). The spoken voices 'energise' the presentation, and allow the 'contradictions, tensions, and ambiguities that are embedded in their lives to emerge' (p. 384). They also reinforce the power of silences, which are juxtaposed with the utterances, illuminating women's experiences of living in a patriarchal culture.

Performance does not just mean drama. There are several forms of bodily expression. Cancienne and others, for example, use dance and choreography to inform qualitative practice. Dance is both a form of expression and a form of enquiry, with the body as a site of knowledge. But the body is not just a text to be read. Cancienne and Snowber (2003: 239) want their audiences to 'sweat, blush, jubilate, and lament while watching a performance'. They want to explore and convey meanings, ideas, experiences and feelings that cannot be done in words. Thus,

The emotions revealed in the 'Women's Work' dancers' sharp movements make audience members alert, and stand in contrast to the sense of monotony and tranquility of repetition in the 'work phrase' and 'washing phrase'. Quick changes between low and high stance and sharp angular motion add to the rush of emotion. This contrast wakens the audience from the trance of circles and plunges them into the world of suspense and attention.

(p. 242)

These authors claim that writing begins in our bodies – how we breathe, think and feel. It is not just a matter of mind and intellect, but of 'bodily attending'. This heightens our awareness and alerts us to new insights.

Bagley and Cancienne (2001) provide one example of how it might be done. They chose to present Bagley's research in the form of Bagley (Performer 1) reading key parts of the text from cue cards, and Cancienne (Performer 2) dancing the data. Here is an extract:

Performer 1: 'An important concern for parents was their child's happiness.'
Performer 2: *Jumps, leaps, turns, skips and kicks her legs side to side and says*, 'If they are happy, they will settle quicker, and they will be more willing to do work.' *Finishing the sentence, she turns sideways, bends her knees slightly, and raises her shoulders tightly into her neck to show tension. She continues, speaking with difficulty*, 'If you have got a child that is unhappy, they get all tensed up and stressed out and will struggle.' *Releasing the neck position slowly, she says*, 'He's very timid, but he's full of beans' (*she jumps and hops around the stage*) 'and' (*standing still facing the audience with arms wide open, face smiling*) 'the school needs to reflect that.'

(p. 231)

Of course, we cannot judge the effectiveness of this through print. If we could, there would be no need for the dance. Bagley himself said that the performance did not change his understanding of the data as they appeared in his written text, but it enabled him to see them in different ways and added new dimensions and depth to his knowledge, bringing all of his senses into play. Audience members attested to how the dance had brought to life the range of emotions experienced by parents of children with special needs; and how these contrasted with the more bureaucratic world of officialdom (2001: 234).

The same critique has been made of performance texts as has been made of poetry. We have all been to third-rate plays, and found the seats uncomfortably hard. Snow and Morrill (1995: 361), ask: 'Do not playwrights and screenwriters have a better eye and feel for that possibility than we do? And why not leave the enactment of our texts to those who are skilled in the arts of the theatre and dramatic presentation?' For some, performances may do too much. One member of Bagley and Cancienne's audience said the written text would have been sufficient for her, and she would have preferred to use her own imagination. Atkinson (2004) has other concerns. He points out that many performative texts share autobiographical literary modes. Half of the examples in Denzin's (2003a) book on the subject are based on biographical pieces, 'part memoir, part essay, part autoethnography', intended to be read aloud. The argument is that, as with some poems, they gain maximum effect by being presented in that way. Atkinson sees a danger here of 'collapsing the social world into one's own lifeworld' and a 'risk of trivialising complex and serious social issues' (2004: 110). He feels that, so far, performativists have taken too narrow an approach and that they might avail themselves of more of the range of performative media that are available. Cancienne (herself a trained dancer) *et al.* show some of the possibilities.

HYPERMEDIA TEXTS

Advances in technology and new media are bringing opportunities that broaden and enrich modes of representation in other ways. Prominent among these are hypertext and hypermedia. Mason and Dicks (2004: 2) define hypertext as 'a form of text that is computer-mediated and contains authored "links" that create associations between different elements in the hypertext'. The term 'hypermedia' is applied to 'hypertexts which incorporate other media such as video, photographic images, sound, graphics and so on' (*ibid.*).

The key feature of hypertext is that it is multi-linear. It does not tell just one story, but offers several different options to the reader, who decides which one to explore (Nielson 1990) or even to create. By clicking on buttons, the reader can go to different points in the data, find similar instances, cross-refer among different kinds of data, tune in to extracts from related literature. These are more examples of 'writerly' rather than 'readerly' texts, enabling readers to 'become, in a sense, authors of their own reading' (Coffey and Atkinson 1996: 10). The author might still construct a number of interpretative pathways. Mason and Dicks (2004: 8) see the reader as 'visitor' with themselves as 'guides':

> In the same manner that a visitor to the heritage museum can take a tour, ask the guide questions, browse around the exhibits, go to the help desk if she gets lost and so on, then the visitor to the EHE [ethnographic hypermedia environment] will always see a help desk on the screen, can click on the tour hall to take a tour, and so on.

However, the author's paths may always be 'supplemented and subverted by the reader' (*ibid.* 2004: 4).

Hypertext gives qualitative researchers more scope to present the complex multi-connectedness of their data. It

> allows many different voices to be brought into creative juxtaposition with each other, through the possibility of incorporating many different

kinds of text and data archive. The fact that the ethnographer can assemble a web-based EHE that is linked explicitly to all kinds of other texts, and through them, ultimately to the rest of the web, means that the field can be more clearly represented as intertextual and interpenetrated than could easily be suggested by the conventional printed book form.

(Mason and Dicks 2004: 3)

It 'creates all kinds of multiple links between both the data assembled and the interpretative texts which comment upon these data' (*ibid.*).

Meaning is no longer carried just by written text with whatever other forms of representation that appear being used simply for illustration. Sound, video, photographs and so on convey *meaning*, and different forms of meaning, in their own right. Mason and Dicks (p. 5) give the example, 'By editing together sequences shot with a digital video camera in the field, particular meanings can be encoded which, when juxtaposed to written text of various kinds, produce quite unexpected and multi-semiotic layers of meaning'. Not only can whole transcripts of interviews be made available, but videos of them also. This enables much more of the full body of meaning to be conveyed – the nuances of inflection and tone, body language, facial expressions and physical context.

There seems little doubt that hypermedia is, or will become, a major growth area in qualitative research. One project currently in progress at Cardiff University is exploring the use of new digital technologies in data collection, analysis and authoring. The research team point out that the combination of visual and print media in the construction of ethnography has been underdeveloped, and that this can be creatively rectified in a hypermedia environment. They aim to produce an environment suitable for both the organisation and analysis of the data by the researcher and the representation of that analysis to a reader. They will develop 'hypermedia narratives', and highlight the range of new skills, expertise and technical resources that will be required. No doubt these will soon feature strongly in qualitative research methods courses. (See the website for the latest developments: http://www.cardiff.ac.uk/socsi/hyper/).

Let us consider one example of a hypermedia production, that of *videopapers*. There has been much debate about the gap between mainstream educational research and educational practice. Hargreaves (1996), for example, controversially argued that researchers had developed their own arcane discourse and had had little impact upon the work of schools and teachers. Part of the discourse entailed the researcher being the knowledge-producer and the teacher the knowledge-receiver (Bartels 2003; John 2003). Other than in teacher 'action research', the teacher had no voice in the production of knowledge that was directed toward improving her own practice.

In consequence, Olivero *et al.* (2004) advocate multimedia representations of educational knowledge which 'integrate the visual, aural, oral and physical cues that are part of the natural world of communication of teachers' which are often lost in print versions' (p. 182). Videopapers contain video, text, slides and hyperlinks, which can all be synchronised. For example,

> When reading the text one can play the part of the video related to it; and when watching the video one can jump to the text describing it. The slides section may contain further explanatory elements thus adding to the video or they can be examples of student work; they might even be interactive Java applets that can be manipulated using a software application.
>
> (Olivero et al. 2004: 182)

Videopapers thus carry some of the advantages noted above:

- They enable readers to interact with the content through the links.
- They give readers control over their reading. They can 'select the pages to view, watch and analyse pieces of video data, pause and expand time as they go along, experiment with other interactive content, conduct further research following the hyperlinks, etc' (Olivero et al. 2004: 184).
- Readers are brought closer to the data, which they can interpret in the light of their own practice.

A teacher involved with the project attests to the authenticity of videopapers:

> This is real. You can see it. When you read some of these journals with research in them, I sometimes think 'did they just make it up' in an afternoon so they could publish something? The writing they do just doesn't link with practice, it's about different things. It makes me suspicious of their motives but with this you can see it's real – there is a real teacher, the kids are real, it's a real classroom – you can see that. She is having real problems, noisy machines, noisy guys, messing around.
>
> (Olivero et al. 2004: 187–8)

Hypertext, hypermedia and digital ethnography will probably become common in time as researchers develop and get used to them, and solve initial problems. They will not replace book or film, which have their own advantages, but they add considerably to the researcher's armoury.

CRITERIA FOR QUALITY IN ALTERNATIVE TEXTS

What makes for adequacy in the kinds of writing discussed in this chapter? There is no single standard. Indeed, Clough (2000) has pointed out that any attempt to establish a common set of criteria would rapidly conventionalise experimental writing. Bearing this in mind, these are some of the qualities that have been variously suggested. They are a mixture of the literary, aesthetic and political and recall the features discussed earlier.

- Some might argue that the same warrants are necessary as for realist texts, based on clarity of claims made and supporting evidence. Experimental writers and performers on the whole, though, are less interested in 'validity' as traditionally defined and are generally wary of hard and fast criteria. We have seen Richardson's (2000: 936) notion of 'crystallisation'. She argues that there is no one 'right' way to present a text, but many different ways depending on our aims and audience. 'Material' is a constant in mass if not in form in her discussion, like 'wet clay for us to shape'. Denzin speaks of 'verisimilitude' which comes from an account that 'gives the context of an experience, states the intentions and meanings that organised the experience, and reveals the experience as a process' (1994: 505).

- Have you captured a likeness, some quality in the social scene or actors under consideration, that comes from an 'enlightened eye' (Eisner 1991: 17)? Typically, this kind of insight and understanding will have been acquired through the intensive methods outlined in the Introduction, and will enable you to portray something 'true to life' (*ibid.*: 108). Lofland (1971) calls this 'deep' or 'intimate' familiarity, Denzin (2003b: 248) 'interpretive sufficiency' and Ellis and Bochner (1996) talk of 'experiential sense' of the events.

- Are you able to communicate this to others, to provoke interest, awaken their interpretive powers, increase understanding, provide new insights, arouse feeling, enable readers to see something that they otherwise would have missed? This is 'representational adequacy' (Denzin 2003b: 248). Ellis (in Ellis and Bochner 1996: 18) talks of using 'narrative strategies to transport readers into experiences and make them feel as well as think'. Tierney (1993: 303) wants to ask of an account, among other things, 'What is learned from the text . . . Are there lessons to be learned from the text for my own life . . . has the text enabled me to reflect on my own life and work?' Whether the writing 'moves' the reader is a key factor, and one that can never be assessed until after the account has been written – though drafts can be tested on colleagues. It is a matter of truth, like beauty, being in the eye of the beholder, and the beholder's ability to convey that to others. There is something here of the potential for relating to others, of 'being at one with others', and in Richardson's terms, 'knowing about lived experiences'. The validity here is in the group recognition, awareness and identification. Since one of the main means at our disposal in this quest is our own feelings, these should be represented in the account. These considerations lead to a further point, about audiences. Scientific research speaks mainly to the academic community. The new genres spread the net more widely. They increase accessibility, speaking directly to the reader's experiences.

- There is no one single, correct way to capture a reality, any more than there is to paint a picture or take a photograph. But the brushwork of the writer will be evident in such qualities as the skilful and accurate use of language, lucidity, linkages and flow, '*les mots justes*', succinctness, how strikingly a point is made, how well a story or account hangs together, how much it 'rings true' within the experience of the reader. Atkinson (1991: 169) refers to ' "lightness of touch" whereby other authors, studies, and empirical parallels are filled in and elaborated on; the appositeness of those comparisons and contrasts; the extent to which they reveal "imagination" and depart from the obvious and hackneyed'.

- Writers need an 'ethical self-consciousness' and should make their own moral and political values clear.
- The writing should be purposeful and useful. It should relate to an issue of public importance and tell us something new. Coffey and Atkinson warn that 'there is a danger in such exercises of producing emotional or aesthetic effects simply for the sake of producing them. They can appeal to inappropriately self-indulgent displays of cleverness on the part of the author' (1996: 129). Eisner (2001: 139) tells of how in one performance presentation at a conference, he witnessed a coffin and pallbearers being used, the significance of which entirely evaded him. This is the criterion of relevance. Walford (2004) gave up an attempt at an autoethnography because he judged it failed this criterion.
- The analytic frame in which the expressive writing occurs should be clear. Lofland (1974: 108) feels that analysis and expression should be 'interpenetrated'. Thus, Payne (1996: 50) tells two stories in tandem: 'a personal narrative of my experience working at a factory over 20 years ago and a theoretical discussion woven around my contemplation of that experience'. Ellis (in Ellis and Bochner 1996: 30–1) feels that analysis might be an intrusion on the emotional experience of expressive writing, but in Payne's case, 'the analytical sections orchestrate an experiential atmosphere', and provide him with a means of 'extricating his body from its ideologically institutionalised inscriptions'.
- How well are the author and others represented in the text? Has the author provided enough information of self and his/her engagement with the research to enable the reader to see how the text has been constructed? To what extent are the voices of others fairly represented in the account, and not modified to fit the author's own tale? Acker *et al.* (1983: 431) feel that 'The first criterion of adequacy in this approach is that the active voice of the subject should be heard in the account'. What implications, then, does this have for the voice of the author? Richardson (1990: 27–8) concludes that 'As qualitative researchers, we can more easily write as situated, positioned authors, giving up, if we choose, our *authority* over the people we study, but not the responsibility of *authorship* over our texts'. In other words, there is a place for both faithful representation of the voices of others and the sociologist's analysis.
- Some prioritise political criteria, emphasising that 'the personal is political' (Ellis 2002: 403). Does the writing empower readers, offering them a form of resistance to the forces that dominate them and hence a means to social transformation? Denzin (2003b: 248) calls this 'authentic adequacy'. He wants an ethnography that 'stirs up the world, that causes trouble, that refuses to give narrative order to a universe which is absurd and often

violent' (Denzin 2004: 731). He wants ethnography to be 'messy, performative, poetic, reflexive, autoethnographical and critical' (p. 734). His
vision of the future sees scholars being committed to

> Not just describing the world, but also to changing it. Their texts will
> be performance based. They will be committed to creating civic trans-
> formations, and to using minimalist social theory. They will inscribe
> and perform utopian dreams, dreams shaped by critical race theory,
> dreams of a world where all are free to be who they choose to be,
> free of gender, class, race, religious or ethnic prejudice or discrimina-
> tion. The next moment in qualitative inquiry will be one where the
> practices of performance ethnography finally move, without hesitation
> or encumbrance, from the personal to the political.
>
> (Denzin 2003b: 261)

You might choose some of these criteria and reject others, or you might
subscribe to most in varying degrees. Some might prioritise literary and
aesthetic criteria, others scientific. Some might have more political intent,
like Denzin; others, like Hammersley (1993) and Flaherty (2002) might feel
the object of their research is to promote understanding of human conduct
and experience, and to produce knowledge. Some, like Lather (1991), in her
concept of 'catalytic validity', marry heightened understanding to action –
you have to understand the world before you can transform it. Your selection
of criteria will depend on your stance on knowledge, and you will need to be
clear about this before you embark on much experimentation.

How can we learn to meet these criteria? We cannot just become novelists,
poets and dramatists. In the USA, where innovative writing is being pion-
eered, those in the forefront of the movement hold conferences, organise
meetings, edit a specialist journal, *Qualitative Inquiry*, produce numerous articles and books. Many run creativity training exercises, writing seminars and
courses for their students, and put on workshops on creative enhancement
and creative writing. The advice would be therefore to undertake courses,
attend conferences, seminars, workshops where they are available, read and
study what has been and is being produced; check online from time to time;
and keep an eye on the journals, especially those that regularly feature examples
and discussion of alternative writing, such as *The Journal of Contemporary
Ethnography, Qualitative Research* and *The International Journal of Qualitative
Studies in Education*. Richardson (2000: 941–3) recommends joining a creative
writing group, working through a creative writing guidebook, enrolling on a
creative writing workshop or class, applying creative writing skills to writing
up fieldnotes, keeping a diary on a narrative of the self, writing a 'writing'
autobiography and other reflexive pieces on your writing, transforming
fieldnotes into drama or an interview into a poem, writing about settings and
studying events from different role positions, writing a 'layered' text, writing
your data in three different ways, writing the same piece of material for
different audiences, collaborative writing of different kinds. Piirto (2002)

thinks that all students should write a poem, a story, a song or a drama; and that generally some arts-based background and experience is advisable. I would say you would have to have a 'feel' for this sort of approach, an arts 'mind', which causes you to identify with and be drawn towards such experimentation. You would have to be prepared to take more risks than is likely in standard writing, and to fail more often, at least in the early stages. Otherwise, I can do no better than repeat the advice given in Chapter 2 to read good literature, poetry, attend plays, go to the ballet or opera, visit art galleries, listen to music. These are enjoyable projects in themselves, but the experience also helps refine our sensibilities, stimulates the imagination, feeds into our appreciation of human expression and possibly enriches our own powers of representation, whether we indulge in experimental writing or not.

CONCLUSION

There is a danger that an 'experimentalist' zeitgeist will promote a belief that 'anything goes', spawning a mass of ill-founded, dilettantish studies. Yet they could be quite the reverse of this, contributing to better understanding and better-founded knowledge. For the quest is accuracy of, and depth of, understanding, and for ways of conveying that to others which keep faith with that accuracy and depth. Many experimental texts are not at variance with the validity model with its reliance on evidence, as outlined in the Introduction. The 'evidence' is in the power and credibility of the writing. It is not necessarily anti-realist. Its warrant lies in its ability to portray different kinds and aspects of realities.

These are aims basic to all kinds of qualitative research. Thus, most researchers, concerned about truth criteria and how you demonstrate validity, do not see these new approaches as a paradigm shift, and adhere to the traditional model, while keeping minds open about new developments. Bailey (1996: 108) notes that these forms of writing 'are not for everyone . . . they are still not the standard style. Many field researchers situate their writing between realist tales and experimental writing'. This is my own position. I see no reason to abandon established criteria of worth in academic representation, but I do feel that some of these new forms promise to reach parts of social understanding that established methods cannot. Denzin (1994: 501) refers to the researcher as writer as a 'bricoleur', who 'fashions meaning and interpretation out of ongoing experience', and 'uses any tool or method that is readily to hand'. As Maines (2001: 109) puts it: 'We should try to find the most useful and appropriate voice, distance, information formats and interpretive frames and devices for the empirical and analytic concerns at hand'. It is a question of fitness for purpose.

It has to be noted, too, that there are times when 'readerly' texts might fit the purpose, that is when writers have something to say, when they want to get a message across and do not wish that to be misconstrued in a variety of meanings that readers might attribute. They do not have to demean others in their texts, whose voices can still be heard and which can strengthen the central argument. But among the readers may be interest groups and people with a particular axe to grind, who will make whatever capital they can out of your text. Politicians and journalists are particularly adept at this. The moral is for authors to make every effort to say what *they* mean as clearly and as fully as possible, perhaps anticipating and heading off some of the alternatives. Richardson (1990: 52–3) avers, 'You cannot finally control how readers will respond to your work, but you can use literary devices to up the odds in favour of others understanding your point of view – that is of responding to what you *intend* to communicate'.

Karl Popper (1968: 226) compares the status of truth 'to that of a mountain peak which is permanently wrapped in clouds'. We might not be able to see it, we might have difficulty getting to it, and we might not even know we are there when we arrive, but we know that it is there. The new methods provide us with some navigation instruments that might enhance our view, and enable us to see a little further through the mist – and to describe what we see when we get there.

5

Style

Ethnography is a game played with words.
(Ellis, in Ellis and Bochner 1996: 26)

The line between profundity and verbiage is often delicate,
even perilous.
(Mills 1959: 243)

I have already touched on how we say things in considering different forms of writing. I wish to enlarge on it in this chapter. This is not just a matter of clarity and conciseness. We might wish to convey a sense of atmosphere, ethos, mood or tone. As discussed in Chapter 4, we might want to represent feelings and emotions, to re-create people's experiences, to transport the reader to a scene in order to deepen understanding. We might want to explore some of our own innermost thoughts and feelings, in a way that promises to cast light on some general aspect of human experience. This is less a matter of categories and themes as presented in Chapter 3 (though these might still be helpful) and more one of expression. Some, such as free-flow or stream of consciousness writing, might be the exact structural opposite of those discussed in Chapter 3. How do you do these things? What forms and figures of speech are used? What textual strategies are there available? How are they used in academic writing? And how can we ensure their quality?

The answer to these questions lies in rhetoric. Qualitative reports of all kinds have traditionally been constructed using a number of rhetorical devices, the intention of which is to persuade the reader of the point of view being advanced by the author (Atkinson 1990). However, rhetoric has both abuses and uses. I consider each in turn before concluding with a note on personal style.

THE ABUSES OF RHETORIC

In components of the text

Among those commonly employed here are:

- *Use of words and phrases subtly designed to persuade without appearing to*, and without evidential support, as in the insertion of frequency or numerical terms such as 'most', 'often', 'seldom' and 'as is commonly recognised'.
- *Misuse of jargon*. We may fall into this in straining to show some theoretical richness in our work which really is not there. Specialist language is often required, but this sometimes runs to excess, and becomes pretentious and opaque. The satirical magazine *Private Eye* runs a column called 'Pseuds' corner'. Sociologists frequently feature in this.
- *Misuse of references*. Citations give an article the ring of academic credibility. Where used appropriately, of course, they are necessary, linking the article to other sources of related knowledge. But they may be peppered about indiscriminately, a technique Bassey (1995: 77) describes as 'sandbagging' – 'adding to a statement inert defences to make it look secure'. Or they may be partially (though not entirely, nor even mainly) relevant to a point. For example, in Hargreaves' (1988: 63) article, he claims that 'As Sikes, Measor and Woods (1985) have found in their life history interviews with second-ary teachers, many teachers regard examinations not as a constraint but as a resource for motivating pupils'. In fact, Sikes *et al.* had a sample of only 40 teachers drawn from science and art departments in two geographical areas. 'Some' teachers would have been a more accurate description. Cita-tions may also be used to indicate a taken-for-granted point, 'what every-body knows', but which still has to be argued for within the context, as with 'labelling' or 'scaffolding' or 'triangulation' . Some of these terms become hackneyed through overuse, and one wonders if their meaning becomes warped as they are passed from one text to another with no actual engagement, rather as in the game of Chinese whispers. In a similar way, 'genuflection' involves 'ritualistic citing of the founding parents of theory' (Bassey 1995: 77).
- *Misuse of quotations*. Quotations enrich a text, but not if they are too lengthy, inappropriate or numerous, or used out of context. By the last point, I mean quoting a piece by, say, lifting a phrase out of a section of text, which by being placed in your text has a different connotation. I was surprised on one occasion to receive a catalogue from a publisher which included in support of one of the books advertised part of a sentence from a review I had written which had been almost entirely critical. Quotations are usually employed because they make a point in a unique and particu-larly telling way; they blend in with the text; they add support and interest.
- *Misuse of acknowledgements and blurbs*. Naturally people wish to thank those who have helped them, but sometimes long lists of these are presented containing a number of highly respected people who may have only had marginal or no association with the construction of the text. Despite the author's claim of full responsibility for the manuscript, those cited nonethe-less lend their authority to the text. Ben-Ari (1995: 135–6) argues that 'acknowledgements . . . may be devised to do a whole range of things like show, report, camouflage, hide, command, beg, maintain, reason, qualify or

inform about a certain order or state'. Wolcott (2001: 146–8) recommends keeping a note of those who have assisted, which resolves the problem of overload, and also the equivalent crime of leaving out people who have lent support in significant ways.

- *Loaded choice of pseudonyms*. Pseudonyms are essential to protect identities, but sometimes the choice carries connotations. 'Mr Megaphone', for example, is one of the teachers in Beynon's (1985) study. The tutors in Riseborough's (1992) ethnography of catering and hotel management students are given names like 'Mrs Hygiene', 'Mrs Metropole', 'Miss Motel', 'Mr Pastry', 'Mrs Silver-Service' and 'Mr Fivestar', while the students are all given proper pseudonyms like 'Ben' and 'Anne'. These are no doubt selected to symbolise the authors' views of the persons involved, but they are loaded views. Mr Megaphone could be regarded as hyperbole – exaggeration for the sake of emphasis or humour. Riseborough's similarly are humorous, but might be seen as demeaning the tutors while upholding the students' rights to be considered more human.
- *Use of subtle, unacknowledged and unsubstantiated rhetorical devices* such as metaphor, simile, synecdoche, metonymy and irony. These are essential tools of the writer's trade, but they need to be recognised and acknowledged, not used subversively.

In using the whole of the text: rhetorical spins

This is where the author, commonly through use of rhetoric, puts a particular, biased construction on a text. Common forms of spin are:

- *Constructing a 'straw person'*. There is a strong temptation to work on a principle of contrasts. Thus, in an attempt to highlight one's own argument and increase its purity and force, you might construct an apology of an opposing one that does not really exist. It is a kind of bastardised ideal type, drawing on the perceived evils of certain positions and gluing them together into a Frankenstein's monster of a case. The straw person typically draws on the work of a number of people and in itself is recognisable as nobody. A similar form of misrepresentation is to seize on only those points within one person's position that serve the present purpose, ignoring their context, which may well modify those points. This is error enough in itself, but the major sin is inadequately contextualising one's own work within the field. It might be argued that the claim by several writers inspired by postmodernist ideas that there is a 'crisis' in representation falls into this category, together with the view that there has been a literary (and/or a narrative, performative and hypermedia) 'turn'. There is a tendency here to overstate the case and to draw battle lines between one kind of writing and another (Tierney 2002: 430). Friedman (2004) identifies a number of different variants of what he calls 'strawmanning', noting how it fails to recognise overlaps and developmental opportunities in some apparently oppositional approaches, and instead encourages the hardening of camps. Of course, people who disagree with the representation of their position and their analysis also, on occasions, shout 'Foul! Straw person!' when it is real flesh and blood.

• *Putting a slant on the text.* Edmondson (1984, reported in Atkinson 1991) draws attention to how this is done in some ethnographies. Thus, Willis (1977), in the book discussed in Chapter 3, arranges his text in the form of engaging, descriptive ethnography in the first half of his book, and rather dense theory in the second. This disposes the reader to be sympathetic to the 'lads" deviant behaviour, which might otherwise be castigated. Further, the more amusing aspects of their culture are placed first before the more condemnatory categories of 'sexism' and 'racism'. Edmondson also feels that examples of the categories, selected perhaps to illustrate typicality, probably, 'exhibit particularly concentrated cases of what happens generally but, perhaps, less remarkably' (1984: 50). He might have added that a disproportionate number of comments came from one lad. Another problem comes from qualitative researchers' heavy dependence on transcripts. As noted in Chapter 4, there is a tendency to select quotations, or parts of quotations, from transcripts out of their original context and meanings to fit the author's preferred account.

• *Being sexist or racist.* At a surface level, this might involve the use of masculine forms such as 'he', 'him' or 'man' when both sexes are indicated. It might permeate the text in deeper ways. Richardson (1993: 705) claims that:

> In sociological research, the findings have been safely staged within the language of the father, the domain of science writing. 'Louisa May' challenges the language, tropes, emotional suppressions and presumptive validity claims of masculinist social science . . . Poetics strips these methodological bogeymen of their power to control and constrain . . . In feminist writings of poets and social scientists, the position of the author is linked aesthetically, politically, emotionally, with those about whom they write . . . [The aim is] knowing about lived experiences which are unspeakable in the 'father's voice', the voice of objectivity.

However, while many traditional research texts may be of this kind, I would say this has more to do with the writer than the approach. Social scientific realist research and writing have made their own contribution to such causes as anti-sexism and anti-racism.

• *Over-claiming.* This often accompanies a straw person. You might get carried away by excitement and enthusiasm as ideas emerge, and in attempting to make the most of the argument in the strongest terms, overstate the case. It is often only when the product is seen in print that this is recognised. The initial exuberance has faded, and a more rational evaluation can take place. There are pressures on us to over-claim which we need to recognise and resist. It has often been remarked that only positive research gets reported. We need to make our research tell and count. We are therefore looking for opportunities to 'excel'.

- *Under-claiming.* This derives from an unwarranted modesty or failure to perceive possibilities. The report may be written 'down' in an inconsequential way, set in a rather lugubrious context with the disadvantages of the method stressed over the advantages, and the weaknesses rather than strengths stressed in conclusion. By oversight, there may be missed opportunities, unspotted connections and relevance. Here especially one stands to gain from the comments of others.

- *Utopianism.* This is an imaginary state of ideal perfection. It is not necessarily a fault if recognised for what it is. At times, however, Utopian suggestions are put forward as practical possibilities. The research then becomes predicated on an otherworldly base and loses credibility. As in the case of the straw person, however, there might be arguments as to what is Utopian and what is not. A form of Utopianism leads, on occasion, to mysticism. Unwilling to commit thoughts to the impurity of the printed page, we may cloak them in obscurity and advance them as an 'ongoing exploration of minds'. Unfortunately it is a journey without end, on which we are likely to be lone travellers.

- *Constructing deficit models.* There is a tendency to identify failings in groups that we study – particularly those with power over other groups, and, having done that, to prescribe what should be done. This might be expected in studies set up to be evaluatory, but in general in social scientific research this is not recommended. It too often sounds as if the target group is inferior, or failing, and the researcher is superior, magisterial and in possession of some all-wise knowledge. Thus, for example, it used to be fairly common to talk of certain working-class children as being from 'deficit cultures', when they were in fact from very rich cultures in their own right. Similarly, researchers have been known to treat teachers as an inferior group. However, it is out of place for researchers to tell teachers what they should do on the basis of research they have done at their school. This is not simply a matter of etiquette – more often than not researchers are not in possession of all the knowledge required to make practical decisions within any one location. They can make suggestions, which apart from anything else might stand more chance of being taken up. It can be a simple matter of certain words that affect the whole construction of what is written and imply deficit on the part of teachers: 'Inadequate . . .', 'Insufficient . . .', 'Failed to . . .', 'It should be remembered that . . .'. The same data, however, can often be treated in positive as well as, or instead of, negative ways. For example, in representing teachers' application of a policy, negatively you might stress what they did not do, rather than what they did. The same points could be made by stressing the positive aspects, and then suggesting where else the policy might be applied. Material can be anonymised or generalised, so that the finger of blame is not being pointed at a specific target. The focus can be on policies, practices and issues, rather than particular people and schools.

- *A related problem is that of tone.* You can meet all the other criteria of good writing and still not be happy with how you are making a point. If it is not said properly it can have the opposite effect to that desired. Perhaps you are being too omniscient, condemnatory, condescending, patronising, facile, superior, unreasonable, unsympathetic, prescriptive, moralistic, evaluatory, judgemental. Striking an appropriate note for the main readership is not an easy task, and it might take several drafts before you get it right. Some examples:

  'It would appear that this was an opportunity lost by the teachers to provide relevant cultural and linguistic support in the classrooms.' (This observation came after a point about bilingual support staff not being asked to work with children in their mother tongue. It could be put more positively in the form of a suggestion, perhaps in the conclusion.)

  'There are also black dolls for the children to play with, though often black dolls have European features, therefore there is a need to seek out dolls who truly reflect black or Asian cultures.' (The last sentence about 'need' is redundant, and patronises teachers – they do not need it spelled out in such a way. Again, it could be rephrased as a suggestion, and used later in a summary.)

  'In this way there was not a clear understanding of the educational benefits of play within the unit.'

  'In this way particular aspects of the ways in which children's thinking changed in relation to these activities were not recognised.'

  'Aspects of children's development remained unrecognised or misunderstood by the educator.' (These examples are in the first instance an empirical matter. Is there evidence to support them? Even if there is, it is unlikely to warrant such sweeping conclusions. Then it has to be asked, even if warranted, if this is the best way of making the point.)

Reviewing one's own past work can be helpful in assessing one's own tone. Diamond (1993), a teacher, educator and researcher, for example revisited one of his published papers, and wondered why it was written quite as it was. There was certainly an over-dominant professorial voice, he concludes. The introduction and the conclusion are a 'little too hortatory . . . Some of the expressions and the appropriations in the paper seem a little too strident . . . the use of 33 citations shows an over-reliance on the voices of others'. He recognises that he has a number of voices, and is 'sorting out which of my voices is the overbearing, silencing one and when my other more tentative voices need to be heard. My third person voice needs to express itself less as a censor and more as a collaborator' (p. 514).

- *Sloppiness.* This is too casual writing, showing careless errors and/or inadequate thought during analysis and planning. There might be wild claims without proper evidence, ambiguities, inconsistencies, non-sequiturs, contradictions. Many of these can be ironed out in later drafts, but if the general structure has not been adequately conceptualised, there is no alternative but to start again.

- *Over-zealousness.* I argued in Chapter 2 for a productive tension between planning and freedom. Too much of the latter leads to sloppiness; too much of the former to over-zealousness. The ideal situation is where the free-ranging mind can produce ideas that are then subjected to methodological rigour. It is difficult to work the process the other way round. Too much concern with the proprieties of method and *le mot juste* at this early stage can lead to a barren product. It is like batting immaculately for a whole session yet scoring no runs, or rigorously scrubbing some clothes – the product ends up scrupulously clean but threadbare. Ideas must be allowed space and time to germinate. They will quickly rot if they are no good, but they will certainly never take root if not sown and cultivated.
- *Over-exactness.* This is too neat an account. There is pressure on us – from research sponsors, publishers and the academic world at large – to be meticulously tidy, to present our work in ordered packages, duly itemised, sectionalised and sequenced. However, as we have seen, qualitative data does not always lend itself to neatness. The problem is how to convey the sense of flux, process, messiness, inconsistency and ambiguity, which is the very essence of everyday life. This is difficult to do while also trying to derive some theoretical order from the material. It is easy to slip into a previous, inappropriate, presentational framework, and make categories and types too sharp and distinct, and the account rather too four-square. The greatest danger of this comes when seeking to use earlier models or theoretical constructions. An extreme example of this I saw once involved a 4 × 4 matrix where the author had felt pressured to produce a type for every square. The result was to make a nonsense of the matrix, for most of the types could have gone anywhere.

THE USES OF RHETORIC

Despite the warnings above, rhetoric is an essential part of qualitative writing. Authors have to be skilled in and conscious of its use. Here is another criterion of quality to add to those listed towards the end of Chapter 4. I consider here three of the potential advantages of rhetoric – in writing for different audiences, metaphor and expressive writing.

Writing for different audiences

Different purposes and different audiences require different styles of writing. Using the same material, we can employ a journalistic style for a brief report in a weekly magazine; an interactional, conversational style for a teaching document; or a theoretical, academic style for a learned journal. Richardson (1990) has a useful discussion on 'writing for diverse audiences'. From the same piece of research on single women involved with married men she produced academic publications and a 'trade book', *The New Other Woman* (1985), written for both lay and professional audiences and designed to have a 'liberatory effect on its readers' (1990: 32). Five major devices shaping the 1990 book were:

- *Encoding*. The language and literary devices that are used. For a trade book this would involve 'jazzy titles, attractive covers, lack of specialised jargon, marginalisation of methodology, common-world metaphors and images, and book blurbs and prefatory material about the 'lay' interest in the material' (p. 32). There would be fewer references. Substantive issues of interest to the audience, and examples, would be brought to the fore. Such an approach thus becomes more humanised. Compare academic encoding, which would follow the lines of the articles discussed in Chapter 3, and of postgraduate theses, and would be theoretical, methodological, and contain appropriate academic terms and references.
- *Narrative stance*. There are many narrative styles – such as letting those studied tell the story through interview transcript, author telling the story or stories, biography or experimental writing. Richardson opted for 'analytical chronologies' (p. 37) – the collective story of the subjects of the research enmeshed in a sociological narrative.
- *Tone*. Richardson was concerned not to appear omniscient, and to have respect for those she wrote about, not treating them as ciphers. So she brings the subjects' voices to the fore, and through her choice of language, terms and quotations, and by intermingling the sociological analysis, she 'decentres' herself as the ultimate authority (p. 39).
- *Structuring quotations and biographical narratives*. Richardson recommends 'variety in format and voice':

  > You can use one-line quotations, sometimes standing by themselves, sometimes in droves; mid-length quotations by themselves or mixed with one-liners; short phrases quoted within the body of the narrative; longer quotations broken into paragraphs . . . Similarly, including quotes with a variety of language patterns, images, slang, and regionalisms makes texts both more alive and more credible. (p. 40)

  Because quotes are often skipped over by the reader, careful attention has to be given to how they are presented and contextualised.
- *Synecdoche*. This is a rhetorical device wherein a part stands for the whole, or vice versa. The whole of Richardson's book is a synecdoche, in that the 'other woman' is seen not as a deviant case, 'but *exemplifies* in very import-ant respects, the lives of normal contemporary women' (p. 47). This, in fact, is often the case with marginal or apparently deviant groups – they reveal in sharp relief characteristics that apply to a whole population. They make good 'critical cases' therefore. A great deal of qualitative research is synecdochal in this way. Richardson thus tried to meet both literary and

sociological criteria, and to make a difference – for the 'other woman' to be better understood, and for all women to feel more empowered 'to alter the civic discourse about and social opportunities for normal women' (p. 48).

Not all authors enjoy the luxury of various outlets for their writing. What, then, about writing for academic and non-academic audiences in the same text? The risk is that neither will be satisfied. It might be too sociological for teachers, with its applications to teaching policy and practice unclear, thus attracting the common criticisms from teachers of being 'woolly', 'opaque' and 'irrelevant'; and/or it may be too atheoretical for sociologists, for them offering little more than 'tips for teachers'. The challenge is to amalgamate the two, and to demonstrate that any recommendations for practice are theoretically grounded. One way to do this is to compose a chapter in the usual way, then to frame suggestions for practice based on the discussion at the end of each chapter. In that way, analysis and practice are separated, but firmly linked theoretically.

It is helpful to have clear criteria to guide your drafting. Your writing should be:

- *Honest to the research and to yourself.* It must be true to the data, and to your own and to generally accepted values of rigour in research.
- *Full.* Part of the honesty, leaving nothing relevant out, and not being unduly selective.
- *Accurate.* The representation must reflect the point wishing to be made.
- *Fair.* This is crucial in this context. A paragraph might be unduly critical of teachers, for example – it is not 'fair'. In an attempt to correct for this, one might move to the other extreme and remove all suggestion of criticism, thus not being 'honest'.
- *Balanced.* Part of the fairness.

Metaphor

> And, Sir, as to metaphorical expression, that is a great excellence in style, when it is used with propriety, for it gives you two ideas for one; conveys the meaning more luminously, and generally with a perception of delight.
>
> (Samuel Johnson, quoted in Lucas 1974: 218)

> Metaphor, a literary device, is the backbone of social scientific writing.
>
> (Richardson 2000: 926)

Among the various rhetorical devices, metaphors are particularly significant. They are 'the life of style' (Lucas 1974: 76). People in ordinary life find them useful in seeking expression or self-understanding, and they are a main source of concepts for researchers seeking to make sense of and to represent data or ideas. Examples of the latter are 'grapevining' (as in Chapter 3), 'labelling', 'scaffolding', the 'ripple effect', 'cultural capital', 'presentation of front', 'front' and 'back regions', 'Balkanisation', 'interaction sets', 'status passages', 'gatekeepers', 'knife-edging' and 'triangulation'. All of these encapsulate the essence of a concept and enable us to see it. It is this ability to see that advances our understanding, sometimes with a 'eureka!' type feeling, since we can transfer our common knowledge frameworks from the one to the other. Thus 'scaffolding' works beautifully for describing and explaining how a teacher incrementally might help children build their own learning until such time when the child's grasp means the scaffolding can be removed; and 'triangulation' transfers the strength of triangles as seen in bicycles, house roofs, gates and astronomy to the enhanced validity of research methods used in a number of combinations brought to bear on the same item.

Teaching provides a fruitful resource for metaphor, because of the manifold, complex, often conflictual and emotionally laden nature of the tasks and roles involved. This is as true for the inmates as it is for researchers. The teacher has been depicted, among other things, as orator, actor, preacher, comedian, artist, child-minder, prison warder, sergeant-major, Hitler, counsellor and parent. Each of these analogies draws attention in an arresting and vivid way to a particular aspect of the teacher's role, as viewed by the one attributing the metaphor. Similarly, schools and/or classrooms have been described as 'mad-houses', 'circuses', 'prisons', 'battlefields' and 'war zones'. In war zones, teachers 'go over the top' when they leave the security of the staffroom for the classroom, have 'battles' with or 'wage campaigns' against groups of pupils or individual pupils, 'shoot down' troublesome individuals, talk of 'winning' or 'being defeated'.

Bullough and Knowles (1991: 123) found the analysis of metaphors to be 'very promising' when seeking to identify the teaching self and the cluster of meanings that compose it: 'The search for metaphors, understood as "picture-preferences" (Bandman 1967, p. 112) or language-embedded images, is central to the struggle to give coherence to experience'. Thus, one of the teachers in their research tried to find himself through metaphor. He wanted to be a caring teacher who taught his subject well, but, in a tough school, felt driven to be more of a 'policeman'. He found himself consequently on a kind of 'emotional roller-coaster' (p. 106). 'I thought of a blind person or a young child or baby, who stumbles and falls, and bumps into walls, gets frustrated easily, and doesn't seem to really know what is going on or sees the bigger picture. No matter how much I realise this lack of perspective, it doesn't come any faster or easier' (*ibid.*). Teaching became for him a 'form of warfare' that had him feeling 'battle weary' and often in a state of 'siege mentality' and hoping for a 'truce' (pp. 108–9).

In more positive vein, Schulz (1998: 181) employed the metaphors of 'path' and 'journey' to make sense of the stories she collected from Nepalese women teachers on being and becoming a woman teacher. She felt the stories showed 'the path taken, the helping hand, the walking without stumbling, the taken-for-granted not seeing of the women, and the new vistas at every step' (quoted in Coffey and Delamont 2000: 66). Schulz had experienced the same kind of journey herself, so the metaphor was not only a useful descriptor, but helped the women teachers and researcher to understand and share a collective narrative. A similar sense of unity came over Aikan *et al.* (2003: 398) as the main author sat on a beach in Hawaii reading about 'third wave feminism' and watching the waves breaking on the shore. She wondered where the waves came from, how they worked, where one ended and another began. Surfers say waves come in threes, and you should go for the third. If miss it, there will be another set of threes soon. They stand with their backs to the shore, looking out to sea in eager anticipation. 'This metaphor for the movements of feminism allows us to keep in motion the fluidity and variation that exists within a single feminine cohort' (*ibid.*). Like surfers, therefore, they look to the horizon with eagerness and expectation as they wait for the next set of waves which will take them to different shores. This shows how a suggestive metaphor can lead the mind in new directions.

Metaphors can be so powerful as to provide the framework for whole articles – as with the 'grapevining' in Chapter 3. An article by Riseborough (1988) is quite instructive in this regard. He organised the whole life history of a teacher on the concept of the First World War, beginning with the title: 'The great Heddekashun war: a life historical cenotaph for an unknown teacher'. He called his teacher 'Tommy Atkins', a name attributed to all British soldiers in the war; and began with a quote from the war poet, Seigfried Sassoon:

> Do you remember the stretcher cases lurching back
> With dying eyes and lolling heads – those ashen grey
> Masks of the lads who once were keen and kind and gay?

Tommy Atkins was a veteran of the 'Conservative education offensive' under Margaret Thatcher which revolutionised the British education system during the late 1980s and 1990s. Riseborough traces Tommy's career from the 'Halcyon days' of his enjoyable early years in teaching, through the 'gathering storm' of falling rolls in the 1970s, which resulted in dangerous kids being taken into his school; to the 'first battle of the bureaucratic Somme: closure' at the end of the 1980s (when the school was closed, for economic reasons); through a 'court martial', when he was reprimanded for circulating a confidential document. He was experiencing 'battle fatigue' (and 'fighting a losing battle'), but eventually found 'peace' and went on 'convalescence to a B.Ed.'. However, this only led to 'The second battle of the bureaucratic Somme: compulsory redeployment to the maladjusted front' when he was sent to 'Flanders Field Maladjusted School' even though he had requested not to be sent to such a school. Problems there led to him having to take 'sick leave'. After this he got into 'Gallipoli FE College' which developed its own 'gathering storm'. But Tommy Atkins is not going to make any more trouble: 'When you are in a trench, best that you stay there, because once you are up and running for the wire, you're dead' (p. 223).

The article consists entirely of transcript, with this metaphorical framing. The metaphor fits well with the words of the transcript, and makes the whole impact more powerful than if it consisted of transcript alone. There is an ironic sense of humour, just as there used to be with the real tommies. And calling him Tommy Atkins indicates a typicality – 'Tommy's "history from below," his accommodations and resistances . . . is produced here as a monument to his generation of "education workers" . . . *Ab uno disce omnes, Mutato nomine, de te fabula narratur!* (from a single instance you may infer the whole. Change the name, and the story will apply to yourself!) (p. 197).

Such metaphors are not neutral. They put an interesting slant on the life history, but the framework for interpretation is seen in advance. Tommy's life of struggle is a consequence of the 'reactionary reconstruction' of the education system under Thatcher. It is class warfare. Riseborough is in danger here of falling into the 'over-claiming' rhetorical spin. But he makes his position clear from the outset, and the responsibility is then the reader's – this is what this man's life would look like, given this theoretical perspective. The man himself does not disapprove, joining in the metaphor from time to time.

This sort of link between theory and metaphor is well illustrated by Shaker (1990) in an article entitled 'The metaphorical journey of evaluation theory'. Over time, he argues, different theorists have depicted the evaluator as:

- superman (reliance on expert opinion: who can do anything, easily)
- controller, comptroller or auditor (objectives based approaches: measuring results against preordained goals)
- detective, scientist or intelligence officer (consumer-based, governed by loyalty to those served)
- judge, art critic or historian (naturalistic theorists: loyalty to abstract principles like truth)
- educator (reflective professional educators, educators of educators).

How do you decide on which metaphors to use? Some of the thought processes are given in the following examples.

Wallace *et al.* (1998: 182–3), in their article entitled 'Learning the ropes: accounts of within-school transition', provide some commentary on how they arrived at this metaphor depicting students' experiences of moving from one year grade to the next:

> We have played with a number of metaphors to conceptualise the dynamics of this process. We mentioned the head who talked of the process of 'finding a way through the jungle'. In other papers we have viewed it as a process of following someone else's script and of navigating the rocks . . . Neither metaphor quite captures the complexity of the students' active interchanges with a changing environment, drawing on family support systems. Here we have chosen the idea of learning the ropes. Learning the ropes (like navigation) has its origins in seafaring. The ropes were the rigging for masts, yards and sails on schooners and

other sailing ships. Learning the ropes was an essential skill if the rigging was to be set appropriately to catch the wind and navigate successfully. Top group students revealed in their responses how their rigging was in place (helped by homes, families and resources) and they were navigating the storms with some skill. The rest could never 'catch up'. Indeed, some preferred the revelling onshore and had never left port.

In seeking to illustrate the 'hidden curriculum' (itself carrying metaphorical overtones), Meighan (1981: 56) talks of the classroom as a 'haunted place'. It is haunted by:

- ghosts of the architects (activity is constrained by building design and space)
- ghosts of the book writers, resource designers and materials' producers (their inaccuracies, distortions and biases are embedded in their writing and designing, and may pass unrecognised and unchallenged)
- ghosts of our ancestors' language and thinking (containing unrecognised and unchallenged limitations, distortions and biases).

Meighan notes some difficulties with this analogy, one being that ghosts are commonly held to be illusory – unlike the hidden curriculum which has very real consequences, but nonetheless feels that

> It helps to locate the causes more accurately. Rather than assuming the malevolence or sinister nature of educators, these analogies suggest the possibilities of unwitting and unintended actions of those concerned and suggest a theory of a complex of causes. They are also optimistic analogies: ghosts can be laid . . .
>
> (p. 58)

What makes a good metaphor? It should help to clarify and to illuminate. It provides interest and variety, and can startle the reader into recognition by its unfamiliarity. It should add to the base description rather than just replicating it, for example by intimating how someone felt, or by making sharp contrasts. It should not exaggerate, mislead, or run away with itself into literary excess (and thus 'over-claim'). When an extended metaphor threatens to take over the description and facts are being modified, however slightly, to accommodate it, then it is time to reconsider its appropriateness. Also, within any one event or experience, where a series of metaphors are employed, they should have a consistency, as in the Riseborough example above. These help to integrate the experience – as a single good metaphor might do. Multiple functions should also be recognised; for example, some of those above might be regarded as coping strategies, creating humour by making surprising analogies. A teacher in one of our researches said the preparations for her school's inspection were like the sex act, 'lots of activity and noise and afterwards we're not fit to do anything else'. This does not really tell us much more about an inspection, other than that it is very exhausting, and it is difficult to see what else the two activities have in common, so it is not a good metaphor from the explanatory point of view. But it is a witty remark and is probably better seen as an example of coping through humour.

Metaphor is a powerful weapon with a hairline trigger. It can go off accidentally or backfire. It can make a loud noise to no effect. But if skilfully used, it can hit the mark.

Expressive writing

From time to time we might wish to employ a number of rhetorical devices to create atmosphere or convey feeling or reproduce an effect. Consider the following examples.

Example 1: Harry Wolcott (2002: 7–8) Sneaky Kid and its Aftermath: Ethics and Intimacy in Fieldwork

> Brad needed to cook. An open fire is slow and quite impractical on a rainy day. One needs a camp stove in order to cook inside a cabin. And fuel. And then a better stove. Cold water is all right for washing hands but it can be a bit too bracing for washing one's hair or torso, especially when outside with the wind blowing. One needs a bigger pan to heat water for bathing. Soap and shampoo. A towel. A new razor. A mirror. A bigger mirror. Foam rubber mattress. A chair. A chaise longue.
>
> One needs something to look at and listen to. Magazines are a brief diversion, but rock music is essential. One needs a radio. Flashlight batteries are expensive for continual radio listening; a radio operated by an automobile battery would be a better source – and could power a better radio. An automobile battery needs to be recharged. Carrying a battery to town is awkward, and constantly having to pay for battery charges is expensive. As well as access to a power supply (in my carport), one needs a battery charger. No, this one is rated too low; a bigger one is needed . . . Cigarettes (or tobacco), matches, eggs, bread, Tang, Crisco, pancake, flour, syrup – supplies get low. An occasional steak helps vary the austere diet.
>
> One needs transportation. A bicycle is essential, as are spare parts to keep it in repair. Now a minor accident: the bicycle is wrecked. No money to buy a new one. Brad 'hypes' himself up and sets out to find a replacement. Buy one? 'When they're so easy to get? No way.'

This is from Harry Wolcott's book mentioned in Chapter 3, and it prefigures a section entitled 'The cultural context of a free spirit'. While Brad claimed to be a 'free spirit' and could largely do without society, he was a product of his society: 'What he had learned to want was a function of his culture, and he drew narrowly and rather predictably from the cultural repertoire of the very society from which he believed he was extricating himself' (*ibid.*). Wolcott could have illustrated this more straightforwardly. Instead, he chooses a style which puts the reader in Brad's place, highlights the way in which one's needs escalate in a consumer society, how one dependency inescapably and rapidly leads to another, and how, if Brad is indeed living on the margins of society, it is still on the side within its orbit. These points are more effectively made here than they would be by any 'straight' writing. Interestingly, the book includes an ethnodrama based on the Brad story, which presents another way of experiencing the complexities involved.

Example 2: Frank McCourt (1996a: 1–2) Angela's Ashes

> Out in the Atlantic Ocean great sheets of rain gathered to drift slowly up the River Shannon and settle forever in Limerick. The rain dampened the city from the feast of the circumcision to New Year's Eve. It created a cacophony of hacking coughs, bronchial rattles, asthmatic wheezes, consumptive croaks. It turned noses into fountains, lungs into bacterial sponges. It provoked curses galore; to ease the catarrh you boiled onions in milk blackened with pepper, for the congested passages you made a paste of boiled flour and nettles, wrapped it in a rag, and slapped it, sizzling, on the chest.
>
> From October to April the walls of Limerick glistened with the damp. Clothes never dried; tweed and woollen coats housed living things, sometimes sprouted mysterious vegetations. In pubs, steam rose from damp bodies and garments to be inhaled with cigarette and pipe smoke laced with the stale fumes of spilled stout and whiskey and tinged with the odour of piss wafting in from the outdoor jakes where many a man puked up his week's wages.
>
> The rain drove us into the church – our refuge, our strength, our only dry place. At Mass, Benediction, novenas, we huddled in great damp clumps, dozing through priest drone, while steam rose again from our clothes to mingle with the sweetness of incense, flowers and candle.
>
> Limerick gained a reputation for piety, but we knew it was only the rain.
>
> (Reprinted by permission of HarperCollins Ltd © 1996
> Frank McCourt)

McCourt would probably not consider himself a qualitative researcher, but his methods in writing a memoir of his childhood are very similar, involving inner reflection, research of his past, comparative analysis and evocative presentation. Observe how in a very few words McCourt conjures up the feel and smell of the prevailing condition of his childhood, the wetness and dampness of it, the discomfiture; how very few words bring to mind a whole area of activity (such as 'dozing through priest drone'). Notice the metaphors, the onomatopoeia, the imagery, the rhythm and cadence of the sentences, the pathos, the gentle ironic humour. There is music and poetry here, clever choice of words and sentences, artfully arranged. There is possibly some slight exaggeration in places but Richardson (1994b: 521) thinks this permissible: 'Because narratives of the self are staged as imaginative renderings, they allow the field-worker to exaggerate, swagger, entertain, make a point without tedious documentation, relive the experience, and say what might be unsayable in other circumstances'. The enlarging therefore contributes nonetheless to the general truth, adding to the humour and humanity of the piece. The whole excerpt hangs together to form a satisfying entity in itself – a prose poem.

We might not be able to emulate this quality of writing in our descriptions. In fact some of our attempts might be truly awful. But this is the nature of experimentation. Many attempts might fail before one works and leaves you feeling that it was all worthwhile. The best preparation is extensive reading of expressive literature, together with repeated experimentation, testing out on colleagues and friends, drafting and redrafting, and jettisoning where necessary.

Example 3: Carolyn Ellis (1996: 241) 'Maternal connections'
Ellis is tending her sick mother in hospital:

> Being careful of the tubes and IVs, I unsnap and remove her soiled gown. She tries to help. I cover the front of her body with a towel, to protect her from cold. 'It feels good when you wash my back', she says, and I continue rubbing. When she shivers, I run the washcloth under hot water. I wonder about washing the rest of her body.
>
> Around front, I wash her belly, noting the faded scars of my younger brother's cesarean birth – and shudder at the reminder that he is now dead – and I look closely at the new scars of the gall bladder surgery. Her stomach is puffy, but almost flat now, not rounded as before. The extra skin hangs loosely. Then her legs. Although her skin is dry and flaky, I admire her thin, almost bony, yet still shapely, legs. Our bodies have the same form, I note. Long, slender, and graceful limbs, fatty layers on top of the hips and belly, and a short and thick waist.
>
> I move to her breasts, still large and pendulous. Now they hang to her waist and, as her shoulders curve forward, they rest on her belly, like mine, only lower.
>
> I take one tenderly in my hand, lift it gently from her belly to wash it, noting the rash underneath. 'Would you like cream on that?'
>
> 'Oh, yes, it's real sore'. She holds her breast while I rub in the cream. Feeling no particular emotion, I observe from a distance. Her body is my body, my body in 36 years. So this is what it will look like and be like. I see.

The accompanying note states: 'In her work on narrative, subjectivity and illness, Carolyn Ellis seeks to write evocative texts that remind readers of the complexity of their social worlds. Writing autoethnographic texts has intensified her life experience; she hopes they also contribute to the lives of readers' (p. 243). She says that she 'didn't want to stay stuck at the level of data.

I wanted to be a storyteller, someone who used narrative strategies to transport readers into experiences and make them feel as well as think' (p. 18). In the piece above, use of the present tense heightens the effect, as does the gently modulated description of her mother's body, the intimacy, and the comparisons with self, the connections between mother and daughter. Though she feels 'no particular emotion' at one point, the reader can hardly fail to be moved by this account. Later in the piece, Ellis reflects on relationships and personal identity, and on some new young fathers eager for a sight of their new babies. The combination of description and reflection, the artfully portrayed intimacy, the powerful bond the daughter feels for her mother, her wistful reflections on her own childlessness at a late age, not only help to convey readers into this private world, but into their own.

Example 4: Paul Willis (1982: 237) 'The Triple-X boys'

> Bill-the-Boot, Sammy, Slim Jim and Bob . . . never wore helmets and goggles. These destroyed the excitement of wind rushing into the face, and the loud exhaust beat thumping the ears. The point of fast driving was the experience, not the fact, of speed . . . On a bike high-speed riding is an extremely physical experience. The whole body is thrown backwards. (At the TripleX club, the boys would often tell one another: 'I was nearly blown off'.) And when even a slight bend is taken at high speed, the machine and the driver need to go over at quite an angle in order to compensate for the centrifugal force. The experienced driver becomes part of the bike and intuitively feels the correct balancing at high speeds . . . The equivalent of gale-force wind is tearing into the living flesh. Eyes are forced into a slit and water profusely; the mouth is dragged back into a snarl; and it is extremely difficult to keep the mouth closed. They make no attempt to minimise the drag effect of the wind. Jackets are partly open and are not buttoned down around the throat; belts are not worn; there's nothing to keep the jacket close to the skin; trousers are not tucked away in boots and socks; and there is nothing at all to prevent the wind from tunnelling up their sleeves.

Willis was able to provide this close description because he also rode a motorbike, and he experienced all these things. He felt the gale-force wind, watery eyes, snarling mouth, heard the thumping of the exhaust, moulded himself to the bike. This 'intimate familiarity' provides him with details that he can convey, such as to transport the reader to the scene and on to the bike. We feel the wind on the face, the tearing at our clothes, the streaming of our hair – and sense the exhilaration of the devil-may-care hurtle through space. Notice how the effect of free-flowing apparel, and an element of the distinctive culture of the group, is heightened by listing as missing accoutrements or arrangements that one might normally expect in their clothing.

Example 5: Pat Sikes (1996: 339–40) in Angela Packwood and Pat Sikes 'Adopting a postmodern approach to research'

> When I went back to work after my maternity leave, I discovered I had changed in some fundamental ways. Although my work was still very important to me, it was no longer my *raison d'être*. It was not just that I was too tired to work for most of my waking hours; it was that I did not want to any more. I did not think that I ought to, and I did not feel guilty about it. This change did not happen immediately. When Robyn was first born, I carried on just as before. I wrote a paper with her on my lap; she attended a friend's inaugural professorial lecture when she was six weeks old; and, four weeks later, I took her to an AERA conference in Boston. Then gradually I began to question what I was doing and came to the conclusion that I did not want and did not have to behave like my childless self. I actually wanted to have time with my daughter. That my priorities could change in this way was something of a shock, but it was nothing to the surprise I got when, in the course of my work, I went into a primary classroom.
>
> Part of my job involves visiting students on school practice. By the time I became a lecturer, I had spent quite a bit of time teaching in both primary and secondary schools as a requirement of one of my research jobs. I no longer hated it as much as I had at college, but I still felt much the same about the children. Now, as a mother, this was no longer the case. I entered classrooms and found that in some bizarre way, other people's children had become my children too. I now cared about the children in a way that I would once not have thought possible. I felt for them; I enjoyed their company; I enjoyed their questions and their attention; I even, in a certain sort of way, loved them.

Here, Sikes, in a clear and straightforward style without embellishment, conveys graphically and movingly a profound change in her persona on becoming a parent comparatively late in life. The narrative, artfully structured, contains a great deal of detail, punctuated by 'change' notes and their accompanying emotions ('did not want to', 'did not feel guilty', 'shock', 'surprise', 'cared', 'enjoyed', 'loved'). In the story as a whole, there are three distinguishable voices – those of researcher, mother and individual. The authors offer the story as

> An example of a postmodern, narrative approach to research in which the multiple voices of the *researcher* are firmly located within the text, interweaving the past with the present, thereby shaping the future. The story told here is of the genesis of the research, the emotional and personal roots to be found in the lived experience of the researcher. We are attempting to present different facets of an individual self and the way in which they impact upon the research process and product. Such a rationale offers the reader the opportunity to understand the subjective

reality informing this particular research process and product. It enables readers to locate the researcher in relationship to those being researched and to the outcomes of the process.

(p. 338)

Example 6: W.S. Dubberley (1988: 119) 'Humor as resistance'

Miss Crabbe recalled an incident to other teachers in the staffroom. [In a superior tone] 'One lad was making funny noises, and he said to me [crude accent], 'I'm not making funny noises – tha' daft. I said [arch tone], 'All right, let's have a competition to see who is daft, me or you.' He said [crude accent], 'I'm not daft.' I said [urbane], 'Well, then, I suggest you go to see a psychiatrist, then. Anyone who makes funny noises and can't hear them must need one.' Of course, all the class laughed at this.'

There were numerous complaints by the pupils, supported by a few of the staff, that teachers often used aspects of the dominant culture, particularly language, code and intonation, social style and urbanity, to put them in their place. One teacher said, 'We should not go down to their level'. Aspects of working class culture and middle class stereotyping of that culture were freely used to parody and ridicule.

Mrs Boyle (arch tone): 'Do you know that awfully tall boy?'
Mrs Roach: 'George Ash?'
Mrs Galton: 'The giant.'
Mrs Boyle: 'Well, he came into my class the other day. I pushed his chest to get him out and then I thought, "Good God, he might strike me".'
Mrs Rice (heavily ironic): 'Oh no – he won't hit a woman. I had him by the neck and he wouldn't hit me.'
Mrs Boyle: 'No – just rape you.'

The insult is multi-layered. This giant is potentially dangerous because of the physical strength he has allied to his dumbness. A Frankenstein monster of the lower orders, through his lack of intelligence he becomes a potential threat, if not by physical violence, then by sexual violence, to his betters, the women.

Here, the author weaves into the account a certain amount of transcript, some reported as said, some as selected phrases, together with the ways in which things were said, and some of his analysis (which contains a startling metaphor). The article is heavily dependent on pupils' and teachers' words, and this extract illustrates one way in which it might be used. The article as a whole builds up an effect of oppositional cultures, largely through what teachers and pupils say, artfully constructed by the author.

Note how these pieces relate to the criteria for adequacy discussed in Chapter 4. Wolcott, McCourt, Ellis and Sikes all include their own feelings.

All the examples meet the literary and aesthetic criteria in various ways. They also link expression with analysis, though McCourt's piece is more of an evocative 'narrative of the self' (Richardson 1994b), in which analysis might get in the way. But it meets the author's purpose of 'showing the face of poverty, the grime and stink of it, without becoming sentimental' (McCourt 1996b: 17), thus making a significant contribution to our social knowledge. Wolcott cleverly interweaves narrative and analysis; Ellis' account is basically about identity, relationships and the sociology of the emotions, and there are indicators to these within the article; Willis' description feeds into theories of identity, as does Sikes'; and Dubberley presents a cultural expression of social class. This is where expressive forms of writing might fit within the prevailing paradigm of qualitative research. In this way, the writing might be both evocative and suggestive of totally new theory or cast new light on existing theory. It might bring together areas of thought, experience or analysis which previously seemed unconnected.

You might not wish to employ expressive writing throughout an article or book. It may be needed to describe key events or incidents, or to evoke atmospheres and feelings at certain moments. Also, apart from its expressive qualities, or perhaps because of them, it helps to make things interesting for the reader – quite a consideration when you are seeking to communicate something (Bailey 1996). Thus in an otherwise analytic piece, it could be used at the beginning, or even intermittently at the beginning of sections or chapters, to set the scene, awaken interest, whet the appetite, give a foretaste of what is to come. It carries the reader into the field setting, providing a stronger base for appreciation of the analysis.

A PERSONAL STYLE

> The poems I was writing were still mainly derivative . . . I had not yet found my own voice.
>
> > (W.H. Auden, in Osborne 1995: 58)

> Developing my own narrative style and voice was what finally made me feel more at home in the academic knowledge-production factory.
>
> > (Foley 2002: 469)

> It took me such a long time to find my own voice. I studied for four years at New York University, but the teaching was useless. And then I went through phases: my Joyce phase, my Hemingway phase. There was a time too when I thought I wanted to write like Evelyn Waugh or Aldous Huxley, write with that cool, brittle sophistication. But it was through being a teacher in the New York state system – teaching children from all ethnic backgrounds – that I learned the value of simplicity.
>
> > (McCourt 1996b: 16)

Denzin (1997: 83) speaks of 'a writing self that creates itself through its writing'. This is a reminder that not only is there a part of ourselves in what we write, but that there is also a becoming in the self as we write. It is a dialectical, developmental activity. Writers, therefore, over time develop a personal style or voice. This might be distinguished by what Golden–Biddle and Locke (1997: 87) term 'authorial persistence' – the tendency for authors to use one particular style in writing up their research; or by 'crafting the atypical' (p. 90) – taking an unusual approach. However, there is much more to style than this – vocabulary, idiom, grammar, ear, literary and academic knowledge, personal history and experiences, values, beliefs, aims, personality – in short, the very person you are. Lucas (1974: 50) in fact, argues that character or personality is the very foundation of style, not technique:

> If you wish your writing to seem good, your character must seem at least partly so. And since in the long run deception is likely to be found out, your character had better not only *seem* good, but *be* it. Those who publish make themselves public in more ways than they sometimes realize. Authors may sell their books; but they give themselves away.

The human qualities that Lucas feels are generally admired are: 'Good manners and courtesy towards readers, like Goldsmith's; good humour and gaiety, like Sterne's; good health and vitality, like Macaulay's; good sense and sincerity, like Johnson's' (p. 66).

We could draw up a long list of characteristics, and while some of us would have similarities, especially through our allegiance to the model of 'institutional scientist' (Golden-Biddle and Locke 1997: 73), there would be considerable differences. Much of this would be to do with values and our conception of the good life and a decent world. Much academic debate seems directed at making others more like us – one of the supreme ironies in a democracy that celebrates difference. However, if this element of style is cultivated within the kind of framework suggested in this chapter, it can add to the richness of our academic literature – and to our democracy – instead of deteriorating into acrimonious and counter-productive debate, as sometimes happens.

You have to be motivated to write. You write because you have something to say. If you want others to take note of what you say, it helps to say it in style.

6

Editing

The larger part of the labour of an author in composing his work is critical labour, the labour of sifting, combining, constructing, expunging, correcting, testing: this frightful toil is as much critical as creative.

(T.S. Eliot, *The Function of Criticism*, quoted in Lodge 1996: 175)

Every author's fairy godmother should provide him not only with a pen but also with a blue pencil.

(Lucas 1974: 88)

THE PROCESS

We now come back to earth! The major part of writing for most people lies not in creatively composing, but in editing – rewriting, rephrasing, reordering, restructuring, moving parts of the text around, adding to and deleting text, clarifying, removing ambiguities, sharpening, tightening, tidying up grammar, and so on. This is even more important in qualitative research, since 'Discursive texts easily become wordy, run-on, repetitive, and redundant' (Sherman 1993: 236). The initial task is to externalise material in the ways, for example, suggested in earlier chapters, and in a form that renders it amenable to editing. The first part might typically represent 10 per cent of the total writing activity, the second part, editing, 90 per cent. Not all authors proceed in this way. I have a colleague who does all the various drafts of his articles in his head then writes an almost finished item. But he is the only one I know who works like this; he takes just as long, if not longer, than others over the process, and he confesses to suffering great mental anguish. Most of us have to carry on 'crafting' the article draft by draft, 'wordsmithing', synchronising, developing, integrating, polishing, refining. Sometimes we do more than this as new ideas come. Better ways of putting things sometimes lead to better thoughts.

Many at the beginning of their writing careers have problems of one kind or another. Perhaps it is to do with spelling, grammar, punctuation (especially where to put commas), sentence construction, saying what you think, or not thinking clearly enough in the first place. But I have seen people improve with a little help to become authorities themselves on the art of writing. It might be helpful, therefore, for you to ask others to read what you have written, and to comment on clarity and accuracy as well as ideas and argument. I learnt a great deal about writing from editors at the Open University, who go through draft teaching units with attention to every detail. I used to think I wrote fairly well, but they made me put myself in the position of the reader and look more closely at my work. They picked out ambiguities which I had not seen, pressed for absolute accuracy and clarity, amended punctuation and spotted repetitions. On occasions they would suggest alternative phrasing, which could be much better than mine or might completely alter the sense. The latter just emphasised the obtuseness of my original construction, and forced me into revisions that left them in no doubt as to the meaning. You might not have the luxury of professional editors in your daily work, but I have also found that friends and colleagues will perform this function – after all, it works on a reciprocal basis. Be sure to ask for whatever comments the reader feels are appropriate, even if they seem ever so small and trivial. These are all important in fashioning a quality product.

A different cast of mind is required from that involved in creative writing, despite the fact that creative thinking might arise. This is neatly reflected in your attitude to the number of words in the text. I am pleased to see these increasing when I am constructing a draft, and equally, if not more, pleased to see them decreasing when I am editing. Editing needs attention to the detail of the means of expression. Each paragraph, each sentence, each word has to be studied fairly intensively as you hone and fine-tune the text. This might help to refashion ideas and arguments in the draft as you find your words or form of words do not convey exactly the meaning you intend. Some ideas and meanings that are not important, or that you cannot find the right words for, may have to be dropped. So again, where anything, however flimsy, might appear in an initial draft, at the editing stage sections are removed where any flimsiness remains or cannot be resolved. Often it is necessary to be quite ruthless with some pet ideas, which, in the cold light of print, just do not work. It also hurts to have to delete material that you went through the pain barrier to write. You go through it again on the way back! But sometimes it has to be done. Creative writing involves taking risks. By the editing stage, it should be clear whether they were worth taking.

The following are some of the considerations. Some recall points made earlier. You might not have succeeded in meeting them all in early drafts!

Insufficient guidance in the Introduction

- Why are you writing this?
- Why in this form (explain the structure)?
- What are the major issues/themes?
- How does it connect to the literature?

- What are the major questions raised?
- How did you set about answering them?

Weak Conclusions

Conclusions are often the most difficult sections to write. There may not be a clear body of material on which they are to be based. They are of a different order from other sections, so you almost have to switch to a different mental mode at a time when suffering from author exhaustion. Yet they are the most important part of papers. They need to be comprehensive if your paper is to have maximum impact, drawing out the full implications. Draw breath after writing the paper if necessary, but set aside time after a day or two to tackle the conclusion. In advance of this, it might be helpful to have kept a 'Conclusions' file throughout the writing up. 'Conclusion' thoughts often occur as you are thinking about and constructing the rest. In this way you accumulate substantial material, and tackling the conclusion is not such a daunting task. The kinds of considerations you might reflect on include:

- How has your paper answered the questions raised earlier?
- What are the strengths and weaknesses of the paper, and how might the latter be rectified?
- What further questions are raised? What indications are there for further research in the area?
- Return to the introduction – what difference has your paper made to the state of knowledge outlined there?
- Often you can provide a new slant on the way the data is presented in the body of the paper. For example, if the paper sets out a number of related categories, the conclusion might look across the categories. This could also be a separate section, but there may not be space for that.
- Evaluation is often left implicit – one approach good, one bad. If evaluation is involved, it needs to be made explicit, and reasons given why one is better than another.
- The conclusion might contain implications for policy or practice if these have not featured in the body of the article.

Similar material in different sections

There is a need to synchronise. Perhaps you have not quite managed to make your categories mutually exclusive. Some of the material may need reordering or editing or deleting, some of the categories may need adjusting, some may need merging.

Theoretical inadequacy

Common forms of this in qualitative research include the following.

Exampling
All that is done is to provide further illustrations of somebody else's concepts or theoretical constructs. Unless deliberately set up as a replication study, or seeking to develop formal from substantive theory, there is little worth in this. What should be done is to re-examine the material carefully to tell us how it advances understanding in these areas. More appropriate, if you knew the research was going to involve these theoretical areas, would be to consider: how might they be tested? What considerations do they omit? How adequate are they as representations of the data? Do my data suggest modifications or development of the concept or theory?

Theoretical lag or mismatch
A good illustration of this 'lag' is the 'characteristics' model noted by Hargreaves (1977) attending much of the early 'interactionist' work in schools, as opposed to a more purist 'process' model. The characteristics model was a hangover from psychological approaches, especially interaction analysis, which had certain affinities with qualitative research. 'Theoretical lag' may come about through our own biography. Steeped in certain methods and approaches by training and experience, we may find it difficult to view the world otherwise.

Under-theorised description
Qualitative research is description by definition, but it is description that is theoretically informed. Under-theorised description is little more than a presentation of the data as it stands, with little attempt to analyse, explain, draw out common features across situations, identify patterns of behaviour, syndromes of factors, and so forth. Seek to bring out the theory behind the facts and the description.

- Reading the relevant literature is essential for this. New theory is nearly always created by the interplay between existing literature and the data. There may be inconsistencies, contradictions or inadequacies in existing theory.
- Seek alternative explanations. Don't be satisfied with the first plausible one. Be your own devil's advocate. Assume an oppositional, critical role towards your own work. Conduct a debate with yourself on the strengths and weaknesses, seeking to shore up weaknesses and undermine claims to strength. Role-play somebody of different values and beliefs from yourself – how would they interpret your paper?
- Test out your ideas on others – show drafts to as many as possible. This is both a test of what you have done, and an aid to further creativity. Others will spot omissions ('Have you read . . . ?'; 'I think you should say something about . . .'); obfuscations ('What do you mean by . . . ?'); inadequacies ('Can you say a little more about . . . ?'); alternatives ('Yes, but what about . . . ?'); unconvincing arguments ('I don't agree with you').

Faulty grammar

With spelling and grammar checks and 'auto–corrects' on computers now, these should be less of a problem, except that most of these checks are set up with American spelling and grammar and by no means everybody has access to such a resource. Nor do these checks pick up all the faults. Common problems are as follows.

- *Sentences*. Not a sentence, or too many in one. Consider, for example, the following:

  > For the bilingual pupils in our study, this lesson represented what we would suggest as being an example of the largely monocultural nature of the National Curriculum as well as the difficulties arising from teachers conforming to this model at the expense of taking opportunities to make their work relevant to their children by means of choosing historical figures with which the children could identify culturally or by using the theme of Boudicca more creatively by inviting children to use the story as a basis for their own imaginative story work rather than an insistence on the retention of facts.

  My comment in the margin was 'Gosh!'. I felt quite breathless when I got through to the end. There is a certain amount of circumlocution here – an indirect way of making the point. My suggested revision was, 'It also shows what is lost by teachers not making the children's work more relevant, for example by using Boudicca as a basis for their own imaginative story work'. The other key points – about monoculturalism and fact retention – had already been made.
- *Sense*. Not clear.
- *Punctuation*. Especially use of the apostrophe and comma.
- *Tenses*. Often not standardised. A common fault is to mix present and past tenses when describing a situation or setting a scene.
- *Order of words in a sentence*. Reading aloud sometimes helps: does it sound right?
- *Consistency of phrasing* (i.e. a second phrase not relating to the right subject in the first phrase).
- *Single subjects, but plural pronouns and verbs, or vice-versa*. For example, 'The child has to learn the cultural expectations of themselves as pupil both in their native culture and the English school culture'.
- *Spelling* (e.g. confusion between 'affected' and 'effected').

Especially in the early stages of your writing career, you might find a dictionary of grammar and usage helpful. A classic is Fowler's (1926) *A Dictionary of Modern English Usage*. I have *An ABC of English Usage* by H.A. Treble and G.H. Vallins (1936), which I acquired from my sister's schooldays, but which I still find useful. They advise on such things as the position of the comma, correct spellings, sentence construction, tenses, cases, 'shall' and 'will', 'which' and 'that', 'might' and 'may', parts of speech, and prepositional idiom. A modern definitive volume is *The Oxford Manual of Style* (Ritter 2003).

Style

Common problems are as follows.

* *Voice.* Use active rather then passive verbs, and 'I' rather than the third person.
* *Repetition.* This includes repetition in transcript material; of points in transcript material and in the text by way of introduction or comment, though sometimes this is necessary; also of the same words or constructions close together in the text. Repetition becomes boring, and is hardly ever necessary where it is not being used for purposes of emphasis. Some examples of constructions repeated are:

> 'After a short time' was repeated three times in one paragraph (you could vary this with 'before long', 'soon' or 'shortly').

> A student was extremely fond of starting sentences with 'In this way' (alternatives: 'so', 'thus', 'similarly' or 'as a consequence').

> The first line below introduces a piece of transcript beginning with the line following. The latter could have been deleted:

> Part of the concern about the examination was the mystery of it all:

> I suppose it is because of the mystery of it all . . .

* *Redundancy.* Use of unnecessary words. See also 'sentences' in above section on faulty grammar. Examples:

> This same type of pressure existed also . . .

> Yet on the whole much of the curriculum . . .

> An example of how teachers sought to make connections is illustrated in the following lesson.

> Teachers were concerned primarily with the children's social disadvantage more so than any other issue.

> . . . rose to a crescendo . . .

> She initially began the story . . .

> The disciplinary measures taken were not adequate enough.

* *Clutter (as against succinctness).* This is the commonest general fault I have found in students' work. There are many kinds of clutter – excessive words, unnecessary names of people or organisations, irrelevant material, unnecessary statements, too lengthy or too many quotes from other people's work, excessive transcript, 'concepting' (i.e. strewing the text with illustrations of concepts that have already been well established in others' work); too many examples of a similar kind – adding to no great purpose rather than triangulating. Faulty organisation can promote clutter.
* *Undisciplined writing.* This is where the author has not thought through the meaning of what he or she is writing. There might be general confusion

uncertainty, second or contradictory thoughts, or 'tributary' writing (wandering off up side streams). A writer might confess to having 'lost it' (i.e. the thread of the argument). This leads to verbosity, stream of consciousness thinking, non sequiturs, conflation of ideas or issues. This is almost like saying, 'I'm not sure what I want to say exactly – perhaps the reader can sort it out'. The solution may reside in preceding stages – data collection and analysis. If the data are good, you may need to return to analysis. Good housekeeping helps correct indiscipline, both on computers and in hard copy. Be very systematic about keeping records; open files for each category, chapter or major item (reviewing occasionally to see if some belong together or need reordering); code data for analysis and so that they cross-relate.

- *Poor expression*. This can come from using clichés, truisms, old, tired or inappropriate metaphors, flowery, over-elaborated writing, 'flat' description and big words. Often what might seem good at first attempt makes you cringe when you come back to it a few days later. This is probably a good feeling to get, as it is a defence against self-indulgence and dilettantism. Consulting others, and insisting they do not pull any punches, is another. A thesaurus and a good dictionary can be useful, not for becoming a slave to or for discovering 'big words', but rather for opening up the mind to new possibilities. Reading good literature also helps.
- *Links between sentences, paragraphs, sections and chapters*. These are important for the 'music' of the text – flow and rhythm. The reader is carried along by conjunctive adverbs and adverbial phrases ('however', 'therefore', 'similarly', 'on the other hand', 'by contrast', 'not only . . . but also', 'in view of this', 'at the same time', 'even so'), and by more subtle ones that draw attention to a particular point ('rather ironically . . .').
- *Lucidity (as against opacity, vagueness, woolliness)*. Drafts need to be read very carefully. Put yourself in the position of the reader. Is everything perfectly clear? Note that it has to be clear to you before you write for others (as opposed to writing for yourself, which can be exploratory). There are also a number of purely editing points that you should bear in mind, for example, sentences beginning with 'This' or containing 'it' – it is not always clear to the reader what these refer to.
- *Accuracy*. Often things are not quite right – a word, a phrase, a conjunction. Sometimes you do have to work hard to say what you want to say, and it may take several attempts. A teacher friend of mine writing his biography told me it took him six attempts to get one chapter right: 'It kept coming out wrong. That's not quite what I wanted to say'. Little points of detail are also important. Compare 'Nor did teachers use any words' with 'Nor were teachers heard to use any words'.
- *Synchronicity*. Sometimes over a number of drafts points can get refined out of synchronism with the original data. This can happen with the alteration of just one word. In some instances you may need to go back to cross-check the draft with your original data.
- *Slang*. Avoid this, unless in quoted material.

- *Consistency.* Ensure that terms and references are used in the same way throughout: 'Y1', 'Yr 1' or 'Year One'? 'Fieldnote 6 February 1995' or 'FN 4/2/95'? 'Science' or 'science'? 'Headteacher', 'headteacher', 'head teacher' or 'head'?
- *Presentational defects.* I am thinking here of the unnecessary use of capital letters, or of aside remarks in brackets, undue emphases, typographical errors, inaccurate or incomplete referencing, faulty formatting, misquotations, messy pages, faint print. Any of these could entail your work being returned to you unread.

Structure

If employing a standard model as outlined in Chapter 3:

- *Organise your paper in sections and subsections*, with an introduction and a conclusion.
- *'Tighten up'*, ensuring that sections are closely linked, lead from one to another, and that there are no loose ends. Look for opportunities for reprises, for cross-references between sections – though do not overdo this, as they can become obscure and/or tedious.
- *Try to secure a developing argument through the paper* – one point leads to another, or raises further questions (as opposed to a structure which is little more than a list of points – ODTAA – one damn thing after another).
- *Display a table of contents* at the beginning to give an overview of the paper – you may wish to reorganise, amalgamate or delete some sections/subsections.

Use of transcripts

Unless there is a special reason for using a complete transcript, or sections of same, um's and ah's and non-verbals and all, and if all that is required is content, then:

- *Edit for sense*, repetition, mannerisms, etc.
- *Use paraphrasing* and reported speech occasionally to save space, perhaps incorporating the key comments into the main text.
- *Check for clarity.* People speak differently from the way they write. You are translating their spoken words into text. There are dangers of adulterating the spoken word in these techniques, but where you have reams of transcript, and much of it in stream of consciousness form, you have no choice. In many cases, respondent validation of your account will be possible.
- *Check for punctuation.*
- *Bear in mind the value of side-by-side analysis* of long pieces of transcript of interview or classroom interaction where these are used (convenient for the reader, but also a useful check on the need for the lengthy extract).
- *Consider alternative ways* of presenting the material.

Misuse of examples

- *All claims need good examples*, preferably more than one of contrasting kinds.
- *Beware of* seeking to prove a point by giving just one example.
- *Examples are subject to the problems listed above.* They take up space. Are they pulling their weight, or are they mainly padding? Can they be trimmed without threats to validity?

Evidence

- *Support all claims* with as strong evidence as possible.
- *Be clear as to what constitutes strong evidence* – triangulation, lengthy and detailed observation, repeated interviews, attention to sampling etc.
- *Beware of speculation ('perhaps', 'may be').* This is acceptable for setting up hypotheses or qualification of your findings, but not usually for the findings themselves.
- *Make appropriate claims*, neither under- or over-claiming.
- *Be sure about what you are and are not claiming.*
- *Significance needs to be established.* Often it is not clear why some piece of data or some findings are significant. Why does it matter? So what?

Bias

This can show in various ways.

- *Slants.* The way the text is written constructs an inference not warranted by the data.
- *Unwarranted and hidden use of 'persuasive rhetoric'.*
- *Unwarranted claims to generality* (e.g. 'Alison at Trafflon sums up what many teachers feel').
- *Use of certain non-neutral, loaded words slipped in unobtrusively* (e.g. 'endured', 'were given', 'unfortunately').
- *Thin evidence supporting strong assertions.*
- *Mind made up in advance and closed to other possibilities* – research used to support what is already known.

Ethics

You need to check carefully for the following.

- *Libellous statements.* What might seem unproblematic in draft can look a lot different in print.
- *False or misrepresenting statements.*
- *Sexist or racist writing.*
- *Pseudonyms being used for people and places,* unless otherwise agreed, and other identifiers removed. The latter point is often forgotten. Even though not

named, it might be obvious who somebody is by the descriptions given or
the language reported.

- *Use of appropriate tone* (see Chapter 4).
- *Contracts being honoured.* For example, if there has been an agreement that
  people featuring in the research would see drafts of papers, this must be
  done. Some researchers might feel the urge, having acquired the data, to
  'cut and run' from the research site to the sanctity of the study. But apart
  from being discourteous, such behaviour could prejudice the chances of
  other researchers being granted access.
- *Adherence to some generally agreed code of ethics.* For example, the British
  Educational Research Association (BERA) has such a guide (1992). Many
  academic institutions have their own guidelines, which prospective
  researchers have to demonstrate how they are going to meet. All academic
  writers would be strongly advised to consult and adhere to at least one of
  these. There is not only wisdom there, but also a certain security.

References and literature

- *Misuse of references.* Precision is needed. Use references to substantiate points,
  but use organically within the text instead of just sticking them in wherever
  possible. There is a need to say exactly how they substantiate points – don't
  just throw them in to impress. Don't be lazy and quote chunks of unre-
  markable text where you yourself should be doing the writing. You might
  be using quotes for:

  a) citing other sources of evidence – but you need to know how strong
     and how appropriate that evidence is
  b) making a point very aptly
  c) the power of the words used.

- *Uncritical use of references.* Interrogate the literature as well as your own data
  and texts. If strongly persuaded by an article, ask what it doesn't do, what
  is wrong with it (there is always something!).
- *Remember to compile a list of full references,* with page numbers for quotes
  used, as you go along. Finding elusive references and page numbers for
  quotes that you have casually noted can be a nightmare at the end of the
  line.

The 'best shot'

Finally, you need to accept imperfection. If you are too much of a perfectionist you will never publish anything. Accept that there will be defects in
the final product. I have seen drafts from students that actually deteriorate
beyond a certain point. How can we identify when we have reached the
optimum, where, all things considered, 'that's the best we can do'? Things to
take into account are:

- *What you have already written.* On balance, is there value in it? Is it reasonably well organised and presented? Does it meet your own criteria of worthiness? Will you be pleased to see this in print?
- *Resources still at your disposal, particularly personal resources.* How is your stamina, interest, sanity?
- *The time factor.* Perhaps you have a deadline, and/or other deadlines are looming. Occasionally a piece of writing 'takes as long as it takes', but we do not always have the luxury of eternal time, and this runs against the basic 'imperfection' point here.
- *Other pressing matters.* Such as other academic work like teaching and administration, the rest of your life, family responsibilities.

Key words

- Reader-friendliness
- Clarity
- Richness (of data)
- Tightness (of organisation)
- Development (of argument)
- Succinctness
- Fairness
- Balance
- Interest
- Worth.

EXAMPLES OF EDITED TEXTS

A text containing transcript

Unedited version
Inspectors drifted in and out of lessons, missing an introduction or leaving just as the activity started and often didn't stay to hear the winding up of the lesson much to the chagrin of the teachers who felt as if they were being treated as functionaries.

> I find that's an incredible attitude, just to walk in whilst lessons are going on. I find it bad manners for a start because if you want to find out about something you don't walk in the middle of the lesson. If you want to see what's gone on before, what the children contributed to the lesson, and what's going to happen, I think most teachers would agree that you'd rather have them in at the beginning of the lesson rather than just wandering in.

The inspector that interviewed Margaret hadn't read her policy and other paperwork before he talked to her. He just gave her a list of questions thirty minutes prior to the interview and proceeded to type very slowly the answers into a laptop computer.

He sat at the table light with his laptop and he just went down the list and asked a question and typed in the answer. I kept saying to him 'am I going too fast'. He stopped me making conversation. Some times I just kept thinking subconsciously 'you're racing Margaret, stop it because he can't write all that'. I remembered somebody came in while he was typing and he didn't even look up and they started to apologise, and he still didn't look up. May be once or twice he may have looked up and then asked me the next question. I think this is why he gave me the questions before hand, so he could get them down and get them in, and I had them in front of me so that we didn't have any delays with me not knowing what he was asking, He didn't look at my files but he asked me if I had any qualifications, or if I done any courses. That is the only one time he did stop, and he was very impressed when I said 'yes' I did the Special Needs course at Christ Church College in Canterbury – 'oh, you did that there – is Joe Blogs still there', he said to me. My reaction was just to get it done and over with. I didn't care once it was over, quite honestly. As soon as I got up to go he said 'take your files' because he didn't want them. When I got up I had them in my hands and walked to the door, but I couldn't get out because of the low and high handles, so I thought 'do I go all the way back', I thought 'no he will open it for me', so I looked around and he was still typing away, so I said 'excuse me, do you think you could open the door for me please, I can't get out'.

Edited version
Inspectors drifted in and out of lessons, missing an introduction or leaving just as the activity started. They often didn't stay to hear the winding up of the lesson, much to the chagrin of the teachers who felt as if they were being treated as functionaries. Margaret found it

> an incredible attitude (and) bad manners . . . If you want to see what's gone on before, what the children contributed to the lesson, and what's going to happen . . . you'd rather have them in at the beginning of the lesson rather than just wandering in.

The inspector that interviewed Margaret hadn't read her policy and other paperwork before he talked to her. He just gave her a list of questions 30 minutes prior to the interview and typed the answers into a laptop computer very slowly. There was no conversation, and Margaret was worried about 'going too fast'. He didn't even look up when someone else came in, only 'once or twice' when asking a question. When she left, bearing her stack of files, she found she could not open the door, and thought he might open it for her, but when she looked around, he was still typing. She had to say, 'Excuse me, do you think you could open the door for me please, I can't get out'.

A marked up text

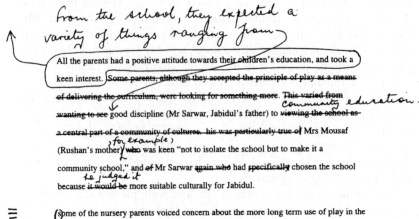

from the school, they expected a variety of things ranging from

All the parents had a positive attitude towards their children's education, and took a keen interest. ~~Some parents, although they accepted the principle of play as a means of delivering the curriculum, were looking for something more. This varied from~~ *Community education.* ~~wanting to see~~ good discipline (Mr Sarwar, Jabidul's father) to ~~viewing the school as a central part of a community of cultures. This was particularly true of~~ Mrs Mousaf *, for example)* (Rushan's mother) ~~who~~ was keen "not to isolate the school but to make it a community school," and ~~of~~ Mr Sarwar ~~again who~~ had ~~specifically~~ chosen the school *he judged it* because ~~it would be~~ more suitable culturally for Jabidul.

Some of the nursery parents voiced concern about the more long term use of play in the nursery. ~~They expressed a preference for a more formal academic approach eventually taking precedence.~~ *favoured* Aleena (Amar's mother) ~~said that she would like to see the children~~ *children's* have a more structured approach during the ~~y~~ last term ~~in the nursery~~ so that they would be better prepared for ~~what she perceived as the more formal systems operating in~~ the lower school. Mr ~~and Mrs~~ Ali (Iqbal's ~~parents~~ *'s father*) ~~considered that once a child had reached the age of four more formal work should begin:~~ *view was*

    ~~I think play to a certain extent in OK but if they're going there to paint, well painting's OK for them, my view is~~ let them play first from three to four then from four they should slowly ~~slowly~~ start breaking them into having some experience of school (*Mrs Ali is nodding in agreement*).

of the children ~~All of~~ the ~~lower school~~ parents ~~interviewed~~ were ~~particularly~~ pleased with the progress their children were making ~~at the school~~ and held high opinions of the teachers. ~~This in part was due to the way their children talked about work they had covered in school, but also through their meetings with teachers at parents' evenings. On these occasions the parents were given written reports on their children which they welcomed. For Hasanan's mother the receipt of her daughter's first report was strongly felt by her mother as an indication of her daughter's progress during her first years at school:~~

Hasanan's mother, for example, was delighted with her daughter's first report.

Figure 6.1   Example of a page of text marked up for revision

The revised version reads as follows:

> From the school, they expected a variety of things, ranging from good discipline (Mr Sarwar, Jabidul's father) to community education. Mrs Mousaf (Rushan's mother), for example, was keen 'not to isolate the school but make it a community school', and Mr Sarwar had chosen the school because he judged it more suitable culturally for Jabidul.
>
> Some of the nursery parents voiced concern about the more long term use of play in the nursery. Aleena (Amar's mother) favoured a more structured approach during the children's last term so that they would be better prepared for the lower school. Mr Ali's (Igbal's father) view was let them play first from three to four, then from four they should slowly start breaking them into having some experience of school (*Mrs Ali is nodding in agreement*).
>
> The parents of the lower school children were pleased with the progress their children were making and held high opinions of the teachers. Hasanan's mother, for example, was delighted with her daughter's first report.

Comment

The first sentence ('All the parents . . .') has been put at the beginning of the whole section, as it is a general comment applying to all the points mentioned about the parents. Other changes are aimed at making the points intended in as clear, direct, and succinct a way as possible.

7

Collaborative writing

> In the 'Lone Ranger' approach, ethnographers have gone out single-handedly into the bitterly conflictual social world to bring data back alive. This approach has demanded considerable strength and courage much of the time and almost always an ability to operate alone, with little or no support and inspiration from colleagues.
>
> (Douglas 1976: 192)

Ethnography, if not all qualitative research, has been by tradition an individual pursuit. The individualism applies to more than fieldwork. The researcher is the main research instrument, investing a great deal of self into research design and data collection, and analysing and writing up in his or her own style and through personal frameworks. The entire research is circumscribed by the person of the researcher.

However, three developments in recent years have assisted the spread of teamwork in ethnography and in qualitative research in general. One is the development of the kind of approaches discussed in Chapter 4, many of which require teams, whether to bring off a performance drama, or to provide the different kinds of expertise needed for mixed media research, or more generally to get away from the sovereignty of the lone researcher and to inject more eyes, ears, voices and views into the research. As Snow (2002: 505) remarks, 'the use of multiple researchers facilitates access to a greater variety of inform-ants and angles of vision and thus more voices and data points . . . we therefore resuscitate the logic and practice of triangulation, particularly with respect to data sources, informants and researchers'. The second development is the advances in computer technology, which have brought the facility of links among team members through email. The third, in the UK at least, is the increased emphasis by funding agencies on teamwork, linked and networked research.

In this chapter, I consider the merits of working in a team for writing up research. I base it on my experiences of working with a research team in the 1990s, consisting of myself and three research fellows, Bob Jeffrey, Geoff Troman and Mari Boyle. We were joined for some of the time by two postgraduate students, Nick Hubbard and Denise Carlyle. For much of the time, they were all working on their own personal research studies within the context of the team; but out of these developed two whole-team, collaborative projects. It is the work on the latter that mainly informs the chapter.

RESEARCH HORIZONS

Teamwork can open up new, unforeseen opportunities for its members. Ideas are often generated and formulated in discussion. They emerge from the interaction as people contribute different perspectives, pool their knowledge, talk round points, challenge and defend arguments. Another's perspective can set off new chains of thought, or enable material to be seen in a new light. They may be comparatively small points – a contrary point of view or different interpretation, the suggested relevance of a sociological concept or piece of literature, a new theoretical slant, the introduction of some comparative material, a suggestion for the next step. It can be comparatively major, as with the generation of our whole-team book on 'restructuring', which drew on the individual projects of members of the team (Woods *et al.* 1997). Common themes that linked the projects had been developed in discussion as part of the 'support' function of the group, but had come to take on a life of their own.

Teamwork also maximises opportunities for dissemination of research. Members have their own contacts and their own favourite venues and journals, for which joint presentations will be made. Since there are a number of people to help with these, a higher number of possibilities and invitations can be taken up than if you were operating alone. Responsibilities and workloads can be shared out among the group, so that no single member is unduly overloaded at any particular time.

Similarly, the numbers of publications produced by members of the group acting in some kind of alliance with each other are rather higher than would be the case if individuals were operating alone. Some of these are internally generated, such as the 1997 book, and methods papers, of which the team papers were two, in addition to books and papers on individual projects. Even with the latter, the prospect of a book on a single project has been much enhanced by the contributions of linked students, as in the 'child-meaningful' research (Woods *et al.* 1999). Some publications are externally generated, coming from invitations, or from personal contacts of team members.

In short, there has been a profusion of outlets for the research. There has been considerable help within the team in reaching these. In a sense, individuals are pulled along by the team in meeting assignments. A high productivity rate becomes part of the group culture. There is a feeling of sustained momentum – there are deadlines, meetings and targets at various levels reaching far into the future. This may, of course, not be suitable for all kinds of research. Some matters may require a lengthy gestation. But for our current mode of research, which we see as highly relevant to policy and issues of the day, a comparatively fast turn-round is necessary if the research is to have any effect in an educational world subject to continuing and rapid change.

MUDDLING THROUGH

Our general approach to analysis is the 'constant comparative' method (Glaser and Strauss 1967). Compared to the lone ethnographer, the use of a team expands the substantive comparative base, and also the interpretive perspectives through which the comparisons are made. Liggett *et al.* (1994: 84) derive two lessons from their experiences here. The first concerns the benefits of 'muddling through' (that is, learning as they wrote rather than planning in detail from the outset), for 'in the "doing" of writing and thinking, we gained an appreciation of the need to have our written thoughts modified'; the other was in 'discovering anew the importance of individual latitude, even in writing'. We would agree with the first point, and partly with the second. Our 'muddling through' includes:

- Shooting a particular rocket into orbit and keeping it there by developing it or letting it fall to earth as a damp squib. This is an essential part of muddling through, in that imagination, spontaneity and enthusiasm are given free rein. It takes a number of damp squibs to get a rocket successfully established in orbit.
- Being left with 'impasses', which then had to be taken up later by email after we had reflected at leisure about the problem. After a few exchanges the impasse either becomes resolved with renewed interest or by the general acceptance of a perspective we can live with. Alternatively, we may drop the idea or material, as we did with a proposed chapter for the 'restructuring' book on changes in pedagogy.
- Presenting a large amount of data with some cursory and tentative initial analysis and allowing the group to give their views on it. This invariably stimulates the originator to do another draft by firming up his or her ideas or generating new insights. We consider it crucial for individuals to be able to work on the data for a significant period before necessarily committing themselves to final analysis, because we are less willing to give up some ideas if we have invested considerable time in analysis. The quality of analysis is enhanced by continual kneading, and the team engagement assists in that process.

COMPARATIVE DEVELOPMENT

We have considered it important for individuals to have a considerable degree of ownership and control of their own projects, and we have had discretion in how we present these, in articles, papers and symposia, relying on the team for 'critical-friendly' comments in the preparation. But we have also written some genuinely 'team' papers, most notably in the 'restructuring' book. Chapter 4, 'Making the new head's role', provides a good example of the processes involved. It is firmly within the traditional model of analysis and organisation, as discussed in Chapter 3 of this present book. In 'Making the new head's role', we consider how three successful primary school heads of widely varying styles were adapting to the radical changes in their role in recent years. We aimed to show some of the 'complicated process' (Smulyan 1996: 186) in such adjustment, as opposed to the 'static models' (*ibid.*) usually proposed, to show there is more to success than any simple listing of factors, and that there is more than one route to that success. Stages in the development of this chapter were:

- The recognition that we had a potentially highly productive comparative base. Particularly interesting headteachers figured prominently in Bob's, Geoff's and Mari's individual projects. Mari's was the subject of an early paper. Several months later, Geoff's featured in a draft chapter of his thesis. Mari's headteacher became even more prominent, and of special interest to Bob (researching the effect of Ofsted inspections), following an Ofsted inspection at her school. Bob thought a joint paper on headteachers would be interesting if the opportunity arose.
- The opportunity came with the book. But on what basis would the comparison be made? We had already characterised Mari's head as the 'composite head', the distinguishing feature of which was her attempt to take on new aspects of the role without relinquishing any of the old. Geoff felt that his headteacher represented an 'entrepreneurial head', marked by the head's self-confident adoption of the new managerial aspects of the role, which were anathema at the time to Mari's head. Arising from discussion, Bob reported that his headteacher (yet to be written about) was unlike both of these, and his description led Geoff to suggest that he was more of a 'reflective realist'. These styles now had to be unpacked, and compared and contrasted.
- We had to find a way of doing this. After several attempts, we decided to structure the discussion around five key aspects of the headteacher's role, as suggested by our research and the existing literature. These were: promoting and guarding the school ethos; gatekeeping; managing; professional leadership; and cultural leadership.
- Applying these to each of the three cases revealed some shortage of data in some areas. Files and transcripts had to be searched, and in some instances, new focused data gathered on specific areas. This follows the classic data − analysis − more data − more refined analysis spiral of qualitative research (Lacey 1976).
- The comparisons revealed other weaknesses in the individual cases. Some arguments needed sharpening, some data needed to be reordered. Other ideas were strengthened, such as that of Mari's headteacher as a 'professional mother' in her management style. Bob's headteacher, who had come late into the frame, had to be re-interviewed to bring the database up to the level of the others.

- The organisation of the chapter went through several experiments. The choice eventually was between presenting the headteachers individually, in succession, or structuring the chapter on the five major categories. In the end, we felt it important to preserve the individuality of the headteachers, examining them along the five categories in turn, but reviewing their styles and their main features in a summary at the end.

REFINING ARGUMENTS

The team also helps in the refinement of arguments. Others can spot weaknesses in cases or see alternative explanations. There have been several occasions where we have debated key points, which have invariably followed the formula:

- introduction of initial argument in a draft paper
- criticism of this on the grounds of insufficient or contradictory evidence, and suggestion of an alternative explanation
- reformulation of the argument with closer reference to the evidence, and perhaps the introduction of new evidence
- if not convinced, a stronger presentation of the alternative case, marshalling evidence from a wider field, perhaps one of the other projects
- further tightening of the initial argument, and expanding on why it was preferred to alternatives.

The interpretation of a headteacher's reactions to an Ofsted inspection in Chapter 5 of Woods *et al.* (1997) proceeded in this way. The issue was whether the joy and elation she felt at getting a good report on her management skills, which had been a matter of some concern to her, was uplifting, enskilling and re-professionalising; or rather marking a move towards managerialism and technicism by abrogating judgement on her abilities to an external agency. The debate was a reminder that an individual researcher could have put up an equally plausible case for either interpretation. As it was, we were forced to make the best possible case for the argument preferred, while admitting the possible relevance of the other if certain factors applied.

These debates take place in face-to-face meetings, but are reinforced, importantly, by email. The exchange of memos among the team enables the debate to continue outside meetings, and forces a different kind of concentration on the issue. In the remainder of this chapter, I draw from email messages that passed among the team during the construction of a book chapter in December 1996/January 1997 to illustrate the advantages of teamwork and technology as I see them.

ENHANCED VALIDITY

Validity was enhanced in the following ways:

- *There is a tone of constructive critique throughout,* and a concern to 'get things right'.

- *Hypothesising.* At times we suggested possible theoretical formulations based on others' data and ideas. This was a way of trying to combine primary analysis with what seemed like appropriate ideas from the related literature; to apply it to the full range of the sample; and to cast it in the theoretical terms we had developed in the previous chapter:

> Bob, A few thoughts on Chapter 3 following the meeting. How about 'Tensions in the New Teacher Role' as a title, taking up the theoretical line of Chapter 2? [In Chapter 2, we had argued that there had been a marked change in teachers' classroom experience from one character-ised by dilemmas which were amenable to professional resolution, to one of 'tension' and 'constraint' marked by less choice and more per-sonal conflict.] We could argue that the standard term of 'role conflict' is not adequate for current developments, and that 'role tension' is more appropriate for our teachers. Many instances of role conflict do not invade the teacher's inner self – they are more situational than per-sonal, and hence dilemmatic. The chapter might then expand on 'role tension' as a theoretical idea, using the data to further our thinking on role theory. What are its properties? How does it arise? How is it experienced? How is it resolved? With regard to the latter, we might develop Lacey's (1977) modes of strategic orientation, particularly as this is taken up in Chapter 5 or 6. Some hypothethical instances might be . . .
>
> (email from Peter, 1 December 1996)

- *Maximising the degree of fit between categories and data.* This had the effect of refining the categories, in this case dividing the 'enhanced' category between those who were more or less unequivocally enhanced, and those who were ambivalent:

> The categories look fine but I'm not sure the examples we have in the first ones [enhancement] are particularly powerful. While Eliza-beth is certainly ambivalent about her role, I'm not sure that she is enhanced by it. In fact, in the transcript there are a number of indications of stress. So real tensions and ambivalence but little enhancement as I see it, though she does say she likes aspects of the managerial role.
>
> (email from Geoff, 2 January 1997)

- *Testing the developing categories on your own teachers* who have not featured in the category generation:

> Simply for reference I would see Theresa [a teacher in Mari's school who features elsewhere in the book] as a supporting conformist, though in the conclusion it may be worth pointing out, as Bob said, that the teachers may exhibit aspects of many of the other categories, and these are not hard and fast sets.
>
> (email from Mari, 8 January 1997)

- *Checking on items that are not clear or complete,* or on which you have doubts:

> I've sketched out an introduction to Chapter 4, suggested a typology that seems to match Bob's and the dilemmas model, and begun to rework and edit the detailed examination of cases. Because of the shortage of time, I'm zapping this through for comment as I continue to work on the rest. Does it look as if it's going to work? The biggest difficulty I have at the moment, Bob, is the 'spoiled self' (constraints) category in your 'Outline D3 note'. I have the rerouters and fragmenters in here. I'm not sure where you see your 'adjusters' fitting in to this framework. How do they differ from 'enhancers' (perhaps they are a third subcategory?) and/or conformists (perhaps a fourth subcategory?)
>
> (email from Peter, 1 January 1997)

- *Seeking to inject balance.* Bob wrote the first draft of the chapter and posed a number of questions to the team:

  - Have I theorised enough?
  - Is the data limited by being drawn on Ofsted material?
  - Are the characters differentiated enough, and if so, what is the conclusion about the differentiation?
  - The methodology section may need pulling out. Is it too negative, and if so, what can we do?
  - Does anyone else have data to support or critique the characterisation/categories?
  - There is not much connection made with the other chapters. This may mean a lot more input.

Bob's critique of his own draft illustrates a typical mode of presentation in the team, and presages the problems to be experienced over coherence and connectedness. The draft was discussed at length at the next team meeting. The data were powerful, but we thought the categories too oriented toward the new managerial aspects of the teacher role, important though they were, and the data too localised within teachers' experiences of Ofsted inspections (the subject of Bob's individual research at the time). The categories also leant heavily in a critical direction (which might have been because of the Ofsted cast of the research) and we wondered if some teachers welcomed the role changes rather more than depicted. There were also questions of the theoretical approach of the chapter and how it would fit within the structure of the book. We debated whether to illustrate general categories by single cases, or to go for identifying subcategories across a range of cases comprising a category. The latter was more difficult, but more analytical, so we opted for it, despite the pressure of time.

ENRICHMENT

There is a potential improvement to quality as a result of input from various perspectives, which might be termed 'writer triangulation'. Individuals bring their own experience, research, knowledge, literature command, personal contacts and insights to bear. They donate new material, and/or develop what is already there, and suggest connections, thus contributing to a spiralling tendency which generates the impetus discussed below. In this way, the typology was developed and integrated with the rest of the text:

Bob,

Thanks for your notes and extra info. I'll get on with incorporating these into a D5. At the same time, I think it would be good if you could add in some of the bits you suggested:

1 *Sinkers*. There might be a point in including these here as a kind of pre-stress group, on the edge of becoming part of Chapter 6 (the stress chapter) but not quite there yet. Because Lucy has left, perhaps she belongs in Chapter 6 (any nice quote from her to include there?). But the other two might qualify. What do you think? I feel the chapter does need some stiffening in that area.
2 *Disturbed conformists and survivors*. Yes, it would probably be a good idea to standardise these with the rest, and include other examples, if you have the data.

(email from Peter, 7 January 1997)

Having maximised input from the various members, the team is then faced with the task of editing and fine-tuning. Again, this process was largely a matter of discussion:

1 I think the cuts are fine except for one element. It seems to me to be important that two of the non-conformists – Clare and Corrine – feel so strongly that they do not fear the sack even though they have made commitments to teaching in the past.
2 Finding more cuts. The ambivalent enhancers might be one possibility for we should emphasise their enhancement and perhaps just make the point about their ambivalence in less elaborate terms, for we see them as enhancers in the first place rather than very disturbed. There is a lot of disturbed evidence from Toni.

With regards to the compliers I think the emphasis should be on 'supportive', 'surviving' and 'disturbed'. In this way we may help deal with the problem of repetition by bringing the reader's attention to these elements rather than the contexts themselves. Some cuts may be possible from the supportive and disturbed (surviving is shorter) and might – to use your terms – harden the edges between them. The diminished seems less amenable to cuts unless it is by cutting longer quotes. Their 'diminishment' needs to be harder edged than the disturbed. Alternatively, cutting the whole 'diminished' section and including it in the stress chapter might be easier to retain 'diminishmentality'.

(email from Bob, 19 January 1997)

In this kind of editing work, the tracking device on the 'tools' menu allows colleagues to insert comments and to make suggestions for changing or refining text on the actual script at the relevant point, and gives others the option of accepting or rejecting them, or to make further changes of their own in the same way. It is so much more efficient and quicker than annotating hard copy by hand and posting.

MUTUAL SUPPORT

The following strategies are evident:

- *Relaying or handing on*, as in a relay race, with the runner handing on the baton to the person doing the next stage. This conveys the sense of sustained flat-out development of the project as a whole, but with points of individual relief following a burst of effort. As individual writers, we proceed in fits, starts and stops. The 'fit' – the product of some inspiration – takes us so far and no further, when we are forced to stop, and seek a new start in the next draft in a few weeks, after we have digested the first attempt, studied more literature perhaps, and come up with some new ideas. In teamwork, we can economise on this process to some extent by handing on a draft we have done to the team to do that kind of in-filling and developmental work, and to sustain inspiration ('Sorry if I'm not being much help but I've puzzled over it for some time and got nowhere really. Some responses to draft four – kicked back up field rather than safely and progressively into touch perhaps. Took an hour off to watch the Leicester v. Toulouse match on Saturday. Very impressive').
- *Portioning – dividing up tasks among the team*. This can operate in a number of ways. For example, you can be working on one section of material, while your colleagues work on others; you may send part of some material through to the rest of the team for evaluation, while continuing to work on other material to bring it to the same level.
- *Sounding*. An individual puts some suggestions to the team, perhaps an outline of how some task is to be approached, and invites responses before making a full commitment to the task. The task can then be approached with a greater degree of security, and perhaps with some refinement to the ideas proposed – part way already to the next draft. Which categories need more data added from more people? Which categories need more work in terms of defining their characteristics? What should I concentrate on next as a priority? Is it looking coherent yet? Have we established the dilemma, tension, constraints distinctions?

- *Encouraging.* As in the relay race where it is customary for the other members of the team to encourage the one running their leg, so in writing. Encouragement is given in words ('This is excellent and done so quickly'); by offering to take over some of the burden ('I'll have a go at 1, 2 and 3'); by promptness of response.
- *Humanising.* Writing is hard and often stressful work, especially if up against deadlines. Occasionally, the messages remind the team that there is another life outside the book and this particular chapter, as in the reference to rugby above.
- *Shared involvement.* Members were brought into the process of analysis and provided with access and insight into the ways others were working with the data. One member felt that this was more comfortable than in a face-to-face situation in that it gave him the opportunity to read, reflect, think, respond – yet at the same time there was the sense of urgency and immediacy created by the context. Further, more face-to-face meetings were impractical – members of the team lived a long way from each other, and were engaged in other project activities. At the same time, the separation was balanced by the strong connections among team members and the occasional face-to-face meeting.

SUSTAINED IMPETUS

All our papers go through a number of drafts, as many as nine or ten or even more, starting perhaps from some sketchy notes or extended memo, then developing and refining arguments, integrating related literature, reorganising, and editing and re-editing. The chapter featuring in the email exchanges above was a key one in the book and it had to be written quickly. We had already had one two-month extension on the book contract, being preoccupied with other chapters. Now, however, having worked our way clear of the incubus of major problems in the other chapters (though editing and refining these still continued), it suddenly 'took off'. It went through nine drafts in two months. This is not to say that the chapter would not have been better had we had more time. There is a point in having 'gestation periods' between drafts, during which interaction takes place with others and with literature, old thoughts become reflected upon and new ones arise. But we did not have that luxury. In the event, we tried to make a virtue of the quick turn-rounds, in that, being able to keep the project in the forefront of our minds from beginning to end, no time was wasted in having to refamiliarise ourselves with the details of the case at the beginning of each draft; while the attentions of the team stimulated the reflection and interaction which normally occurs. Further, you might claim that the way things were combined – emails, access to the data, team meetings, telephone conversations – provided a strong sense of sociology over technology, the latter being a vehicle for the strengthening of the ethnography, providing a wider access to conducting the analysis than if we were looking only at hard copy drafts.

Thus there was a sense of sustained continuity from inception to conclusion, until the construction of the chapter was resolved. This was much aided by modern technology. Drafts of papers and comments on them were instantly sent around members of the team, allowing swift exchanges, such that mental concentration on issues could be sustained, and an almost continuous discussion maintained on them throughout their development. There is no need for central typing, correcting, retyping and printing. There is pressure to respond, balanced by the knowledge that you are actually saving time by cutting through to the nub of issues, and the feeling that you are all making progress through some difficult problems. Further, home computers are no respecters of institutional opening and closing times, or of public holidays. There was consequently a blurring of the distinctions between work and non-work time, and public and private arenas. The fact that the university closed down for a week over the Christmas period did not affect progress. We were needs-driven, rather than timetabled through an institutional calendar. There is only you, the task and the computer. The only constraints are those that derive from human fallibility in, and aversion to, writing – and even those are eased by the team and the technology.

STYLE

We notice two particular aspects of style in our email exchanges. One is the sense of wrestling, struggling, agonising, speculating, experimenting, grafting, consolidating. These are the very same kinds of emotions and actions we go through when writing individually, the fact that they are unarticulated contributing to the stress of the activity. Externalising and sharing our feelings in this way makes writing a little less of a stressful activity.

The second aspect is the economy of words used in the emails. There is a 'distanced directness'. In some ways, working by email is a far more streamlined mode of operating than face-to-face meetings where there is invariably a great deal of exploration, experiment and embellishment – not always to the point. There are one or two asides in the emails, but for the most part they are succinct and to the point – qualities required for writing. The email device forces us to concentrate on the matter in hand as closely as possible, saying what we have to say, with little of the human and relational interface that might blur these messages in face-to-face meetings.

PROBLEMS AND SOLUTIONS

There can be problems with both team and technology. Teamwork does not suit every purpose, every group or every individual. Some attempts have foundered on the very basis of individual differences (Platt 1976). Teamwork is expensive in terms of time and cost (Liggett *et al.* 1994), and continuous and harmonious communication is sometimes difficult to maintain. It is easy to see how responsibility might become shifted and not accepted among individuals in the group, and how a team might be used to divert account-ability. In another context, teamworking can be a managerial device for securing functional participation of members, similar to the 'contrived collegiality' that has been observed in schools (Hargreaves 1994). Bell (1977) describes the tensions, conflicts, frustrations, stress, mistrust and acrimony that can arise from an ill-assorted, 'contrived' team. There might be exploitation of those with less power, who may do more than their fair share of the work but receive less of the credit and benefit. There might be divided loyalties to the team's concerns, and different career projections which could affect those loyalties. There could be personal problems among team members, clashes of temperament, different competencies, varying paradigmatic and theoretical allegiances, all leading to factionalism and counter-productive fights and strug-gles over whose view prevails. Some might feel that teamwork stifles their individuality and originality, and is against the very spirit of ethnography if not of all qualitative research (Beidelman 1974). As Ellen (1984: 208) remarks, 'The fieldworker who regards the discipline of social anthropology as akin to the art of the novelist is likely to find the presence of other researchers distracting and irrelevant'. If they do produce something worthwhile, they might be fiercely protective of their work against other team members. The 'cult of individualism' still survives (Erikson and Stull 1998: 28). Questions of team size are also relevant. Ellen (1984: 210) notes considerable logistical, organisational and intellectual problems with teams larger than two, and that 'the degree of personal commitment of the lone anthropologist is likely to be much greater than that of an anthropologist . . . who is the member of a large fieldwork team' (p. 98). Interdisciplinary teams 'can provide unrivalled breadth and depth of authoritative data, but often lack theoretical impulse and ana-lytical focus' (p. 212).

Clearly, the composition of research teams and the relationships among their members are crucial. Despite the general 'multiplier effect', they might also represent constraints for certain individuals, rather than liberation. The group itself might set up its own constraining parameters, beyond which it becomes difficult to move due to the volume of work generated – a victim of its own success. Democratic procedures and a respect for individuals, and ensuring opportunities for purely individual advancement and products would seem sensible, to go side-by-side with the various kinds of teamwork we have identified here. Questions of balance have to be borne in mind. To what extent, for example, was our team initially de-feminised? To what extent was it de-racialised? A research team cannot represent every con-stituency – but it can be reflective of its composition, and aware of the implications.

Liggett et al. (1994: 81) refer to a 'common bond' or 'mindset' among their core team, which, despite their varied perspectives, sustained a collect-ive commitment to their study and ensured a 'common framework' in presenting their work to others. Ely et al. (1997) go so far as to claim that they 'write as a team and often think as a team' (p. 1), and that their writing demands 'more we-ness and less I-ness' (p. 3). We adhere to the former rather than the latter position. There has been little 'writing as a team' as such among us. Rather, the joint preparation of material usually takes the form of somebody taking the main responsibility for it, with others making comments and contributions. But we do have a 'common framework', consisting of complementary theoretical and methodological approaches, the use of similar concepts in our work, and the addressing of similar issues. The application of this framework has an integrating effect, and adds more depth to individual work. We have our differences, but these complement rather than disrupt, broadening perspectives, checking and balancing. The pains and pleasures of writing, the demands and pressures of preparing, presenting and defending papers at conferences and symposia, have cemented relationships within our team, developing a team spirit marked by mutual trust and collegiality. The serious intent of matters is also cushioned by the general good humour shared by team members. A few jokes along the way not only help us through long meetings, but also make individuals feel easier in situations that might otherwise be threatening to them. It is well known, also, that humour promotes group solidarity (Mealyea 1989). As a significant feature of the group's culture, humour acts as a humanising and binding force, reminding us that people, and the bonds between them, are more important than abstract issues. In several ways, therefore, the team helps to counteract the traditional loneliness of the long-distance ethnographer.

Many of the problems some research teams have experienced in the past appear to have arisen from the undemocratic nature of the relationships among members of the team. Platt (1976: 76) notes that 'no team is completely non-hierarchical'. This was certainly true of ours – we held posts of different status and permanence for a start. Beyond this, however, and especially in 'whole team' meetings, we operated in a democratic manner. This was aided by our 'immersion' in issues of common interest. Olesen *et al.* (1994: 126) use this concept in explaining how their team was able to raise the analysis to 'a higher order of abstraction or generality', as we feel we did with the 'restructuring' project:

> In part we could realise this because of our long mutual immersion in the study of self-care. That immersion honed our analytic skills, and also provided a safeguard against any team member, faculty or not, dominating the analysis or manipulating agreement; others simply knew too much and too well the subtleties of self-care ethnography readily to agree even on nonproblematic categories or themes.

As for email, like computer technology in general, it can have its drawbacks. There is a danger of loss of individuality, individual style and the personal touch of qualitative work. Email is not a recipe for all circumstances. We need to bear in mind Platt's (1976: 91) criticisms of the use of the computer – 'sophisticated solutions to problems we could hit with a hammer', and 'as the computer becomes fascinating, sociology becomes less fascinating'.

In other words, we can become more involved with the means of commun-ication than the communication itself.

Clearly, also, while we have celebrated the communicative capacity of email, by the same token it can constitute an invasion of private life. Email can take over your life. There is a compulsion to look at it, and then to answer the messages immediately, even if schedules are full. You thus might spend too long receiving and answering messages, and there may be too many interruptions, splitting up the day. Some find its 'rapid response feel' a real problem, developing 'email guilt syndrome' if they do not respond quickly. In short, email can disrupt our carefully constructed and delicately balanced working routines and coping mechanisms. One colleague reported how, on returning from a spell of study leave, he found over 500 email messages on his computer. His method of handling these was simple – he deleted them at the touch of a button – a masterstroke which enabled him to get on with more pressing matters, but which nonetheless might have lost him some important items.

All this indicates the need to establish protocols before you start, and to situate the email resource among the other resources and responsibilities of individual members of the team. Success has probably a great deal to do with size of the team and relationships among them. There needs to be agreement about rates of exchange, priorities of task, working hours, nature of the exchanges and nature of team involvement. In this way, you can control the resource, rather than becoming controlled by it.

8

With what do we write?

Peter Woods and Andrew Hannan

The presentational task of ethnography is sometimes held to be 'painting pictures in words', 'capturing a likeness', re-creating the 'very feel' of an event, evoking an image, awakening a spirit, or reconstructing a mood or atmosphere (see Chapters 4 and 5). What tools do we use in applying these methods? Are they as important to the qualitative researcher as they are, say, to the artist, musician or sculptor? What effect do they have on the process and on the finished product?

The advent of the computer has revolutionised the writing process for many people. This book was written on one – though using a sheaf of hand-written notes. Is there much more to be said? Well, yes, if only because different people have different preferences. Wellington (2003: 24) found that 'people seem to vary widely in how they actually write, what they write with . . .' This is not just a technical matter. Writing is not a mechanical, linear, exercise involving simply placing what is in one's mind on paper, the writing tool – whether pen, typewriter, computer or whatever – simply being the recording device. It is a more complicated activity in which the whole writer's self is engaged. Writing is an expression of the self. The writing tool, as an extension of self, is central to the psychological processes involved. We consider this first, before going on to discuss the uses of computers and pens. We draw on our own experiences, on those of colleagues, and on the literature.

THE RESEARCHER'S SELF AND
THE WRITING IMPLEMENT

The qualitative researcher tunes in to the 'life of things', at every turn jotting down notes, fashioning *aide-mémoires*, scribbling memos, experimenting at analysis, constructing drafts, making corrections, recording ideas. The researcher is never without pen or pencil, and, increasingly these days, some electronic recording device, such as a laptop, palmtop or wireless handheld computer. Data press and crowd the memory, ideas form and float in the mind, playing games like 'catch me if you can'. The writing tool concentrates the mind wonderfully.

These implements make both a material and symbolic link between writer and written. One possible explanation for newscasters, who, laptop in front of them, pen in hand, end the news by screwing the top back on the pen and putting it in their pocket, is that the pen gives the newscaster a sense of connection of self with the news. Sitting in a TV studio reading from a teleprompter under the glare of bright lights is an unnatural situation. The pen and laptop are lifelines that make it seem real. The symbolism is that the newscasters are writing the news that appears on the screen. It gives them more of a sense of control, and of self-identification with the viewer.

It is not uncommon for artefacts to become extensions of the self. Willis (1978), for example, gives a graphic description of the motor bike and its meaning to the 'motor-bike boys': 'The roughness and intimidation of the motor bike, the surprise of its fierce acceleration, the aggressive thumping of the unbaffled exhaust, matches and symbolizes the masculine assertiveness, the rough camaraderie, the muscularity of language, of their style of social interaction' (1978: 53). In another analogy, a potter 'becomes an extension of the clay, experiencing its plasticity, feeling its willingness to go in certain directions, sensing how far and how long it can be worked without collaps-ing . . . It is hands and mind and spirit concentrated on extracting from the clay its most poetic possibilities' (Bevlin 1970: 125). Similarly, Herbert Read portrays sculpture as 'not a reduplication of form and feature; it is rather the translation of meaning from one material into another material' [1931] 1949: 185).

Can the same be said of our writing implements? Compared to a motor bike, a pen is an uncomplicated, almost insignificant piece of equipment. But that is part of its beauty. It can be secreted in a pocket, or in a hand, or behind an ear. It sits in the hand naturally, like an extension of it, an extra digit. But what an explosion of riches can emerge from it! It has affinities with the researcher, therefore. In the field it is unobtrusive, mostly hidden from view, in fact. Yet it is to hand, ready to act. It channels thoughts in an uninterrupted flow from mind to paper. It may be a simple object, but it can be aesthetically pleasing in itself, a pleasure to hold and to look at – as might be said of its product, which undoubtedly bears the individual hallmark of the writer. It is also amazingly multifunctional. It can do words, shorthand, notes, sketches, diagrams, figures. In this way it offers a kind of penmanic triangulation.

Computers can do all these things, too, and other things besides. There are a variety of them, designed for different purposes or situations. Some are so neat and compact they can fit within the pocket. Some researchers have become so skilled in their use that they have largely replaced the pen for them throughout their research. We have seen worn-out keyboards on hand-held computers through constant use during the day. Once you have gained reasonable keyboard skills (soon developed through usage), you will find computers can process material faster. Your notes are simply transferred electronically to your main computer, saving time and the drudgery of keying them in. You can also access the internet and use email from tiny hand-held computers while in the field, so that they are a link not only to what you are writing, but to other sources of information, enormously enriching the research situation. If the pen is an extension of the arm, the computer lends more strength and skill to it. Together they are a formidable resource.

THE COMPUTER AS A WRITING AID

Computers have brought enormous benefits to writers. They have had a liberating effect for some. Gabriel Garcia Marquez found writing easier 'since I made the greatest discovery of my life: the word processor . . . If I'd had this machine 20 years ago, I'd have published two to three times as many books' (Hamill 1988: 51). Marshall Cook, an unlikely convert to computers, has found, like many others, that they are wonderful aids to his creativity and productivity – though he cautions, '. . . never lose your ability to create with blunt Crayola on paper sack while riding the bus to work . . .' (1992: 99).

Consider this testimony from somebody who used to find writing his 'worst nightmare':

> I did not learn how to write until I learned how to use a computer . . .
> The computer helped me to discover that there was more to writing than just spelling. First of all, the computer was something new and different and was a relief from pencil and paper. All my life pencil and paper had been a nightmare. When I picked up a pencil and paper to write, my stomach would automatically tighten, and my nightmare would begin. The computer helped me view writing in a different way. It helped me to shed my fear of the pencil and paper. Sitting down in front of a computer was not nearly as frightening to me as sitting down with a pencil and paper. For this reason. I immediately saw the computer as a sign of hope. I had never been able to put down the right words with a pencil, but sitting at a keyboard seemed to free my mind. A pencil was like a piece of dead wood in my hands, and trying to make this stick form letters always seemed awkward and difficult. When using a keyboard, however, the letters seemed to come out through my fingertips. The writing seemed to be closer to my brain . . . The computer allows me to be inventive, to go beyond the simple words I know.
>
> (Lee and Jackson 1993: 23–8)

Here is clear expression of the computer as an extension of self, and indeed as a means of discovery of self. The computer, for some, has catalytic qualities. Through its use they discover skills they did not know they possessed. They find a way to do things that have been obstructed to them for years, not through any complete personal deficiency, but because they have not found or been presented with a method that works for them. The same may well be true for some researchers, brilliant data-gatherers and analysts, but struggling writers, who have found new chances with the computer.

Snyder (1993: 62–3) concluded from his extensive research on the matter that 'most writers, regardless of age, enjoy writing with word processors, and believe that their use enhances composing and revising strategies, as well as the quality of their writing', through

> the formulation of thoughts and their expression at all levels, from the juxtaposition of words and ideas to the logical development of para-graphs and cohesion of argument or narrative. Because word processing takes over much of the mechanical operation involved in the writing process, the student is released to concentrate on the logic, organization and clarity of the piece. The computer increases the range of work practices available and offers more control over the final product.
>
> (p. 55)

We (PW and AH) can type much faster than we can write, and we can change things much more easily. That being so, we make more changes, more often, which ought to mean a better product. There are physical limits to the extent that one can cut and paste with pen and paper, but no such limits with the computer. There are also those marvellous facilities for compiling tables and diagrams through the use of spreadsheets. So one can work on the integrity of a piece to a higher level. It is also very easy to incorporate and work on other material (e.g. transcripts of tapes) that may have been created by somebody else on a compatible machine. With ever-increasing space on computers, whole libraries of material can be stored and be available for immediate access and use. There are also voice recognition programs whereby you can speak text directly into a computer for it to convert into a document. Bob Jeffrey has found this very useful for sorting out rough fieldnotes, transferring parts of taped transcripts which would have been too expensive to have transcribed, and for summaries of books or quotes. However, the text produced needs to be carefully checked by the writer as we do not speak in the same way as we write, and the computer does not always 'hear' as intended.

Computers may be machines, but there is a strange compulsion about working with them, learning about their mysteries and limitless capabilities, mastering the skills involved and internalising their processes. The engage-ment starts with switching the machine on to welcoming noises and images, through to the thrill of seeing the finished work emerge from the printer. It has something to do with control both of the writing process *and* of the machine. One is practising a dual skill, and the more the computer skills are worked on, the more second nature they become, but also the more other, more difficult, skills come within reach. Nick Hubbard used to feel hostile to computers as a 'negation of the mutual reliance central to democratic modern-isation' (thus requiring human interaction), but discovered their usefulness almost by accident. He writes: 'There is no doubt that having the "knowledge" helps me to feel that I am not excluded from the modern project, that as a middle-aged person on the road to discovering technology I am under-going a process of renewal which denies the central image of old age and its propensity for a reactionary view of the world'. Here we have computers assisting in a renovation of self. We live in a technological age, and through these machines we keep in touch with the developing world, open to any new advantages for self-development that may arise.

Let us review in a little more detail the various ways that computers can help the qualitative researcher with writing at all stages of the research process.

Literature review

A preliminary search on the internet by topic using one of the search engines, such as 'Google Scholar', can reveal lots of information of variable quality, amidst which may well sit some gems. More systematic searches of electronic databases, such as the British Education Index, of web-based journals, for example *EducatiON-LINE* (http://www.leeds.ac.uk/educol/), and of a multi-tude of traditional journals now available online can provide the starting points for further enquiry. Searching the Qualidata site (http://www.esds.ac.uk/qualidata/) can reveal what other qualitative researchers have previously found in your field of interest. Of course, the beauty of being able to do all this without the trouble of leaving your computer means that you can easily integrate what you find into your growing account, selecting, copying and pasting relevant passages into your own text with all the bibliographic acknow-ledgments, details of which are readily to hand. This saves an enormous amount of time which is freed up for the more creative aspects of writing. Access to sites on the internet can be a problem if you are not a member of an academic institution that subscribes to the various services, but enough is openly and freely available to make the internet a wonderful source of material. Searching for an author by name or for a specific paper by title can yield exactly what you are looking for at minimal expense and with no delay. Waiting for the library to get you a copy of an important article and paying a fee for inter-library loan may not be entirely eliminated, but its frequency is likely to be significantly reduced.

Data collection

Digital audio recorders and digital cameras that capture both still and moving images, the latter with audio, are sufficiently user-friendly to encourage their employment in qualitative research even among those who are not techno-logically minded. Video and audio files can be recorded directly onto a computer. These can then be annotated and indexed using software such as

AnnoTape (http://www.annotape.com/) rather than delaying all analysis until they have been laboriously transcribed. You can scan text in the research situation with an unobtrusive, pocket-fitting pen scanner, though this as yet has not been fully tested in the field. Being able to transfer such data directly to a computer for editing and analysis brings considerable benefits. Hand-held computers and lightweight laptops offer the possibility of notes being recorded electronically, even in handwritten form for those who prefer to use a pen of sorts rather than a keyboard. The big advantage here is that the data can then be saved on a computer for later perusal and analysis.

Survey research is also increasingly being conducted via computer, using email or web-based questionnaires, the responses to which are often analysed by means of both quantitative and qualitative data analysis software (Hannan 2002; Saxon *et al.* 2003). A particularly interesting example is the survey of undergraduates conducted by Ruth Woodfield, which followed students through their first year experiences by means of their responses to email 'prompts', which combined to form something akin to an interactive and virtual diary (Woodfield 2002).

Data analysis

Researchers have long been aware of the power of computers when it comes to the analysis of quantitative data, hence assisting the organisation of their writing. Software for qualitative data analysis is a more recent invention, but already proliferates. A good place to find information about what is available is the Computer Assisted Qualitative Data Analysis Software site (at http://caqdas.soc.surrey.ac.uk/). Packages such as HyperRESEARCH (http://www.researchware.com/), ATLAS.ti (http://www.atlasti.com), NUD*IST and NVivo (http://www.qsrinternational.com/) are intended to promote theory-building as well as enabling sophisticated content and theme analysis. Importing data into one of these programs is obviously not the same as poring over typed transcripts or handwritten notes with different coloured felt-tipped pens. However, they do have the great advantage of flexibility, with virtual selecting, copying, cutting and pasting being a lot less bother than the real-life versions once the tricks of the software have been mastered. It is also possible to combine the old and the new approaches by printing hard copies of the data to be read off-screen and even scribbled on before decisions are made about coding devices and grounded hypotheses. The qualitative data analysed by means of computer software is easily incorporated into word-processed accounts. AH has made use of software for handling qualitative data in several of his projects, analysing both responses to open-ended items on questionnaires (Hannan 1995) and transcripts from semi-structured interviews (Hannan and Silver 2000). Advice on how to use NUD*IST and NVivo can be found in David and Sutton (2004: Ch. 19). There are also courses regularly on offer initiating researchers into the use of qualitative data analysis software (see e.g. http://caqdas.soc.surrey.ac.uk/events.htm).

Presenting reports of qualitative research

One of the problems of presentation for qualitative researchers has always been that of giving the reader access to the analytical processes that have taken place before the report is published. For someone relying on quantitative data it is relatively easy to provide tables that give a summary of the findings alongside the various measures necessary for a statistical analysis. For the qualitative researcher the problems of space necessitate a more selective and illustrative approach, where evidence is used to build an account that reads well and conveys meaning. Avoiding accusations of selecting quotations to support the case being made and ignoring those that do not is a problem that computer-aided analysis can help to overcome. This can be done by giving an indication of frequency, easily derived from the use of qualitative software, when offering a quotation that illustrates a certain response or position. Better still, the whole of the suitably anonymised original data can be made available online for others to look at along with the classificatory devices used through the chosen software for others to check. Such transparency, however, is an ideal that is often aspired to but, as yet, infrequently practised.

Communications and collaboration

As discussed in Chapter 7, networked computers make it possible for authors to work together with almost instantaneous exchanges of information while many miles apart. Email with easy-to-use copying and forwarding as well as attachments, instant messaging with several co-authors discussing their efforts in their own chatroom and various other networking devices make collaboration at a distance a lot easier than relying on telephones, the post and the very occasional meeting. As noted in Chapter 7, when word-processed drafts are exchanged as email attachments any changes suggested by one author can be marked and traced through a 'tracking' device under the 'tools' menu, with the other authors having the option to accept or reject the amendments and being able to propose changes of their own. Putting together several parts of a conference paper, an article or even a book is greatly facilitated by the electronic merging of parts and of the editing of the whole.

Drafting

The great advantage of word-processing is the ease with which changes can be made. Unfortunately, the computer is still seen by some in the same way as a typewriter once was: that is as the means by which a final version is produced, rather than as an almost infinitely flexible tool for redrafting. Many teachers get their students to write early drafts of their work with pen and paper before typing up the final versions on the computer so that they can be printed and displayed. Education researchers who have had the benefit of working with assistants who do their typing for them have come to see the typed form as at least the penultimate version, to be corrected with marginal adjustments before being finalised. The finality of a typed version is, however, very different from the fluidity of its word-processed counterpart. Authors who can treat the text as adjustable from their very first sentence, who are prepared to attempt things in different ways, to change the order of sentences and paragraphs to try and achieve the maximum effect, are capable of deriving great benefits from the computer. Again, though, a combination of the old and new methods is possible, with consecutive drafts being saved to a different title (by number or date), printed as hard copies for ease of reading and critique, annotated by pen, adjusted on the computer and re-saved to a new title. In this manner it is possible to return to previous drafts in order to retrieve an approach mistakenly abandoned or to find early ideas once thought unusable but later seen as crucial. We say more about this later.

Editing

In the old days, one common mode of procedure was to write one's initial draft in pen and type it up, or have it typed up, afterwards. Revisions to the typed-up draft took the form of correcting typing errors, writing directions for changes on the script and in the margins, and 'cutting and pasting'. PW was fortunate enough to have the services of a secretary, who described his amended drafts as being like games of monopoly – 'go to . . .', 'do not . . .', 'delete . . .', 'insert . . .', 'replace by the attached . . .', 'see over . . .', with a multitude of arrows, deletions and corrections. The draft would be amended, cut up and pasted if reordering was involved, and photocopied to give a copy of the new draft, which would then go through a similar process. All of these things, and more, can now be done, and much more efficiently, at source by computer, with no need for checking and double-checking typing errors. Cutting and pasting are done at a click of the mouse, insertions and deletions by selecting text and moving accordingly. Computer devices can also check for spelling and grammar. These are not without their flaws, but they can be made to work in ways especially useful for those not trained as typists and who are prone to errors that can be automatically corrected while they work. It is easy, too, to find things and to monitor for unwanted repetition in your work. By feeding an appropriate word or words into the 'find' device under the 'edit' menu, you can discover exactly where in a text they occur at the click of the mouse. Similarly, the terrors of referencing can be overcome by the use of software such as EndNote or Reference Manager. These are bibliography-makers that format citations while the text is being composed with templates that can be adjusted to fit the requirements of the most finicky of editors or publishers.

Publishing

Finally, recalling the discussion of hypermedia ethnography in Chapter 4, and anticipating the discussion of ejournals and ebooks in Chapter 8, it would appear we are only at the beginning of what computers and other technology can do for us as writers. They can improve our own process of writing. They are also opening the way to radically new conceptions of the product, new avenues for representation and new opportunities for publishing.

SOME USES OF THE PEN

Writing, let alone ethnography, is a very individual matter. We build up a whole plethora of processes and materials, some of which may be trivial to others but central to us, to aid in this hardest of tasks. It is a question, there-fore, of what tools suit the individual and the most productive relationship that can be set up between them. Some authors might prefer a PC, some an Apple Macintosh, some a desktop, some a laptop. Some, like Alan Bleasdale, might prefer using an old-fashioned Imperial 66 typewriter. Some prefer working with pens and pencils, and very particular kinds. One may need a 'Mont Blanc Solitaire', with ribbed German silver stem and 18-carat gold nib; or perhaps a 'Tomboy Zoom', a cigar shaped Japanese pen; or an 'Élysée en Vogue'. It might be that a 'platinum Man from Uncle Special' does the trick. We don't know of anybody still using a quill pen, but Shakespeare for one didn't do too badly through its use. Pens and pencils have served many fine writers in the past. Philip Larkin used nothing but Royal Sovereign 2B pencils, scribbling his way through countless drafts (Motion 1993). Solzhenitsyn selected from a range of pencils to suit the mood of a paragraph. William Faulkner said that the only tools he needed were pen, paper, tobacco, food and whisky. The composer, Robert Simpson, uses the gold pencil that belonged to Carl Nielsen to work on his symphonic scores.

What then are the main benefits of the pen or pencil for the writer?

Ease and economy

Bruce Mason, a computer expert (see e.g. Mason and Dicks 2004) still finds

> . . . a notepad and pen to be the most flexible noting tool there is for fieldwork, but I am gradually becoming more open to using a PDA [personal digital assistant]. Thing is, for £10 I can buy all the pens and paper I will need. I can use multi-coloured pens, annotate, draw and cross-reference, and do so in a way which is a lot less obtrusive than noting on a PDA. The batteries aren't going to run out and I don't have to learn and run several different programmes.
>
> (Personal communication)

PW uses Parker biros. They are comfortable, with a good flow, reliable, and they suit his style of handwriting. He has a number of these situated in strategic places all over the house and in every coat pocket and briefcase, together with notepads and backs of envelopes. They are ideal for jotting down ideas and thoughts while out walking the dog, having a bath, digging the garden, or doing anything, anywhere.

Identity and cultural uses

Nick Hubbard uses a Parker 51 which his wife bought him in 1972. It is both an 'aesthetic object' and 'a central means by which I record my ideas on paper'. He comments, 'I have always used black ink because it looks bold and permanent. Somehow using the same pen with the same coloured ink for all these years has given the act of writing a sense of status and personal identity' (Personal communication). Nick sees a symbolic link between writer and pen, and notes a cultural significance:

> Most important is the notion that a pen is an emblem of cultural identity drawing one closer to an interaction with the text one is creating and indeed reading. The 'material and symbolic link between writer and written' as an act of personal culture is very strong. It creates a personal engagement with a text which is physical as well as mental. There are opportunities for a direct interaction involving underlining, inserting and recording ideas and impressions alongside the text. In this way the read text and the written response create a bond . . . Another aspect of this is represented by my response to learning another language. I go to a French class once a week. I quite consciously handwrite my homework. For me to be able to 'write' another language is to engage not only with it from a technical point of view, but also to provide a means of re-creating and imbibing, through one's own developed skills, a culture which one wants to understand and identify with. The relationship becomes that much closer. In writing, one is using a skill which is ancient, which has been handed down and again is culturally significant. It is how many of our forebears recorded their lives and somehow it is one of the few personal skills left to us, enabling us to maintain our autonomous self.
>
> (Personal communication)

The overall effect of a longhand draft, even with corrections, may be aesthetically pleasing. There is only one of these, and it records the pain as well as the joy of creation. It is a distinctive expression of self, like a signature. Lawrence Stenhouse once produced a beautifully handwritten draft for a conference (later published in Burgess 1984). It seemed particularly meaningful, being more of a personal statement, and appropriate to the content of the paper which was 'an autobiographical account'. There is a closeness, almost an intimacy in such a presentation, as there is in private letters that we write and that we wish to imprint with something of our selves, as contrasted with business letters that we type or send by email. Eisner (1991: 36) talks of 'the presence of voice in text . . . We display our signatures. Our signature makes it clear that a person, not a machine, was behind the words'. For others, of course, the computer offers similar identity chances, as earlier testimony in this chapter shows.

As therapy

> Assist me some extemporal god of rime, for I am sure I shall turn sonneter. Devise, wit; write, pen; for I am for whole volumes in folio.
>
> (William Shakespeare, *Love's Labours Lost*)

A pen can become highly personalised, a tried and trusted friend, a companion countering the loneliness of writing. In PW's wishful, adolescent days, like Shakespeare's Armado in *Love's Labours Lost*, above, he used to fondly imagine a magic pen that answered all examination questions perfectly. All that was required was for the pen to be laid on the paper and it was away! One of the hard lessons of life is that there is no such magic other than what you accomplish through your own efforts. However, a pen that has been through those efforts with you has acquired some of those 'magic' properties. Words have flowed from it before; it has experienced pauses, some of them lengthy; it has gone on false trails, doodled, been chewed and sucked, used as a chin or back scratcher; but it has always, in the end, delivered the goods. There is something very reassuring about, at the beginning of a writing session, just picking up a proved, successful pen.

However, as noted earlier, the pen does not act as a liberator for everybody. In fact it can be quite the reverse. It is a matter of personal choice.

As psychological and physical relief

There are psychological and physical advantages to having a variety of tools available. The problem of RSI (repetitive strain injury) is well known and a growing hazard with increasing computer use. Bob Jeffrey finds that word processing for any length of time causes a tightening across the shoulders. He finds a voice recognition programme relaxing. He can sit back, look out of the window if he chooses, proceed at a slower pace but still make progress. Using a pen to make some notes or annotations on printed scripts can have the same effect.

As gleaner

> When I have fears that I may cease to be
> Before my pen has glean'd my teeming brain,
> Before high-piled books, in charact'ry,
> Hold like full garners the full-ripen'd grain.
>
> (John Keats, 'The Terror of Death', 1817)

To 'glean' is 'to collect what is thinly scattered'. Granting Keats the customary poetic licence, the pen is useful whether the mind is alive with activity or faintly twitching. In the latter case, by 'doodling' – experimenting with words, new formulations, sketching figures and diagrams, annotating transcripts and other documents – the pen helps to stir into life, to formulate and to collect an idea here, one there, a shape here, a possible connection there. Writing can be very untidy in the early stages: arguably the more creative, the more untidy and chaotic. We may have internalised more formalised models of writing, like the teachers in a design project who only wanted their children to produce 'neat' work, consigning their experimental scribblings on odd pieces of paper to the wastebasket before anybody could see them. However, these scruffy sketches were the items the architects, who were assisting in the project, were most interested in. They were the most creative products.

Where the mind is 'teeming', the pen serves as a means of selection and discipline, sifting and refining, putting a brake on excesses, encouraging the more likely ideas, concentrating the mind. Thoughts have to come through a communication channel. They have to be intelligible and coherent, to yourself as well as to others. The pen represents a way in which the writer can have a conversation with the self. Perhaps it is well, at times, that it can only move so fast – it reins in the galloping, potentially stampeding mind to a more viable pace. Where there is need to register a suspected valuable thought while the pen is already engaged on externalising others, there are strategies available, such as a scribbled word in the margin. This 'gleaning' is an artistic, creative process. Eric Newton (1962), speaking of art itself, though his words apply to all forms of art, states that

> Every artist knows from experience, but few laymen ever realize, the constant inter-play between mind and hand as a work of art progresses ... The original imagined image is actually far from complete, and as soon as the artist sets to work his medium begins to modify and clarify it; unless he is a bad artist, he will accept and take advantage of these modifications.

Such a view is consistent with a view of qualitative research, in part at least, as an artistic activity.

As a listening and reading aid

Some researchers are nervous about using tape recorders, or even taking notes during an interview. In some instances, however, a researcher taking notes is seen as a compliment to the interviewee. One aims in qualitative interviewing for naturalism, rapport, unobtrusiveness, as in participant observation; but too much concession to informality and relaxation can be counter-productive, affecting the interviewee's motivation to tell the tale, raising doubts in their mind about the quality of and interest in what they are saying, devaluing the discussion to the plane of casual and passing conversation (though there are times in qualitative research when those kinds of conversation are needed). Note-taking in interviews therefore is not just a matter of recording information, but of anchoring the discussion through the communicatory outlet of the pen, and of motivating the interviewee. You can also scribble down prompts to future questions you might want to ask that come up serendipitously in the course of the interview without faltering in the attention you are giving to the current answer. It thus aids the quality of the researcher's listening as well as the interviewee's talking.

Nick Hubbard marries this point to a function of the doodle:

> I am an inveterate doodler as I talk with people, listen to them or have conversations with them on the telephone. These doodles usually take the form of interconnected triangles which can end by enveloping the page in front of me depending on the length of the conversation or telephone call. Doodling for me represents a link between what a person is saying and what sense I make of it. It helps me to listen, to think and interpret and I can lose concentration without it.
>
> (Personal communication)

For others, perhaps, doodling is a sign of lack of interest. If using it as an aid, therefore, in somebody's presence, you would need to be careful to use other responses, such as eye contact and understanding and appreciative noises, to avoid your doodling being interpreted by your interviewee as the opposite of what you intend!

Sue Waite, a colleague, finds the pen a useful reading or thinking tool: 'When reading through something, a pen in hand helps bridge the gap between the writer and the reader because it enables you to interact with the text through marginal notes, asterisks, exclamation marks. This is why reading, whether for editing or an original text by another, is so much easier when printed off' (personal communication).

As a promoter of ideas

For example, making mind–maps (drawing branches, tracing interconnections, identifying patterns in the data); brainstorming (noting down free flow of ideas); freewriting or speedwriting (to overcome 'writer's block'); bubble outlining; 'bricklaying' (Cook 1992); jotting down ideas wherever you might be.

As an aid in drafting

Despite our earlier comments on the benefits of the computer in drafting documents, there are some who find it an impediment in this respect. One respondent in Wellington (2003: 25), says,

> I find that using pen on paper is much more 'organic' in terms of the relationship between thinking and writing. It's almost going down your arm, from your head and onto the paper. I write on wide-lined paper every second line, write 5000 words, then go through it scribbling in the spaces, changing, adding and pruning. What you end with looks

terrible, but you know it's a first draft. If you do that on a computer it comes out looking great – but it's still a first draft. It looks better than it is. But with hand-written stuff, it actually is better than it looks.

P.J. Woods (1995: 180) makes a similar point:

I still have the Waterman pen with which I used to compose texts in large, outdated diaries . . . The crossings-out on the handwritten page represented either a failure of literary intent on my part, arising perhaps from fatigue or lack of inspiration, or – and more comforting for the truly creative artist – a denial of the alternative expressions welling up from the competing liminal authors . . . When using a word-processor the denial may be more permanent, but the penned corrections were useful reminders of the presence of 'ghost-writers'. This is why I still prefer to write in pen and ink rather than seated before a word-processing screen. Regrettably, convenience and lack of time mostly dictate that I adopt the latter *modus operandi*.

Greenlaw (1996: 23) adds a related point:

I do not write on a computer as I like to see what I have crossed out. A computer offers the seductive image of printed text. You may forget that what you have on your screen is a rough draft. The ease with which you can move, delete and revise your words can be deceptive and disorientating. Try to stick for as long as possible with paper and pen.

This of course, is all in the perception, and not intrinsic to computers. As we noted above (p. 120), such views are possibly influenced by the old handwriting-typewriter model that many of us have grown up with. By contrast, some writers have become almost completely dedicated to the computer in drafting, finding pens cumbersome and unnecessary. Many of us, we suspect, use a combination of the two in a variety of ways. Sue Waite, for example, finds that she edits by computer at paragraph or sentence level, and uses a pen for phrases and single words. Wolcott (2001: 14), whose writing 'sometimes flows easily, sometimes slows to a snail's pace', still finds that 'when the words don't come easily, I leave the computer keyboard and retreat to my Bic pens and yellow pads to push words on to paper one at a time'. These days PW rarely does totally handwritten or totally word-processed drafts. In general, it is so much easier, more efficient and quicker working on the computer. Changes are recorded, and all drafts kept in a file on the computer for later inspection if needed. But he still tries to recapture the provisional nature of drafts as he is used to seeing them by printing them off and quickly reducing their pristine appearance by scribbles, deletions, insertions and reorganisations. These are also kept, in a 'hard' file so that the whole career of a paper or chapter is available across the two locations. Writers who have used computers from the very beginning might not need to do this, but PW has found it a useful amalgamation of styles, gaining benefits from use of the computer while retaining something of the rhythm of production from his previous mode of working.

As an enhancer of quality

Using longhand or a word processor may have an effect on quality. Some writers have found the computer a constraint on creativity (see e.g. Amis in Hammond 1984; Murdoch in Hammond 1984). Many of these are successful writers who have established highly productive ways of working with other tools and see no need to change them. Their pens, typewriters or whatever have become indispensable parts of their selves which the computer threatens to disrupt. Some, who may feel compelled to use them, may not be best served by them. PW has seen PhDs produced by students on a computer strewn with errors (one had an extraordinary variety of dash and hyphen), badly spaced, inconsistently laid out and poorly printed. Wolcott (2001: 25) also, himself a convert to the 'genius of computers' and 'word processing as an indispensable tool in writing up research', notes that

> word processing has created some problems of its own, one of which has become evident in reading student papers (and occasionally, read-ing colleagues' papers as well). The ease of production often results in faster rather than better writing. Computer capabilities for easy revision, even checking for spelling errors, are often ignored. Hastily written and hastily proofed first drafts are tendered as final copy; printout is equated with 'in print', the sketch proffered in lieu of a more careful rendering.

Of course, it is not the fault of the machine. The point here is that in the increasingly distant past secretaries were paid to type the final draft of a PhD and nowadays it is a do-it-yourself job. Being able to produce a high-standard text is a very worthwhile transferable skill for which tuition should be pro-vided as part of the process of research training.

As noted earlier, many find the quality of their writing improved by the use of computers. We count ourselves among them. But equally, some will, like Nick Hubbard, 'sometimes become so tied up with the process of learn-ing the ins and outs of the technology that it tends to interfere with the ideas I want to get down' (personal communication).

CONCLUSION

It is a matter of personal choice. We need to find out what tools we are most comfortable with, what best facilitates formulating what we want to say and getting it down on paper. Some need the typewriter to bash (Bernard 1990). Some prefer to write longhand (Trollope 1994). The pace of writing is closely geared to one's thought processes. For some, the computer has speeded this up, enabling faster, more productive thought. For others, the flow of the ink, the scratch of the pen, the contact with paper, the handwriting (a personal signature), the way the pen shapes a particular word, may all be important. Most of us, we suspect, use a combination of implements in ways we have personally developed. Sharples and Pemberton (1992: 325–6) conclude, 'There is no single best approach to writing . . . Computer systems to support the writing process will be of most help if they fit the writer's perception of the task and assist whichever strategy the writer chooses to adopt'.

Researchers need to bear in mind the powerful resources that, in this computer age, are continually becoming available. And for those who feel uncomfortable with computers, or have not yet settled into their use, we would urge them to persevere. The potential rewards are considerable. Bruce Mason writes:

> Ubiquitous computing, technology such as the iPOD and so on, even the mobile phone, are likely to become central tools for any fieldworker . . . Solid state audio recorders are on the verge of a massive price drop and the passion for mobile integrated devices with computer connectivity means that we're already seeing devices which are cameras, phones, web browsers and organizers all at once. Of course, this is just a roundabout way of saying, as people have for at least twenty years, that the appropriate technology is just round the corner.
>
> (Personal communication)

In the last resort, writers, having considered the resources available, will choose those implements, or combination of implements, that best enhance their selves, their writing styles and their rhythm of production.

9

Writing for publication

Research needs to be disseminated, and the main avenue for this is through publication. There is added pressure on academics in the UK to publish at the moment because of the 'Research Assessment Exercise' (RAE) which determines research funding for institutions (and therefore jobs), status and research careers. There are fears that while this might increase the quantity of published work, it might decrease the quality. Writing could become more instrumental in such a performatist climate as pressure mounts and as writers acquire more streetwise knowledge of how to get things published. This is a case of pressure to publish from without, rather than inspiration from within. We need to be aware of the dangers. Research – and that invariably means publishing – is part of an academic's job and, if done well, one of the most rewarding, since it means that your work is esteemed and that it will reach a wider audience. If done badly, however, it can be savaged by your peers in reviews, and/or moulder on library bookshelves for evermore. The two main routes for publication of research are through academic journals or via books. I consider some of the issues involved in each of these.

ACADEMIC JOURNALS

Weiner (1998: 4) reports the role of academic journals as being to:

- provide a means of up-to-date thinking and current research at the cutting edge in a particular discipline
- challenge entrenched assumptions, encourage divergent thinking and develop a critical approach to the establishment
- exchange information, provide work which can be used for teaching and learning, showcase high-quality work, offer an outlet for publication and dissemination, and act as a forum for campaigning on important issues.

Given this, what are the considerations when preparing material for submission to a journal?

Know your own product

You must have something worth publishing. Is it suitable for an academic journal? Criteria would include high academic content, involving a contribution to knowledge – which can be research findings, research methods or an original review of the literature. Your work might show a theoretical advance, an unusual approach, cast new light on a field of research or make a distinctive contribution to a current debate. Book chapters, though in fact they may turn out to be better, are rated below journal articles in academic circles, since most of the latter are subject to a strict form of evaluation by your peers, usually people who are chosen by editors as experts in the subject area concerned. There is no better preparation than studying the journals to which your research is relevant to get the 'feel' of an academic article. So it would be useful if you had already sought the views of others on your paper. Some may advise 'this is a journal article', and say how it might be enhanced as such. Watch out for 'calls for papers' for special issues of journals. If an issue is in your area, it increases the chances of your article being accepted on the grounds of 'suitability', though all other criteria still have to be met.

All theses of master's level and above should contain at least one potential article. After all, the main criterion in their assessment is 'making an original contribution to knowledge'. It might be based on a particularly exciting chapter, or a combination of chapters representing the core of the argument. I often advise my students to construct a paper on their whole thesis, primarily as an aid to integrating the thought behind the whole of the work, but also as a prospective journal article. Such a paper adds to the thesis in that it reveals the 'theoretical spine' of the work. It captures the essence of it in a single article, while thesis chapters are filled out with data and extensive references.

The same applies to any comparable piece of research. For example, if the main product is to be a book, there may still be an article there which encapsulates the theoretical line in a tighter form, and which stands to reach a different audience. As Richardson (1990: 54) notes, 'It is usually not until you have finished writing a book that you have digested, expanded, and theorised your work sufficiently to be able to compress it or reframe it for submission to a major social science journal'. Note that where you use substantial amounts of the same material in more than one publication, albeit in a reworked form, it is customary to ask permission from the original publisher. This is usually freely given.

There are also what I call 'spin-offs' – papers developed from quality material which cannot, for reasons of space and/or coherence, be worked into the main means of dissemination, but which have enough substance, coherence and relevance to make an article. Thus, in the course of our 'creative teaching' research, while the main focus was on teachers and teaching, we accumulated a great deal of material on students. Opportunities arose to publish articles based on this material, through invitations to contribute first to a conference, and second to a book on pupils. Such invitations might suggest ways to present your work which have not yet occurred to you, and these in turn might lead to new research. These 'pupil' papers, for example, fed into the planning of a new research project on 'creative learning'. Writing up in this sense is more of a process than an end point. Thus the file on the research should never be closed, as you don't know what further opportunities might occur. Furthermore, the thought and organisation that goes into writing up is not just retrospective, but can inform your plans for the future.

A particular kind of spin-off is one that might arise from adversity. Everything that happens during a research project has potential relevance. If things do not go well for you during your research, it is a good idea to analyse the reasons; the results might be of interest to others as well as to you. Geoff Troman (1996), for example, encountered difficulty gaining access to a school for his PhD research, for which he had been awarded a three-year contract, and used up valuable time in the attempt. But he turned his problem to good account by writing an article in which he analysed his experiences within the context of sociopolitical trends in recent years and their effect on schools. The article was duly published in the *British Educational Research Journal* – and made a useful contribution to his thesis. This kind of reflexiveness – in this case on the problems of access – is invaluable methodologically and also from a knowledge point of view, providing a sociological analysis of the situation giving rise to the problem. I never throw research materials away, however irrelevant or useless they may seem at the time. All data are capital and should be stored, since:

- There might come a time when you are invited to reflect on your past research experiences. This might be in a special edition journal, or an edited book focusing on your area, or an invited conference paper. You could be asked to give a talk which might then become the basis for a further article.
- You might wish to revise your first analysis in the light of later thinking and research and others' comments. This can be quite illuminating for your own development, and such a process would command considerable general interest.
- It might come in useful as comparative material to later research.
- It might provide part of a 'composite' article – one drawing on material from a number of other projects. Here you would be identifying themes that they all had in common – a similar process to that discussed in Chapter 3 as applied to one paper, but now offering opportunities for wider application and theorisation. Similarly, there might be composite articles which focus on methodology (such as 'New developments in action research'), a particular approach ('A postmodernist approach to educational study') or a review of the literature ('Educational ethnography in Britain').

Know your journal

> The form of academic literacy required by journals is not neutral.
> (Weiner 1998: 17)

Considerations here include whether the journal is suitable in terms of its usual content. Has it published articles before in the general area of your research and method? It is not much use submitting an article on quantitative research to the *International Journal of Qualitative Studies in Education*, or a highly theoretical paper with no clear practical applications to *The British Journal of Inservice Education*. And if you have been involved in a particular form of presentation, such as experimental writing, for the best chance of publication you must seek out journals where that is welcomed (e.g. *Qualitative Sociology, Qualitative Inquiry, Qualitative Research, The Journal of Contemporary Ethnography, Sociological Quarterly* and *Symbolic Interaction*). Your article might refer to articles or to discussions or debates that have appeared in a particular journal. Most journals have clearly defined areas – such as gender, educational policy, comparative education, special education – though some have more general fields, such as *The British Educational Research Journal*. What guidance do the editors give? Most specify the criteria inside the front or back cover of the journal – empirical research, theoretical discussion, methodological debate, disciplinary approach – in what areas and in what format, under which they invite submissions. Some write introductions to each issue (as in *Research Papers in Education*). Some write articles about their editorial experiences (e.g. Sherman 1993; Donmoyer 1996; Gargiulo and Jalongo 2001). Most are keen to encourage new authors. Some editors have difficulty finding papers of sufficient relevance and quality and canvass submissions, though others are over-subscribed. You could be reasonably confident about getting a quick and sympathetic judgement from the former, which unfortunately is not true of all journals.

Is the journal suitable in terms of status? Journals vary considerably in this respect. In general, the higher the status, the more stringent the scrutiny, and thus the more difficult it is to have an article accepted – though if it is, the kudos is commensurate. Refereed journals are considered more highly than non-refereed ones, but even among those there are big differences. The highest-status journals are the leaders in their particular field, for example *The British Journal of Sociology of Education, The British Journal of Educational Psychology* and *The British Journal of Sociology*. At the other end, there are journals which seek shorter articles, perhaps of a less theoretical and more immediately practical nature (such as *English in Education, Topic* and *Educational Action Research*). Included here are the educational press, such as the *Times Educational Supplement, Education Guardian*, and *Education*. Most journals lie between these two extremes.

What are the refereeing practices of the journal? You can obtain this information by writing to the editor. A typical checklist sent to referees is given in Figure 9.1.

Referees are asked to bear the following in mind when assessing papers for inclusion.

We want *BERJ* to represent the best of educational research and so it is important that referees are rigorous and demanding, taking into account the status of the journal as a premier international publication.

Articles are welcomed on all kinds and aspects of educational research, and addressing any form of education, formal or informal.

It is the policy of the journal that articles should offer original insight in terms of theory, methodology or interpretation, and not be restricted to the mere reporting of results. Submitted work should be substantially original, recent in reference and previously unpublished. It is expected that articles should have a clear intellectual argument demonstrating the significance of the work, that authors demonstrate a good grasp of the literature in the relevant field and have a critical stance. The methodological approach should be argued, not simply stated or assumed, where relevant to empirical work.

It is important that referees pay particular attention to the appropriateness, accuracy, consistency and accessibility of tabular data, and the specified referencing protocols.

We welcome original ways of presenting research findings, and support accessible, well-written accounts.

It is important that referees are decisive in their judgements of submissions.

In writing up their comments on articles submitted to the journal, referees are asked, *in a minimum of 250 words or so*, to address whatever is relevant in the following:

- Offer a brief critical résumé of theoretical, methodological, or substantive issues raised by the author.
- Assess how adequately the research is located in terms of previous relevant research.
- Make a reasoned appraisal of the overall quality of the submission in terms of its significance, contribution to knowledge, or originality.
- Provide feedback useful to the author (a) for resubmission (b) more generally in terms of the further development of the research. It is helpful in the resubmission process if specific numbered points are made by referees and addressed by authors.
- Indicate where appropriate any limitations on their ability to comment.

We also expect referees to be able to report on submissions within a three-week period. It is important that these deadlines are respected. Articles published in *BERJ* include information on 'date received'/'date resubmitted'/'date finally accepted' and we do not wish to exhibit unprofessional delays between receipt and acceptance/resubmission/rejection.

Figure 9.1 *British Educational Research Journal*'s Notes for referees, 2004

Some recommend tailoring your material towards a specific journal, rather than writing an article first and then looking around for a suitable journal. Walford (1998) relates how, in one particular project, he knew from the beginning that he wanted to publish some academic articles, and then base a book around them. As the research progressed, he 'divided the various parts of the research into articles, each linked to a particular journal' (p. 190). While this might indeed facilitate publication, you would have to take care that such a strategy did not have undue influence upon the research – a case of the media being mightier than the message.

Authors should include the growing area of online journals within their purview (I'm grateful to Andrew Hannan for his suggestions in this area). The internet has radically changed the whole idea of publishing. What used to be an expensive and time-consuming exercise is now very cheap and almost immediate. Anyone can create a website and publish whatever happens to be at hand. There is no guarantee to the readers that what they see is any good – they do not have an intermediary in the form of an editor or publisher to vouchsafe its high quality. All they have to go by is their own critical faculties unless, of course, the website is an online journal with some sort of refereeing process. These are the ones I am concerned with here. At the time of writing, there are 190 of these as listed on the American Educational Research Association Special Interest Group website in 'Communication in research' (http://aera-cr.ed.asu.edu/). The organisers state, 'To the best of our ability to discern, we have included only links to electronic journals that are scholarly, peer-reviewed, full text and accessible without cost. We have excluded professional magazines that are largely not refereed, and commercial journals that may only allow access to a very limited number of articles as an enticement to buy. By restricting membership in this way . . . we hope to do what little we can to promote free access worldwide to scholarship in education'.

Note the twin principles of 'free access' and 'scholarship'. We might add the advantage of 'quick turnaround' compared to print journals. Also, electronic publishing is well suited to the kind of hypermedia approaches discussed in Chapter 4. There are possibilities of more writer-reader interaction, of using a variety of presentational approaches, and even different languages. Some can cope with a range of academic offerings at various stages, thus giving a wider view of the research process and opening it up for discussion. One of these is Education-line, an indexed, full text, electronic archive of conference and working papers, reports, policy and discussion documents and early research results in the field of education and training. There is evidence that such online journals reach a wider audience – different groups, different countries (Glass 1999). There are more people with access to the internet than to academic libraries. And you can see how many times your article has been visited. Weiner's 2001 article had been retrieved 7417 times up to November 2004. Not many paper articles achieve that strike rate. If you publish in a print journal, you may have your article cited by others, or you may not. You may wonder if all your hard work has been worth it.

There is much debate at the moment about the proliferation of print journals, the commercialisation of the area, the cost to individuals or libraries to buy, the pressure on academics to publish from the research assessment exercise, the quality of articles, and systems of refereeing and review (see Weiner 2001 for a discussion of these issues). Abbott (1999) feels that journals are becoming more routine and bureaucratised, and are opting for 'safe' publications. New outlets through different media are welcome, therefore. How, then, do we get a quality article published in an online journal? All of the above advice about knowing your product and your journal still applies, as does the general advice on writing. But it might be helpful to see how one online journal reviews submissions through peer-reviewing. A good example of this is the *Journal of Interactive Media in Education* (*JIME*) (http://www-jime.open.ac.uk/), which describes its reviewing process in Figure 9.2.

This system has strong similarities to the qualitative approach, with a far more open system of review in which accounts can be challenged from different perspectives and the generation of discussion is seen as valuable. The means by which the final version of a paper is constructed are thereby more transparent and the contested nature of the piece is more readily apparent with the views of reviewers and readers made known.

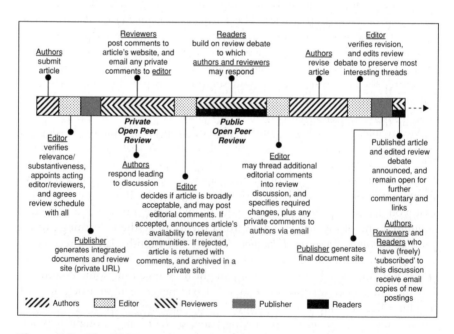

Figure 9.2   The *JIME* open peer review lifecycle, showing the private and public review phases, and the active stakeholders at different points (*Journal of Interactive Media in Education*: http://www-jime.open.ac.uk)

The psychological set

If your article is accepted, you might feel exhilaration. Invariably, however, even with experienced writers, the first response from the journal editors is not one of outright acceptance. Currently, only 9 per cent of articles submitted to the *British Educational Research Journal* (*BERJ*) are accepted as they stand; 25 per cent are rejected; the rest are referred for revisions that range from minor to major. As in any form of writing, therefore, the writer's approach needs to be resolute and patient, ready for all kinds of comment, extensive or minimal; and particularly criticism which can be insightful, helpful and constructive, and/or sarcastic, devastating and destructive. The standard of refereeing ranges from excellent to abysmal. Even worse, perhaps, is hardly any comment at all apart from a one- or two-line judgement. Outright rejection, with no sympathetic or encouraging comments, is the most hurtful – as it is in failed research proposals. This can be profoundly depressing, representing the difference between the 'arrived academic' with an exciting future of a stream of articles, and the 'struggling applicant' with still a great deal of work to do before arrival. It is easy to get disheartened after a rejection. It is hugely disappointing, and can seem as if months of work have been wasted. You will want some evidence of worthiness from others, perhaps your colleagues, as encouragement to persevere, refining the article and trying elsewhere. Refereeing can take an age. The *BERJ* currently has a year of stacked up articles. The *International Journal of Qualitative Studies in Education* accepted one of our articles but was unable to publish it for another year. That was over two years after its initial submission, which entailed some very minor revisions, done within a week. You might ask, therefore, for an estimate when you submit the paper. For an article containing material that is likely to date rapidly – not uncommon in a field such as education – an ejournal may have advantages.

Meanwhile, you will be constructing other papers. You might develop some contingency plans for the journal article, so that all is not wasted. There are alternative uses to which it could be put, and which might yield further useful feedback – a conference paper, a chapter in a book, a teaching document – or you may have a shortlist of journals. If you are convinced that you have a quality product, you should leave no stone unturned. I submitted one of my articles, 'Towards a theory of aesthetic learning', to the journal *Research Papers in Education* (*RPE*). Six months later I received a cursory note from the editor, without any referees' comments, saying that it was not considered 'suitable'. They might have given me some comments, but the judgement was probably sound. I had never seen an article in *RPE* anything like the one I had submitted – so I had not taken my own advice offered above. I am on the reviewing panel of *RPE*, and thought it would be rather nice to submit an article to them. Clearly, there is no room for sentiment. I then sent the paper to an American journal, *Aesthetic Education*, which at least from its title was highly appropriate. I was not too sure, however, about the style of articles in past numbers, what you might term the 'discourse' of the journal. In due course, I received a reply, again devoid of referees' comments, saying they would be prepared to publish a shortened account in their 'Research reports' section. I was not happy with this, as I felt the article was quite tightly constructed, and would forsake some quality in any abbreviation, so sent it off, again unchanged, to *Educational Studies*, who accepted it as it stood within a matter of weeks. I have to admit that the article was inappropriate for both the first two journals, but sits quite happily in the third. I might have saved myself, and the editors of the first two journals, time and effort if I had studied the suitability of the journals a little more closely in the first place.

Strategies

There might be numerous journals in your area of research. Shortlist those that look as if they might be suitable, then scrutinise some recent numbers for content and discourse. Seek advice from experienced academics in your field. It is essential to study the criteria a journal specifies for submitted articles, and its 'house style'. 'Notes for contributors' give the optimum dimensions and format of the article, and guidance on how it should be submitted. These should be followed to the letter, otherwise your article in most cases will not be considered. Often, but not always, there is a note about content. Where none is given, look through recent editions of the journal to familiarise yourself with the subject areas and discourse. Presentation should be meticulous – clearly written, no or very few mistakes (grammar, spelling, typographical), well set out and printed. Sloppy presentation usually means poor content and is very irritating to referees.

It is a good idea to get your article assessed by others first, if possible. Start with friends, who can be relied upon to give it a sympathetic read; then other colleagues who might have an interest in it for one reason or another. When you are confident the paper is in reasonable shape, you might use it to lead a seminar or present at a conference, where further feedback would be forthcoming. At some point, if you were brave enough, it would be interesting to test it out on a known opponent of the stance you are taking – as long as they were somebody who would not simply condemn it out of hand. The range of viewpoints that are brought to bear broadens your own outlook. They enable you to see things that you would not otherwise have noticed.

Once it is submitted, you can continue to work on the article, looking out for new relevant literature and discussion. A paper is only finished when the final copy is handed over and any queries on it have been answered. You might well anticipate some of the referees' comments, and thus be better equipped to respond to them. It is also a good idea to begin fashioning a new paper, if your material justifies it. Since it might take years from inception to acceptance of a paper for publication, it is useful to have more than one at different stages of completion.

I advise my postgraduate students to regard their oral examinations as seminar situations, and to bear in mind that they know far more about their theses than their examiners. The same counsel applies to journal articles. In a situation where you receive a reply from an editor saying they are prepared to reconsider the article if you take the referees' comments fully into account, it is necessary to *engage* with the comments, not just reject or accept them without question. The important thing is that you consider them carefully and give a reasoned response to all the points made. The main points deserve a comment each, but some you might be able to deal with collectively ('I accept all the other points'). Some things you are urged to do you might have good reason for not doing – perhaps something else more valuable might be lost, or it might lend a different slant to the argument from that you wish to make, or you might not consider it relevant. Sometimes, referees' comments contradict one another, but both can be of use in redrafting. For example, one referee might prefer a different explanation to that being advanced, while another very much likes it. Giving reasons why you prefer one to the other can only strengthen the paper.

Assistance

Though your article might have your name only on it, invariably a number of other people will have contributed to it – friends, colleagues, referees.

Some of the most helpful comments I have received have been from journal editors. My first journal article was in the *British Journal of Sociology*. The article I submitted was greatly overlength (a common failing in qualitative research) – some 12,000 words compared to a recommended 7000 – and might have been rejected on these grounds alone. But the editor was gently encouraging, feeling that the article would actually be improved by some abbreviation. Though at first disappointed that I had to lose some of my 'valuable' material, I confronted the pain barrier once more and cut the article back to the required length. Having gone through this discipline, I had to admit that the article was better – much tighter in argument, much more focused on the issues, the least relevant data trimmed, more succinct expression, tangential material excised.

I learnt other valuable lessons from Gabriel Chanan, co-editor of a book published by the National Foundation for Educational Research (NFER), which included one of my early articles. Gabriel took a lot of trouble over my ill-formed article, and made many detailed suggestions on the manuscript – clarifying points, supplying alternative ways of saying things, linking sentences, requesting explanations, pointing out ambiguities – taking care to say that they were suggestions, and that the final decision in all instances was my own. These were the first two articles of mine that were published. I learnt a great deal from the people involved in the process, and this equipped me well for writing future articles.

If you receive an outright rejection, all might not be lost. Most editors try to be helpful, and act in the spirit of all being members of an academic community rather than simply in the interests of their own journal. Sometimes a more suitable journal is recommended, or some hints might be given on how the paper could be improved. If no comments are sent, write back and request some, pointing out that they will help you. Ponder on comments that are sent. More often than not these will be helpful and to the point, concerned with quality of data and argument, knowledge of the literature, research methods, presentation and organisation, and relevance to the journal. Sometimes, however, they may be more contentious – ideological ('not Marxist enough' or 'too Marxist'); epistemological or paradigmatic ('too modernist'); atheoretical ('what use is this?'); or idiosyncratic and peremptory ('I just don't think this article should be published'). It is useful to identify the nature of comments, and of your own product, so that you can defend it against them.

A selection of critical comments on journal submissions

The following extracts from reports convey the main faults I have found with some of the articles submitted to journals sent to me in recent years to referee. Again, they mostly recall points made earlier – but here they are put into operation!

Inadequate methods or explanation of methods

'It is based on a very small, and rather unbalanced, sample – only 20 per cent by my reckoning followed through to the classroom observation. This, then, may be a self-selected sample given to a certain mode of response by their willingness to contribute. Yet the authors still claim their sample to be representative of a whole population.'

'We do not know how long the interviews lasted, where they took place, how they were recorded. There are no extracts given from these interviews. They are treated quantitatively in the analysis. Similarly, the observations are claimed to be "naturalistic", but we do not know how long the researchers spent in the school, how many lessons were observed, and how observations were noted. There seems to be an assumption that you can walk into a lesson and observe "natural" behaviour. Some qualitative researchers spend years gaining entry, in the interests of penetrating the outer layers of reality to the innermost meanings. There is no attempt to do that here. Validity therefore is suspect.'

'The main problem is that the research does not seem to match the subject, i.e. "active learning". The research methods employed are too crude and closed for ascertaining views and feelings, and there is questionable validity and reliability. For example, students might be expected to rate themselves highly, but did they really? What meanings were being attached to the questions that were being put to them, and how are we to frame their answers? The paper is unidimensional, where it needs to be multiperspectival. The selection of the sample is not explained, nor what is meant by "exemplary". The main problem is that the research questions are too huge for such a small scale study.'

Limited or misused data

'The data seem thin. No examples are given in the first category. Where examples are given, we are rarely given the questions that were asked to elicit the response, so context is lacking. Examples consist of little more than one or two sentences – not much to go on in considering intellectual development. We know nothing about the people making the statements (age? sex? position? etc.).'

'Data are limited, and appear to be based on two interviews which are presented as "in depth" research. Not enough is known about the two subjects. There is no background, nothing of their previous lives – life histories would have helped here. The literature shows that clues to teachers' careers often reside in these earlier periods.'

'. . . the failure to link long extracts of transcript adequately to the text (the assumption presumably being that they almost speak for themselves), making unwarranted assumptions (such as that a kind of "progressive pedagogy is most conducive to equity education").'

Inadequate theory

'The paper is weak theoretically. Presumably the subject is teacher culture, but there is no discussion of this concept. There is no recognition that there can be a dialectical relation with a culture, whereby individuals both contribute to and draw from a culture, and that it is a dynamic, living, processual thing. The data might contribute to an interesting discussion along these lines, but fall well short of it.'

'Much more definitional work needs to be done. For example, it is not clear what is meant by "structure". In one place, social class is offered as an example, elsewhere a school or university; and later, reference is made to "macro". There seems some conceptual confusion here.'

'"Analytical dualism" is held out as a solution to the structure/agency problem, but we are told very little about it, and its application to the case study is obscure and superficial.'

Inappropriate journal

'I wondered if the article would be more appropriate in a psychology journal, such as *BJEdPsych*. It bears on both disciplines, so is suitable for either, but I would recommend a submission to a psychology journal if no place is found for it in *BJSE*.'

'Alternatively, the author might prefer to try a journal like *School Organisation*, or *School Effectiveness*. In some ways, the character of the article may be more suited to those.'

'It is, perhaps, more suitable for a journal that is more immediately practically based, such as the *British Journal of Inservice Education*, or *Educational Action Research*.'

Presentation and style

'The tone adopted is one of exhortation rather than argument and analysis.'

'Inadequate because of the verbose and highly repetitive style in which it is written (which includes making simple points sound very complicated), the use of labels (such as "conservative" and "progressive") in spite of the argument for complexity and contradiction.'

'There may well be a worthy article here, but it needs a lot more work clarifying and sharpening the argument, editing out the clutter, making more of the evidence.'

'Organisation of the article is also suspect. There is no sectioning, with clearly identified themes, which increases the sense of it being rather a rambling discourse. I was left wondering what the aims of the article were, and what the author was trying to achieve. The abstract was no help in this respect.'

'It all seems rather superficial, rising little above elementary textbook level in places – see Sections 2 and 3 for example on "teachers' lives" and "theories of intellectual development". These are central to the issue, and need examining in much more detail.'

'Lucidity is lost in places (e.g. mid. p. 8), there are non sequiturs (e.g. p. 9); instances of bad fit (e.g. between claim made and supporting quote e.g. p. 9); exaggerated claims (e.g. pp. 8, 9, 10, 11, 13); key matters unexplained (e.g. "exclusions"); and undue speculation (e.g. p. 14). It is not clear that there are two "systematic" discourses operating in the school. Even the dominant discourse has not been adequately documented.'

Unacknowledged bias
Ideological bias:

'A pervasive problem is "hegemonic masculinity" – the author takes this for granted, so it is not explained, nor argued for. If you accept this as a given, then there may be fewer problems with the paper. Often, no evidence is presented to support an assertion. I found myself writing "How do you know?" and "Evidence?" in the margins. There are unqualified claims from the literature. Alternative explanations are not considered. Some examples given do not clearly and unequivocally support the argument, and some just do not fit the claim made. It is very speculative in parts.'

Author dominance:

We need much more of the teachers' voices, more extended quotations from them, so that they speak through the material. Here, they appear to be stifled, and very much under the control of the author.

Selective data to fit a favoured theory:

Do we get a complete enough picture of the children's mental processes? Might there be other factors unconnected to social class operating? What are the criteria for testing this argument? To what extent is the theory driving the data collection and analysis? To what extent can the theory be said to be 'grounded' in the data? Are there other theories that might be brought to bear on the data, possibly at odds with those that have been chosen? The reader is not given enough to formulate an independent judgement, nor to assess the strength of the argument. We are forced to go along the lines the author takes us. I want to know more about these children and their discourse – I want to widen the framework of the debate.

Inadequate knowledge

'The presentation is too simplistic in the light of the existing literature on pupil perspectives on effective teachers and teaching. Much of the conclusions here have been well established in British, American, Australian and French studies, and more sophisticated discussions made of their interrelationships. None of this work is referred to in the article.'

'A fair range of literature is cited, but it is dealt with in a very shallow way, usually by mentioning a single point, which only begs a range of other questions – for example, they say "evidence from a similar study supported our decision to consider our sample as representative". They do not say what this "evidence" is. To this reader, this only demonstrates the inadequacy of the other study. There is no critical engagement with this literature, nor does it always seem to support the point being made (e.g. p. 15, studies are quoted about first-year teachers when the sample is third year); nor do they always link together, being presented in list-like fashion, as in the introduction.'

'There is a wealth of sociological and educational literature that would appear to be relevant to points made. For example, on pp. 5–6, the author seems to be talking about "role", though this is not mentioned, but leaves out of account the notions of "role style" and "role modification", and of course the huge literature on the subject. Instead, we are offered a lesson in very elementary sociology. The ensuing discussion leaves out of account the growing literature on implementation theory and the equally growing literature on teachers' adaptations to recent government measures.'

'Some of the conclusions are not new (e.g. several of the points made on pp. 17–18 are sociological clichés) . . . It is reporting on a worthy project which no doubt has much to contribute. But this article does not do it beyond making a strong central point which in itself is not original.'

'One of the continuing problems in sociology is that some favour structure in their approach, others agency. There are few that consider the two together. I was hoping that this article might provide a few pointers, but it does not even get as far as clearing some of the introductions out of the way. Consequently it is a little reminiscent of some of the writing of the early 1970s that came out of the counter-productive positivism v. nonpositivism divide.'

'There is more on pressures on teachers than on solutions, and these, as presented, are not news. Nor is their desire for practical help.'

Limited analysis

'This article is almost purely descriptive. There is some primary analysis, organising data into categories, but it is limited, and it is not clear where the categories come from (author or subjects?).'

Inadequate discussion

'There are dubious arguments, elementary arguments, and unconvincing arguments.'

'There is no consideration of gender, personality, or "side-bets", all of which have been shown by other studies to be powerful factors in teacher careers.'

'Much of the data is unidimensional and some of it is superficial. What lies behind the level that is presented? There are examples in some of the literature above. Werthman and Marsh *et al.* explored the rules underlying the pupil perceptions; Gannaway teased out the interconnections among his (similar) categories, showing a flow-chart of priorities; Turner found, in his case, that students' definitions of "interesting" were related to the marketability of subjects and teachers' ability to deliver the goods.'

'There is a major sociological faux pas on p. 10 where it is asserted that "most staff operated rather childishly". A sociologist would treat this, not as a fact in itself, but as an unusual and surprising matter in need of explanation. In skirting over such points, the article is resonant of some of the "effectiveness" literature of which it is so critical.'

'The recommendation is unrealistic, with no recognition of the politics involved in these matters.'

Dubious ethics

'I am concerned about the ethics of the approach, i.e. asking pupils directly about their teachers, and their problems in keeping order. The possibility is that the research might compound their difficulties by cementing pupils' possibly ill-formed views of teachers who have more difficulty than others. The problem is not got round by not referring to "efficiency" or "inefficiency". The research questioning is still cast in terms of particular teachers, moreover in polarised form – good or bad. An alternative approach would be to try to identify components of styles that might apply variously to some degree or other to all teachers, depending on factors and circumstances to be identified. Did the teachers know they were being discussed in this way? What were the terms of the contract, written or unwritten, between researchers and school? Has any feedback been given to the teachers, if so, with what result?'

A supported submission

Let us conclude with a positive report on an unusual article:

'I enjoyed this paper.

It is a product of the "literary turn", reflective, poetic, exploring feelings and relationships, and mode of representation. The strength is in the expression. This is so easy to overdo or misjudge, and requires just as much skill, though of a different kind, as in more scientific accounts. The author avoids mawkishness, and shows a depth of feeling, and a sure artistic touch in conveying it to the reader.

Some may consider the paper a self-indulgence, and in a way it is. But the point is, does it have relevance for others, and does it deal with a worthy subject? I would say incontrovertibly "yes", since the "caring" element in teaching (associated with Noddings, and Nias, for example) has become submerged beneath the welter of research activity that is subsumed within the current dominant managerialist, marketisation and technicisation trend, and needs reviving. It is a reminder that, among all the instrumental activities, there is something more at the heart of teaching.

The paper must meet certain criteria of quality. Among these, depth of insight and understanding, the appositeness of representation, and the power of the account to "move" the reader are important, and I think the author meets these.

If it has a weakness, it is more about the author's family life than about school and relationships among teachers and students. If it is thought unsuitable for *TAT*, the author might try one of the American-based qualitative journals that have trailed the way with this kind of article (such as *Symbolic Interaction, QSE, Journal of Contemporary Ethnography, Qualitative Inquiry*). Also, the author states that he does not like schools, but it is not altogether clear why, and it also raises the question of whether schools in his preferred image are possible. How are we to educate our young? How are we to handle the many material considerations? Advocating the power and practice of love can also have its dangers in the education of the young.

Even so, I would recommend publication. It is a refreshing approach, and I am sure would create a lot of interest and debate.'

BOOKS

Much of the above applies also to the writing of the chapters of a book. In this section I shall therefore consider matters relating to a book as a whole.

Background knowledge

Do you have the material for a book? Considerations include:

- *Do you have enough material?* A book can be the equivalent of six to eight articles – a major enterprise.
- *Substantial, original, high quality material.* Origins might include a postgraduate thesis, a sustained research project, a course of teaching, a series of lectures or a number of related articles that have already been published.
- *Likely to be of wide interest.* Publishers generally are not interested in theses as they stand because they are too academic and too specialist, and will not sell well. They might be on esoteric topics, and/or half the content might be taken up with introductory material on research design, methodology, theory and reviewing the literature. A book has to be marketable – a huge consideration. Books are unlike articles in this respect. Having said this, PhDs often do contain books, and exceptionally good ones, unsurprisingly in view of the quality of the research. They have to be tailored to a different audience, condensing the introductory material into a single introductory chapter, and focusing on the major findings.
- *Substantial and innovative experience in a particular area*, for example, research methods.

Do you have appropriate knowledge of yourself? For example, do you have the time, resources and inspiration to write a book? It will inevitably impinge on family and social life and on other areas of your work.

Do you know your publisher? It is possible to publish a book yourself. Indeed, Wellington (2003: 124) has noted an increase in self-publishing recently; also, the uses of the internet in making work available at comparatively low cost. But he notes you would still 'need to buy in marketing, promotion and publicity'. If such a book does well, a publisher might offer to take it on under their own imprint. That, however, happens rarely, so do not count on it! Publishing your own book in print is not usually recommended since it is costly, and also, publishing houses have developed expertise in the production and especially marketing of books. Also, your book will have higher credibility going through a publisher in the usual way, as your proposal and final text will have gone through a strict evaluation and publisher's editing process (see below).

Books are likely to become increasingly available in electronic form. Ebooks are currently in their infancy, but could take off dramatically once the software and hardware have been refined and developed, and once writers have seen the possibilities. Ebooks will provide rapid access to knowledge, easy searching within texts, the choice of downloading just those parts of a text that are required, and the ability to store whole libraries within your computer – and to take them about with you on your laptop or PDA. Ebooks also offer creative potential in that, for example, they might contain links to other websites and material, and even audio and video clips, making them a useful outlet for the kind of hypermedia approaches discussed in Chapter 4. To get a feel of ebooks and issues related to them, you can consult any publisher's list (The Taylor & Francis eBookstore website, for example, is www.eBookstore.tandf.co.uk). Ebooks, however, will not replace printed versions, which will continue to be the main outlet for most writers for the foreseeable future.

So which publishers should you approach? In the educational field in the UK, the leading publishers at the moment are generally regarded as being Routledge, Open University Press and Continuum. There are specialist publishers in particular areas, such as Multilingual Matters, Virago Press (women's studies), Christian Education and Whurr (special needs). There are publishers more exclusively interested in books that are of immediate practical value to teachers, such as Chapman (now part of Sage) and David Fulton. Trentham Press has expanded in recent years and has a growing reputation in the educational field. There are those that will facilitate the publishing of your book with your help, such as Avebury. For a full up-to-date list you would need to consult a text produced annually such as the *Writer's and Artists' Yearbook*. Publishing is subject to market forces, and things change rapidly.

It is as well to be aware of current trends in publishing. For example, at the time of writing most educational publishers are requiring more books of a practical nature, and being more wary of disciplinary books – for example, those that take a sociological view without drawing out the practical implications. Teachers need all the help they can get, but we might ask whether this need should dominate the market, particularly if it is met in an uncritical manner. This is quite a problem currently for the educational disciplines, since those working in these areas are averse to simply providing 'tips for teachers on how to teach the National Curriculum' without adequate context. They would like any such advice to be theoretically and critically informed. This does not mean that you should simply follow trends and pander to the current vogue. There are ways, for example, in which sociologists can lean in the direction of practical recommendations without losing sight of the basic discipline (see Chapter 5 for one such approach). I agree with Nixon and Wellington (2005: 99) who argue that efforts need to be exerted by all to ensure the continual publication of books in the educational sphere that are 'intellectually challenging and engaging, generous in respect of their reaching out to diverse publics, and uncompromising in respect of their promotion of educational values'.

As a first step, you would need to write to the commissioning editor to see if they were interested in receiving a proposal from you. An alternative is to contact the general editor of a series of books if you see your topic fitting within that series. It would be a good idea to discuss the process, and the pleasures and pains involved, with colleagues who have experience of it. Watching the educational press and studying publishers' catalogues will also keep you informed of trends in publishing.

As in all things, it helps to have a measure of luck and be prepared to act on it. I was fortunate with my first book in being encouraged and assisted by an able and sympathetic editor at Routledge, who happened to be an ex-colleague. On one of his visits, he urged me to put in a proposal. He continued to be very helpful throughout the project.

Should you have an agent? In principle, an agent should be able to help you first find a publisher, and then secure you a better deal. However, agents are unusual in academic publishing. Academic books on the whole simply do not make enough money to warrant or interest an agent. If your book is good enough you should be able to place it with one of the relatively small group of educational publishers, and it is fun negotiating the terms yourself – not that it makes a great deal of difference given the small sums involved (see below).

Preparing a proposal

As with a research proposal, it makes sense to spend some time on this. A contract may depend on it, but also it involves important and necessary planning. It forces you to think about aims, content, style, organisation and the logistics of producing a book. A publisher will usually specify the criteria they employ in judging a proposal (see Figure 9.3), but they all revolve around the central point of 'will it sell?' For this, a book needs to be of high quality, original, with no or few competitors, have a clearly defined audience and promise to be a product they can market at a reasonable price. If a commissioning editor likes the proposal, they will send it to a number of referees for comment (see Figure 9.4 on their guidance for referees). As with articles, responses can reflect a range of opinion. The proposal might be rejected if there is not a fair degree of support, but if there is some the editor might invite your reaction to the comments that have been made. Some of these might be critical but lead you to see ways in which the book might be improved. Others might seem to be urging you to go in directions to which you are averse, requiring a different kind of book altogether. As with articles, you might treat this as a seminar situation and engage with referees' comments in the spirit they were intended. As long as you meet all points reasonably, if you have reached this stage your proposal stands a good chance of being accepted.

At the end of this chapter, I give a sample proposal. It is not the only kind – I have seen much different and much shorter ones accepted. But it is a successful model I have worked with over the years.

Submitting a proposal
Guidelines for authors

Introduction
Taylor & Francis are keen to consider proposals for new books. Mainly publishing at University level, our list includes everything from core text books to research monographs. We are able to offer:

- *Global distribution and marketing.* Unlike many UK publishers, the majority of our sales come from overseas. We have a strong presence in the US with our sister company, Taylor & Francis Inc., and a dedicated international sales team.
- *Quality design and production values.* Our books are produced efficiently, quickly and attractively using the latest technology.
- *Prestige.* We are one of the world's leading academic publishers with a reputation for cutting-edge and ground-breaking books. We are the publisher of many of the leading figures in the Western intellectual tradition including Bertrand Russell, Freud, Wittgenstein, Einstein and Foucault.

The proposal you submit will be the basis on which we judge the book's suitability for publication. Therefore it needs to be organised in a way that provides the right information to us and to referees. The following notes should help you prepare your proposal, and your co-operation in following our recommendations will ease the task of evaluation. We would suggest a proposal between 3–4 pages in length, although this should be supplemented by sample chapters, or a draft manuscript, and curriculum vitae.

Figure 9.3   Taylor & Francis' guidelines to authors on submitting a proposal

Four main areas need to be addressed:

1 **A statement of aims including 3–4 paragraphs outlining the rationale behind the book**
   - Quite simply, what is your book about?
   - What are its main themes and objectives?
   - What are you doing differently, or in a more innovative way, or better than existing books?

2 **A detailed synopsis and chapter headings with an indication of length and schedule**
   - Please list working chapter headings and provide a paragraph of explanation on what you intend to cover in each chapter. This may be all that the reviewer has to go on, so a list of chapter headings alone is not enough.
   - If sample chapters, or a draft manuscript are available, please send them or let us know when they will be available.
   - How many tables, diagrams or illustrations will there be (roughly)?
   - Roughly how many thousand words in length will your book be? Does this include references and footnotes? Most of our books are 80,000–100,000 words long.
   - When will you be able to deliver the completed typescript? Please be as realistic as possible.

3 **A description of the target market**
   - Who is your book primarily aimed at? Who will buy it? Who will read it?
   - Is it aimed at an undergraduate or postgraduate student audience?
   - What courses would the book be used on?
   - Is it a research monograph that will sell primarily to academic libraries?
   - Is the subject area of the proposal widely taught, or researched?
   - Would this subject have international appeal outside your home country? If so, where?

4 **A list of the main competing books**
   - We would like some indication that you are familiar with competition to your proposed book. What are their strengths and weaknesses? What makes your book better then the existing competition?

It will also be necessary to include:

1 **One or two sample chapters, or a draft manuscript, if available**
2 **A curriculum vitae of all authors, and notes on any other contributors**
   Additional questions for edited collections
   - Is the book of a consistent academic quality?
   - Should some of the weaker chapters be excised?
   - Are the chapters structured logically and integrated around a coherent central theme?

Figure 9.3 (*Cont'd*)

- Will you be providing a detailed introductory chapter and a conclusion?
- Is there a balance between theoretical/methodological and empirical chapters?
- Will the case studies (if appropriate) appeal to an international audience?

How we evaluate your proposal, or manuscript

Evaluation by commissioning editor(s)
The proposal will be considered carefully by the most suitable editor. The editor will ask several questions: is the content of this book of a high academic standard? Is there a market for a high-quality book on this subject? What evidence is there for this market? If there is a gap in the market, is this the right book to fill it? Will the book sell internationally? If the editor is satisfied at this stage, then the proposal will then be evaluated by academic experts.

Evaluation by independent referees
We ask respected academic specialists in the field to give us independent advice on the content, quality and potential market for a finished book based on your proposal or manuscript. We normally solicit 2 or 3 reports from academics. This process should take 6–8 weeks but can take longer as it is sometimes difficult to find suitable reviewers, and reviewers some-times interpret deadlines rather loosely.

Editorial board meeting
If the reviews have been positive, then the editor puts together a written proposal including your proposal, the referees' reports, and projected pro-duction costs and revenues. These are circulated to all members of the editorial board in advance of a regular meeting, where each proposal is discussed and either approved, rejected, or provisionally passed, subject to certain revisions. The editorial board consists of editors, a publisher (who manages a team of editors), marketing and sales managers.

Contract, desk editorial and publication
If your proposal is passed then we will issue a draft contract. Once we have agreed on terms you sign and return the contract with an agreed date for the delivery of the manuscript. Once the book has been written and delivered, you will liaise with a desk-editor over the copy-editing and pro-duction process. We will then publish, market and sell the book.

If you would like to submit a proposal, or have any queries, or concerns, please contact:
The Relevant Editor,
TAYLOR & FRANCIS GROUP, 2 Park Square, Milton Park, Abingdon, Oxon OX14 4RN
Tel: 020 7017 5000. Fax: 020 7842 2298

Figure 9.3   *(Cont'd)*

Guide to referees of a synopsis

The questions below have been selected for two purposes:

(a) To help us decide whether an author is to be encouraged to proceed with this projected book – we hope to learn at this stage whether the project meets a need in the marketplace and whether it is well-conceived.
(b) If the project is to be encouraged we would welcome your suggestions for any necessary revisions of structure, content or approach.

Organization and content

1 Do you agree with the choice and weighting of topics?
2 Do you agree with the order in which the topics are treated?
3 Are any subjects or topics not covered which, in your opinion, form a necessary part of a book on this subject and with this proposed market?
4 Is there any material which you consider superfluous to the objectives of this project?

The market

1 To what groups of students could this book be recommended for purchase? (e.g. first year university undergraduates).
2 What would be its importance to these students? (e.g. main text, all first year, one of several texts, third year option course supplementary reading, library only).
3 How widely is the subject taught?
4 To what extent do you think there would be an international market for the book?
5 What are the competing books? (Please quote the books you consider would be its principal competitors, with comments on them.)
6 What would you consider to be a reasonable price for the book?

Conclusion

Is this project, either in its present form or with the modifications suggested in your report, to be encouraged?

Identification

It would be most helpful if when you submit your report you could indicate whether you wish it to remain anonymous.

Figure 9.4   The Open University Press guide for referees of book proposals

Negotiating a contract

Harry Wolcott (2001: 176 *et seq.*) likes to write his book first before seeking a publisher, but I consider this is a risky business for most of us. I know of three people who did this and could not find a publisher. I agree with Denscombe (1998: 224) that 'the process of research is not complete until the findings have been written up', but there are many ways of doing this – reports to sponsors, journal and magazine articles, conference papers for some. Writing a book is hard and time-consuming work, and my view is that it makes sense to seek whatever guarantees of publication may be on offer. Seeking a contract also forces you to think hard about the form and content of the book, its audience and the style in which it will be written. Once a contract is secured, you can be reasonably sure that your book will be published as long as you meet the terms of the contract.

A contract is not so much, therefore, about the author maximising profit. Academics are not in the writing business for commercial reasons. One or two research books have become best sellers, but most are specialist items, many being acquired only by libraries. A standard print run in the UK is for 2000 copies or less, and sales of 750–1000 in the first year are considered good. Compare this with the 7295 copies of the 1998 Booker Prize winner, *The God of Small Things* by Arundhati Roy, sold in one week in June 1998! So refrain from demanding half a million in advance, as Martin Amis did for one of his books, and don't plan to retire on the royalties you receive! Having said that, it makes sense to try to get the best terms you can. There is some good advice on negotiating contracts (see Caute and Graham 1983; Germano 2001), so I just refer here to some basic points.

• A standard rate is 10 per cent of the published price of the book for each copy sold. Most publishers these days offer 10 per cent of the money they actually receive from sales, which of course is somewhat less. You might try for higher royalties as sales rise, say 10 per cent on the first 2000, 12.5 per cent on the next 3000 and 15 per cent thereafter. On the other hand, do be reasonable. Publishers' offers are guided by the marketing advice they receive, and you may have to settle for less if you wish to see your book published. Well-known, highly successful authors will command higher royalties. An unknown author with a risky manuscript (in marketing terms) might be offered less. Also, there are other considerations than royalties, such as the appearance of the book, marketing arrangements and relationships with the author. You can find out about these aspects by looking at books produced by the publisher and talking to some of their authors.

• Do try to secure an advance. Most publishers will agree to one, typically half on signing the contract and half on acceptance of the delivered manuscript. This may help with some of the costs of preparation, but more important, perhaps, is that an advance signifies the publisher's commitment to the project.

- Do examine all the clauses of the contract. It might be difficult seeing your book turned into a film, or serialised on Radio 4 or in *Readers' Digest* – but you never know which one of such scenarios might arise. 'Translation rights', for one, are quite important. A book can earn more from translation than in its original language as, for one reason, it may not have as many direct competitors in the translated language. Try for 80 per cent in these clauses, and don't settle for less than 50 per cent.
- Try to get as many free copies of the book as you can. I usually ask for ten paperback and ten hardback.
- Allow yourself enough time to write the book. I have once or twice had to request a two-month extension because of unforeseen circumstances that arose. Publishers do not usually mind a short extension as long as they are given sufficient warning, but not delivering on time is technically a breach of contract. Publishers have their own schedules, deadlines, catalogues, lists etc. The longer the delay, the more the possibility that publishers might reconsider producing the book.

Strategies

As with a PhD, writing a book is a huge project, and for me has to be tackled piece by piece, chapter by chapter, and not necessarily in the order in which they are to appear. One way is to write a series of journal articles first, then bring them together into a book. I did this with my first authored book, *The Divided School* (1979). Six of the ten chapters had been published in journals or collections of articles between 1975 and 1979. The book was a trimmed down version of the PhD, which also appeared in 1979. Some of the parts that were taken out, however, had appeared in Open University teaching material. So *The Divided School* had had a thorough grounding in other outlets, and I wonder if it would have been written otherwise.

Once you have written one book, as with articles, you have acquired a knowledge of the processes involved. It remains the hardest work as an academic that I have experienced, but at least you know what lies ahead and what has to be done, and can plan more securely within the frame of other responsibilities. I always like to get some material 'in the bank', as it were, as soon as possible. This may be based on existing material. Of the rest, there may be some chapters that are essential and easier to write than others. I intersperse these with the essential harder chapters, leaving other chapters to the end. These may never get written. It is easy to overestimate what you can get into a book. Some chapters may have to be omitted, therefore, or substituted by new, exciting possibilities that may occur to you within the lengthy time period it usually takes to write a book. As with articles, you may also find the need to review the structure of the book as you get into the writing of it. The book proposal does not have to be strictly adhered to. I have not written one book that follows the proposal to the letter. This does not mean that you cannot plan seriously from the beginning.

I find it useful to allocate a number of words to each chapter, and to keep track of how many words I actually write. I can then see if I am likely to overshoot. In a standard book of 80,000 words there might be, say, seven chapters of 10,000 words each, with 10,000 left to cover introductory material and references. This is only a rough guide, since chapters may need to end up at variable length, but it helps to provide a measure of self-discipline. Thus, if my chapters begin to come out at 15,000 – as they might do with large sections of transcript, for example – I might have to rethink, but not before I have done a thorough job of editing the chapter and ensuring that every word left in is absolutely necessary. Invariably this brings the wordage down significantly, and yields a much tighter chapter.

As stressed earlier, editing becomes the most important and most time-consuming activity. In general, the onus has always been on the author to present as accurate and complete a copy to the publisher as possible, in line with the house style. This is becoming even more essential. With my first book, I received valuable aid from an in-house editor, who made constructive comments on the submitted text. I even went to London to discuss some points with her. My ex-colleague also made some comments, including pointing out some potentially libellous material. Such a service today is a luxury. In fact, you may find yourself having to de-edit a manuscript after it has had the attention of an editor. Manuscripts are often sent out to independent copy-editors who format the material for the printer and check the references. They might pick up some errors, and ask for clarification of some points. Usually this job is professionally done and enhances the book. But some might make changes without alerting you. They might only be small matters of punctuation or a slight alteration of word, which nonetheless cause large changes of meaning. Especially in view of this, it is essential that you read the proofs with great care. This may be the nth time you have read your book and you may be becoming a little tired of it, but it is an essential task as it is the last opportunity to put things right. If necessary, demand to see a second set of proofs incorporating your corrections. Also, make sure to ask to see the publisher's design for the front cover, and their blurb for the back cover. Publishers are usually cooperative over these matters and send them to you for approval as a matter of course. I have rejected one or two designs, but I did slip up over one back cover blurb that was not sent to me, and this spoilt my pleasure at seeing the final product.

Child-Meaningful Learning

The Experiences of Bilingual Children in the Early Years

A Book Proposal

From Peter Woods, Mari Boyle and Nick Hubbard

Background

This book is based on original research material collected over the last two and a half years by sustained, in-depth participant observation in a primary school and its nursery unit, and in a contrasting nursery school. Both schools had high proportions of Punjabi-speaking children. The main aims of the research were to:

1 Study the theory and practice of teachers' approaches to teaching young bilingual learners.
2 Consider the meanings that the children attached to their learning.
3 Consider the children within their own social frameworks.
4 Make recommendations for future school policy and teaching practice.

Key issues were:

• access to the National Curriculum for bilingual pupils
• the principles that guide the teaching in the schools; how they relate to teachers' practice, and how that practice is experienced by the children
• factors constraining the teachers' practice
• how young bilingual children accomplish the transition to institutional life in English society, and how they accommodate to the diverse cultures of their experience
• the relationship between bilingual children's home and school lives.

The theoretical bases of the research were:

Social constructivism

This theory of learning derives from Vygotsky (1962) and has been developed by Bruner (1986) and others (Donaldson 1978; Edwards and Mercer 1987; Wood 1988; Mercer 1995). There is emphasis on the cultural and communicative aspects of the context in which children learn; on cooperation – with both teachers and other pupils; on negotiation with the teacher over learning tasks; on the teacher as facilitator who helps construct a 'scaffolding' for children's mental explorations; on the 'handover' of control of learning to pupils once this cognitive edifice is secure; and on the resulting 'ownership' of knowledge by the child. In primary schools this

Figure 9.5   A specimen book proposal

theory has largely displaced the 'child-centredness' associated with Piaget and the Plowden Report (1967). Yet, without appropriate 'conceptual and empirical testing', it is in danger of becoming the same kind of ideology – operating at the level of ideas rather than practice – as 'child-centredness' (Alexander 1984, 1992).

In our previous research, we have developed the related notion of 'creative teaching and learning' (Woods 1990, 1993, 1995; Woods and Jeffrey 1996). This features innovation (which refers to the teacher's powers of invention, or the child's learning something new), ownership (of knowledge), control (of pedagogical or learning processes), and relevance (operating within a broad range of accepted social values while being attuned to pupil identities and cultures). The initiation of the young bilingual child into the world of school seemed to offer a stringent test of these criteria, while the theory in turn might prove fruitful for school policy and practice.

Intensification and coping

Any such recommendations for schools would have to take into account the constraints that currently operate on teachers. Prominent among these is the intensification of teachers' work. The theory of intensification (Apple 1986) derives from Larson's (1980) discussion of the proletarianisation of educated labour. As advanced capitalist economies seek to maintain and promote efficiency so the sphere of work narrows, high-level tasks become routinised and there is more subservience to the bureaucratic whole. At the chalk-face, there is more to do, including a proliferation of administrative and assessment tasks, less time to do it in, less time for reskilling and for sociability, few opportunities for creative work, a diversification of responsibility, and a reduction in quality of service. As with the constructivist theory, however, the intensification theory requires opening up for empirical and theoretical inspection (see Hargreaves 1991).

We have done this through combining with it another theoretical area, that of 'coping strategies' (Woods 1979; Pollard 1982; Hargreaves 1984). This notion combines structure and agency, system and individual, constraints and creativity. Intensification implies an increase in the constraints, and greater pressure on the ability to cope, producing a range of reactions from stress and burn-out to personal adjustment and accommodation (Lacey 1977). The school of our research made an interesting test case for these theories.

Multiculturalism

This term, though still the preferred one within schools, has been somewhat discredited for failing to deliver equality of opportunity in relation to 'race',

Figure 9.5 *(Cont'd)*

for promoting complacency and for failing to acknowledge that the issue is a structural one, persistently reproduced by racism (see Stone 1981). Here, teachers who are sensitive to such criticisms are reaching toward new policies and strategies. They do not appear to be helped by the National Curriculum (NC) which 'effectively marginalises community languages and mother tongues' (Reid 1992: 18) and crowds the timetable with statutory subjects. How, then, do highly aware teachers promote mother tongue teaching in such circumstances? How can bilingualism be seen and developed as a resource within the context of the NC? How can the 'entitlement' implicit in the NC be made a reality for all children? Again, our schools made a critical case for testing the theoretical frameworks both of multiculturalism and of the NC. For example, if there were few opportunities for such activities, the argument for the NC being a centralising, intensifying, monoethnic instrument would be strengthened. Opinion, and the research evidence on the NC in this respect, is currently divided. On the one hand, it seems to be introducing more constraints (Campbell *et al.* 1991; Broadfoot *et al.* 1991; Pollard 1991); on the other, there appear to some to be new opportunities (Webb 1990; HMI 1991; Wragg 1992). Our research contributes to that debate.

Relevance of the research and of the book

A number of factors make this subject of study a pressing current issue:

a) Primary school pedagogy has been a major concern for some time, but even more so since the Alexander, Rose and Woodhead (1992) report. This called for more whole-class teaching, an end of 'dogmas' about 'child-centredness' and urged acceptance of the subject-based NC as a *fait accompli*. It is seen by some teachers (wrongly perhaps) as a threat to their basic personal, practical philosophies. There is a great need here for clarification on both sides. The issue has been a matter of debate for some time. It always seems to be presented in polarised terms ('traditional-progressive', 'whole-class teaching – individual work', 'child-centred – knowledge-centred'). It surfaces and induces a moral panic every few years, featuring more politics and ideology than evidence and reasoned argument. As Alexander (1992) argues, therefore, there is a clear need for the application of 'conceptual and empirical tests' (p. 194). Halpin (1990: 31) argues for 'the development of an archive of case studies of attempts by progressive schools and teachers to sustain their existing priorities in the light of, and despite, the requirements of the Act'.

b) The NC has little to say about equality of opportunity. With the great demands on teachers of what *is* prescribed and the pressures on their time (Campbell and Neill 1990), there is a danger that such issues will become marginalised. This will be exacerbated by the demise of the

Figure 9.5 *(Cont'd)*

LEAs, some of whom have kept such issues in the forefront of policy. Equality of opportunity, therefore, needs bringing back on to the agenda.

c) The increased pressures on teachers in recent years have lent weight to theories of intensification, deskilling and demoralization (Apple 1986). There are said to be crises of confidence in professional knowledge and in the teacher role. Some fear the loss of work that is most meaningful to them (Lawn and Grace 1987; Nias 1989). There are three implications here for this book:

   i) If the research helps teachers to articulate their 'personal, practical philosophies' (Connelly and Clandinin 1985), and to evaluate what they consider to be their best work, it might help, to some degree, to restore confidence.

   ii) Through the strong representation of teacher voice in the book, teachers may be encouraged to defy any 'technical-rationalist' threat in recent developments and to develop their roles as 'reflective practitioners' (Schön 1983).

   iii) Points (i) and (ii) might help teachers accept and act upon the points of criticism advanced in the book, which will be offered in a balanced, constructive, and collegial spirit.

Readership

All those – teachers, students, governors, inspectors, academics, teacher trainers – involved in 1. Early Years' education; 2. Primary education; and 3. The teaching of bilingual children and minority ethnic groups. We would envisage the book being used for professional studies, policy studies and educational research components of initial and inservice courses for teachers; also management training initiatives in education, for example the new government-sponsored deputy headteacher and headteacher training schemes.

Level

We aim to present a highly readable book, soundly based in academic research, but aimed at practiitioners and policy-makers rather than academics. We would hope that it would be a recommended text on courses for student teachers in the areas indicated.

Competing books

We are not aware of any other book that represents the young bilingual child's point of view, or studies these subjects at this school level, in such fine detail.

Figure 9.5 (Cont'd)

Length and timetable

We would aim for a maximum of 80,000 words, the text to be completed by 28 February 1998.

Authors

Peter Woods is Professor of Education at the Open University. He is the author of numerous books and articles on education and research methods. He is the director of the research project on which this book is based. Mari Boyle is a Research Fellow at the Open University. She has taught in primary school. She has a master's degree in computer-based information systems. She has published and made conference presentations in the area of teachers' and pupils' work in lower schools. Nick Hubbard is a former primary school headteacher. He is a school governor and school consultant. He has a master's degree in 'child-meaningful learning in two nursery settings'.

Structure and contents

Introduction

This will explain the nature of the research on which the book is based. We discuss how the research sought to develop previous research on 'creative teaching and learning' with reference to the experiences of young bilingual children at the very beginning of their educational careers. Apart from promising to illuminate the theory on 'creative teaching and learning' in particular ways, the subject contains a number of issues of current concern, such as the adequacy of, and access, for all pupils, to the NC; methods of teaching in the early years; providing for diverse cultures and languages; inducting the learner into the system; and relationships between school and community. We shall outline the methods of the research, schools and personnel involved.

[There followed 1000-word summaries of each of the following chapters]:
Chapter 1: Curriculum and culture
Chapter 2: Teaching approaches and methods
Chapter 3: The children's perspective
Chapter 4: The parents' perspective
Chapter 5: The educational significance of books and stories for bilingual children
Chapter 6: Bilingual children in transition
Chapter 7: The social and cultural worlds of the children
Chapter 8: Recommendations for policy and practice

[There followed a number of extended examples illustrating points made in the outlines of the chapters.]

Figure 9.5 *(Cont'd)*

The book eventually appeared like this:

Introduction
Chapter 1 Teacher perspectives (Chapter 2 above)
Chapter 2 Teaching the National Curriculum (Chapter 1 above)
Chapter 3 Creative teaching (a new chapter, suggested as we re-analysed the
          material)
Chapter 4 The educational significance of stories (Chapter 5 above)
Chapter 5 Bilingual children in transition (Chapter 6 above)
Chapter 6 Children's perspectives (Chapter 3 above)
Chapter 7 Children's identities (Chapter 7 above)
Chapter 8 Parents' perspectives (Chapter 4 above)

The logic of this was that the first four chapters were about teachers and teaching, the next three about children, and the last about parents. We decided
to make suggestions for policy and practice at the end of each chapter, so the
old Chapter 8 disappeared.

In conclusion, I quote from a document on the National Literacy Strategy
(Standards and Effectiveness Unit 1998). Literate primary pupils should:

- read and write with confidence, fluency and understanding
- understand the sound and spelling system and use this to read and spell
  accurately
- have an interest in words and their meanings and a growing vocabulary
- know, understand and be able to write in a range of genres
- plan, draft, revise and edit their own writing
- be interested in books, read with enjoyment and evaluate and justify their
  preferences
- through reading and writing, develop their powers of imagination, inventiveness and critical awareness.

Here is a recipe for us all!

Suggested further reading

General

There are number of excellent texts on writing, written from the authors' various viewpoints, including:

Becker, H.S. (1986) *Writing for Social Scientists: How to Start and Finish Your Thesis, Book or Article*, Chicago: University of Chicago Press.

Ely, M., Vinz, R., Downing, M. and Anzul, M. (1997) *On Writing Qualitative Research: Living by Words*, London: Falmer Press.

Holliday, A. (2002) *Doing and Writing Qualitative Research*, London: Sage.

Van Maanen, J. (ed.) (1995) *Representation in Ethnography*, Thousand Oaks, CA: Sage.

Wolcott, H.F. (2001) *Writing up Qualitative Research*, 2nd edn, Newbury Park, CA: Sage.

General qualitative research texts which contain useful guidance on writing include:

Coffey, A. and Atkinson, P. (1996) *Making Sense of Qualitative Data: Complementary Research Strategies*, London: Sage.

Delamont, S. (2001) *Fieldwork in Educational Settings: Methods, Pitfalls and Perspectives*, 2nd edn, London: Falmer Press.

Delamont, S. and Atkinson, P. (2004) *Successful Research Careers: A Practical Guide*, Buckingham: Open University Press (useful advice on writing and publishing).

Denscombe, M. (1998) *The Good Research Guide: For Small Scale Social Research Projects*, Buckingham: Open University Press.

Hammersley, M. and Atkinson, P. (1995) *Ethnography: Principles in Practice*, 2nd edn, London: Tavistock.

On getting going

Dillard, A. (1998) *The Writing Life*, 2nd edn, New York: HarperCollins.

King, S. (2000) *On Writing: A Memoir of the Craft*, New York: Scribner.

Maisel, E. (1999) *Deep Writing: 7 Principles that Bring Ideas to Life*, New York: Tarcher/Putnam.

Moxley, J.M. and Taylor, T. (eds) (1997) *Writing and Publishing for Academic Authors*, 2nd edn, Lanham, MD: Rowman & Littlefield.

Perry, S.K. (1999) *Writing in Flow: Keys to Enhanced Creativity*, Cincinnati, OH: Writers' Digest Books.

Standard approach

Denscombe, M. (2002) *Ground Rules for Good Research*, Buckingham: Open University Press (pp. 50–63 for guidance on literature review).
Gilbert, N. (1993) 'Writing about social research', in N. Gilbert (ed.) *Researching Social Life*, London: Sage (Chapter 16).
Hammersley, M. and Atkinson, P. (1995) *Ethnography: Principles in Practice*, 2nd edn, London: Tavistock (p. 209 *et seq.* for a discussion of the generation of categories etc.).
Strauss, A.L. (1987) *Qualitative Analysis for Social Scientists*, Cambridge: Cambridge University Press (Chapter 10).

Alternative approaches

There is a great deal of literature now available in this area. On writing and new approaches, see:

Bochner, A.P. and Ellis, C. (2001) *Ethnographically Speaking: Autoethnography, Literature and Aesthetics*, Walnut Creek, CA: Altamira (for a discussion of different kinds of autoethnographic texts).
Dadds, M. and Hart, S. (2001) *Doing Practitioner Research Differently*, London: Routledge/Falmer.
Ellis, C. and Bochner, A.P. (eds) (1996) *Composing Ethnography: Alternative Forms of Qualitative Writing*, London: Sage.
Goodall, H.L. (2000) *Writing the New Ethnography*, Walnut Creek, CA: Altamira.
Richardson, L. (1990) *Writing Strategies: Reaching Diverse Audiences*, London: Sage.

On debates about the 'crisis in representation', see:

Flaherty, M.G., Denzin, N.K., Manning, P.K. and Snow, D.A. (2002) 'Review symposium: crisis in representation', *Journal of Contemporary Ethnography*, 31(4): 479–516.
International Journal of Qualitative Studies in Education (2002), 15(4) (special issue on ethnographic writing).

To keep up to date with these debates and other issues in qualitative research writing, see recent editions of the above two journals, and also *Qualitative Sociology, Qualitative Inquiry, Qualitative Research, Sociological Quarterly* and *Symbolic Interaction*.

On use of the visual in ethnographic representation and electronic hypermedia, see:

Hine, C. (2000) *Virtual Ethnography*, London: Sage.
Pink, S. (2001) *Doing Visual Ethnography*, London: Sage.

Style

Atkinson, P. (1990) *The Ethnographic Imagination: Textual Constructions of Reality*, London: Routledge (for the use of rhetoric).

Ritter, R.M. (ed.) (2003) *The Oxford Manual of Style*, Oxford: Oxford University Press (for basic grammar, punctuation and construction).
Trimble, J.R. (2000) *Writing with Style*, Upper Saddle River, NJ: Prentice-Hall.
Zinsser, W.K. (1998) *On Writing Well*, 5th edn, New York: Harper & Row.

Writing and computers

There are a number of excellent texts that describe the accomplishments and potential of the computer in the analysis and presentation of qualitative work. They include:

David, M. and Sutton, C.D. (2004) *Social Research: The Basics*, London: Sage.
Fielding, N.G. and Lee, R. (eds) (1991) *Using Computers in Qualitative Research*, London: Sage.
Fielding, N.G. and Lee, R. (1998) *Why Use Computers in Qualitative Research?* London: Sage.
Palmquist, M. and Zimmerman, D. (1999) *Writing with a Computer*, Boston, MA: Allyn & Bacon.
Tesch, R. (1990) *Qualitative Research: Analysis Types and Software Tools*, London: Falmer Press.

On writing and the Internet, see:

Dorner, J. (2000) *The Internet: A Writer's Guide*, London: A & C Black.
Dorner, J. (2002) *Writing for the Internet*, Oxford: Oxford University Press.
Lee, R.M. (2000) *Unobtrusive Methods in Social Research*, Buckingham: Open University Press (pp. 115–38).

See also the English Centre's online guide at http://ec.hku.hk/writing_turbocharger, *Sociological Research Online* at http://www.socresonline.org.uk/socresonline/.html

On publishing academic texts

Canter, D. and Fairbairn, G. (2005) *Getting Published: A Guide for Researchers*, Buckingham: Open University Press.
Day, A. (1996) *How to Get Research Published in Journals*, Aldershot: Gower.
Gargiulo, R. and Jalongo, M.R. (2001) 'Writing for publication in *Early Childhood Education*: survey data from editors and advice to authors', *Early Childhood Education Journal*, 29(1): 17–23.
Germano, W. (2001) *Getting it Published*, Chicago: University of Chicago Press (view from an editor).
Noble, K.A. (1989) 'Publish or perish: what 23 journal editors have to say', *Studies in Higher Education*, 14(1): 97–102.
Wellington, J. (2003) *Getting Published: A Guide for Lecturers and Researchers*, London: Routledge/Falmer.

On the internet

Use one of the research engines such as 'Google Scholar' to research any aspect of writing you wish. This is probably the best way of keeping in touch with the array of material that is becoming increasingly on offer in print and online.

References

Abbott, A. (1999) *Department and Discipline: Chicago Sociology at One Hundred*, Chicago: University of Chicago Press.

Acker, J., Barry, K. and Esseveld, J. (1983) 'Objectivity and truth: problems in doing feminist research', *Women's Studies International Forum*, 6(4): 423–35.

Adams, N., Causey, T., Jacobs, M-E., Munro, P., Quinn, M. and Trousdale, A. (1998) '*Womentalkin*': a reader's theatre performance of teachers' stories', *Qualitative Studies in Education*, 11(3): 383–95.

Aikan, H., Erickson, K. and Moore, W.L. (2003) 'Three women writing/riding feminism's third wave', *Qualitative Sociology*, 26(3): 397–425.

Altheide, D.L. and Johnson, J.M. (1994) 'Criteria for assessing interpretive validity in qualitative research', in N.K. Denzin and Y.S. Lincoln (eds) *Handbook of Qualitative Research*, London: Sage.

Anderson, E. (2003) 'Jelly's place: an ethnographic memoir', *Symbolic Interaction*, 26(2): 21–37.

Atkinson, P. (1990) *The Ethnographic Imagination: Textual Constructions of Reality*, London: Routledge.

Atkinson, P. (1991) 'Supervising the text', *International Journal of Qualitative Research in Education*, 4(2): 161–74.

Atkinson, P. (2004) 'Performing ethnography and the ethnography of performance', *British Journal of Sociology of Education*, 25(1): 107–14.

Bagley, C. and Cancienne, M.B. (2001) 'Educational research and intertextual forms of (re)presentation: the case for dancing the data', *Qualitative Inquiry*, 7(2): 221–37.

Bailey, C.A. (1996) *A Guide to Field Research*, Thousand Oaks CA: Pine Forge Press.

Ball, S.J. and Vincent, C. (1998) '"I heard it on the grapevine": "hot" knowledge and school choice', *British Journal of Sociology of Education*, 19(3): 377–400.

Bandman, R. (1967) *The Place of Reason in Education*, Columbus, OH: Ohio State University Press.

Bartels, N. (2003) 'How teachers and researchers read academic articles', *Teaching and Teacher Education*, 19(7): 737–53.

Barthes, R. ([1970] 1990) *S/Z*, trans. R. Miller, Oxford: Blackwell.

Barton, D. and Hamilton, M. (1998) *Local Literacies: Reading and Writing in one Community*, London: Routledge.

Bassey, M. (1995) *Creating Education through Research: A Global Perspective of Educational Research for the 21st Century*, Newark: Kirklington Moor Press.

Becker, H.S. (1971) Footnote added to the paper by Wax, M. and Wax, R. 'Great tradition, little tradition and formal education', in M. Wax, S. Diamond and F.O. Gearing (eds) *Anthropological Perspectives on Education*, pp. 3–27. New York: Basic Books.

Becker, H.S., McCall, M. and Morris, L. (1988) 'Performing culture: local theatrical communities', performed at Northwestern University Theatre and Interpretation Centre, Evanston, IL, 15 January.

Beidelman, T.O. (1974) 'Sir Edward Evan Evans-Pritchard (1902–1973): an appreciation', *Anthropos*, (69): 554–67.

Bell, C. (1977) 'Reflections on the Banbury restudy', in C. Bell and H. Newby (eds) *Doing Sociological Research*, London: Allen & Unwin.

Ben-Ari, E. (1995) 'On acknowledgements in ethnographies', in J. Van Maanen (ed.) *Representation in Ethnography*, Thousand Oaks, CA: Sage.

Berger, P.L. (1966) *Invitation to Sociology*, New York: Doubleday.

Bernard, J. (1990) 'A woman's twentieth century', in B. Berger (ed.) *Authors of Their Own Lives*, Berkeley, CA: University of California Press.

Bernstein, S. (1978) 'Getting it done – notes on student fritters', in J. Lofland (ed.) *Interaction in Everyday Life*, Beverly Hills, CA: Sage.

Bevlin, M. (1970) *Design Through Discovery*, New York: Holt, Rinehart & Winston.

Beynon, J. (1985) *Initial Encounters in the Secondary School*, Lewes: Falmer Press.

Blishen, E. (1980) *Shaky Relationships*, London: Hamish Hamilton.

Blumenfeld-Jones, D. (2002) 'If I could have said it, I would have', in C. Bagley and M.B. Cancienne (eds) *Dancing the Data*, New York: Peter Lang Publishing Inc.

Bochner, A. (1997) 'It's about time: narrative and the divided self', *Qualitative Inquiry*, 3: 418–38.

Bochner, A.P. and Ellis, C. (1996) 'Talking over ethnography', in C. Ellis and A.P. Bochner (eds) *Composing Ethnography: Alternative Forms of Qualitative Writing*, Walnut Creek, CA: Altamira Press.

Bochner, A.P. and Ellis, C. (1999) 'Which way to turn?', *Journal of Contemporary Ethnography*, 28(5): 485–99.

Bolton, G. (1994) 'Stories at work: fictional-critical writing as a means of professional development', *British Educational Research Journal*, 20(1): 55–68.

Bradbury, M. (1998) 'Authors are born, not made', *The Observer*, 29 November: 5.

British Educational Research Association (BERA) (1992) *Ethical Guidelines for Educational Research*, Edinburgh: BERA/SCRE.

Bruner, J. (1993) 'The autobiographical process', in R. Folkenflik (ed.) *The Culture of Autobiography: Constructions of Self Representation*, Stanford, CA: Stanford University Press.

Bucknell, K. (ed.) (1996) *Christopher Isherwood Diaries Volume 1: 1939–1960*, London: Methuen.

Bullough, R.G. and Knowles, J.G. (1991) 'Teaching and nurturing: changing conceptions of self as teacher in a case study of becoming a teacher', *International Journal of Qualitative Studies in Education*, 4(2): 121–40.

Burgess, A. (1992) *A Mouthful of Air*, London: Hutchinson.

Burgess, R.G. (1984) *The Research Process in Educational Settings: Ten Case Studies*, Lewes: Falmer Press.

Cancienne, M.B. and Snowber, C.N. (2003) 'Writing rhythm: movement as method', *Qualitative Inquiry*, 9(2): 237–53.

Caute, D. and Graham, G. (1983) 'Contacts and contracts', *Times Higher Educational Supplement*, 2 December: 14–15.

Charmaz, K. and Mitchell, R.G. (1997) 'The myth of silent authorship: self, substance, and style in ethnographic writing', in R. Hertz (ed.) *Reflexivity and Voice*, Thousand Oaks, CA: Sage.

Clough, P.T. (2000) 'Comments on setting criteria for experimental writing', *Qualitative Inquiry*, 6(2): 278–91.

Coffey, A. and Atkinson, P. (1996) *Making Sense of Qualitative Data: Complementary Research Strategies*, London: Sage.

Coffey, A. and Delamont, S. (2000) *Feminism and the Classroom Teacher: Research Praxis and Pedagogy*, London: Routledge/Falmer.

Cook, M.C. (1992) *Freeing Your Creativity: A Writer's Guide*, Cincinnati, OH: Writers' Digest Books.

Cooper, P. and McIntyre, D. (1993) 'Commonality in teachers' and pupils' perceptions of effective classroom learning', *British Journal of Educational Psychology*, 63: 381–99.

David, M. and Sutton, C.D. (2004) *Social Research: The Basics*, London: Sage.

Davies, B. (1982) *Life in the Classroom and Playground: The Accounts of Primary School Children*, London: Routledge.

Delamont, S. (2001) *Fieldwork in Educational Settings: Methods, Pitfalls and Perspectives*, 2nd edn, London: Falmer Press.

Denscombe, M. (1998) *The Good Research Guide: For Small Scale Social Research Projects*, Buckingham: Open University Press.

Denzin, N.K. (1989) *Interpretive Interactionalism*, Newbury Park, CA: Sage.

Denzin N.K. (1994) 'The art and politics of interpretation', in N.K. Denzin and Y.S. Lincoln (eds) *Handbook of Qualitative Research*, London: Sage.

Denzin, N.K. (1997) *Interpretive Ethnography: Ethnographic Practices for the 21st Century*, Thousand Oaks, CA: Sage.

Denzin, N.K. (2003a) *Performance Ethnography: Critical Pedagogy and the Politics of Culture*, Thousand Oaks, CA: Sage.

Denzin, N.K. (2003b) 'Reading and writing performance', *Qualitative Research*, 3(2): 243–68

Denzin, N.K. (2004) 'Review of P. Atkinson, A. Coffey, S. Delamont, J. Lofland and L. Lofland (eds) *Handbook of Ethnography*', *International Journal of Qualitative Studies in Education*, 17(5): 731–5.

Denzin, N.K. and Lincoln, Y.S. (eds) (2000) *Handbook of Qualitative Research*, 2nd edn, London: Sage.

Diamond, C.T.P. (1993) 'Writing to reclaim self: the use of narrative in teacher education', *Teaching and Teacher Education*, 9(5/6): 511–17.

Donmoyer, R. (1996) 'Educational research in an era of paradigm proliferation: what's a journal editor to do?' *Educational Researcher*, 25(2): 19–25.

Donmoyer, R. and Yennie-Donmoyer, J. (1991) 'Introduction: special issues on reader's theatre in education', *Literacy Matters*, 3(1): 1–3.

Donmoyer, R. and Yennie-Donmoyer, J. (1998) 'Reader's theatre and educational research – give me a for instance: a commentary on Womentalkin'', *Qualitative Studies in Education*, 11(3): 397–407.

Douglas, J.D. (1976) *Investigative Social Research: Individual and Team Field Research*, Beverly Hills, CA: Sage.

Dubberley, W.S. (1988) 'Humor as resistance', *International Journal of Qualitative Studies in Education*, 1(2): 109–23.

Edmondson, R. (1984) *Rhetoric in Sociology*, London: Macmillan.

Eisner, E.W. (1991) *The Enlightened Eye: Qualitative Inquiry and the Enhancement of Educational Practice*, New York: Macmillan.

Eisner, E.W. (2001) 'Concerns and aspirations for qualitative research in the new millenium', *Qualitative Research*, 1(2): 135–45.

Ellen, R.F. (ed.) (1984) *Ethnographic Research: A Guide to General Conduct*, London: Academic Press.

Ellis, C. (1995) *Final Negotiations: A Story of Love, Loss and Chronic Illness*, Philadelphia, PA: Temple University Press.

Ellis, C. (1996) 'Maternal connections', in C. Ellis and A.P. Bochner (eds) *Composing Ethnograph: Alternative Forms of Qualitative Writing*, Walnut Creek, CA: Altamira Press.

Ellis, C. (2002) 'Being real: moving inward toward social change', *International Journal of Qualitative Studies in Education*, 15(4): 399–406.

Ellis, C. and Bochner, A.P. (1992) 'Telling and performing personal stories: the constraints of choice in abortion', in C. Ellis. and M. Flaherty (eds) *Investigating Subjectivity: Research on Lived Experience*, Newbury Park, CA: Sage.

Ellis, C. and Bochner, A.P. (eds) (1996) *Composing Ethnography: Alternative Forms of Qualitative Writing*, London: Sage.

Ellis, C. and Bochner, A.P. (2000) 'Autoethnography, personal narrative, reflexivity: researcher as subject', in N.K. Denzin, and Y.S. Lincoln (eds) *Handbook of Qualitative Research*, 2nd edn, London: Sage.

Ely, M., Anzul, M., Friedman, T., Garner, D. and Steinmetz, A. (1991) *Doing Qualitative Research: Circles within Circles*, London: Falmer Press.

Ely, M., Vinz, R., Downing, M. and Anzul, M. (1997) *On Writing Qualitative Research: Living by Words*, London: Falmer Press.

Erikson, K. and Stull, D. (1998) *Doing Team Ethnography*, Thousand Oaks, CA: Sage.

Filer, A. (ed.) (2000) *Assessment: Social Practice and Social Product*, London: Falmer Press.

Filer, A. and Pollard, A. (2000) *The Social World of Pupil Assessment: Processes and Contexts of Primary Schooling*, London: Continuum.

Fine, G.A. and Deegan, J.G. (1996) 'Three principles of serendip: insight, chance, and discovery in qualitative research', *International Journal of Qualitative Studies in Education*, 9(4): 434–47.

Flaherty, M.G. (2002) 'The "crisis" in representation: reflections and assessments', *Journal of Contemporary Ethnography*, 31(4): 508–16.

Foley, D.E. (2002) 'Critical ethnography: the reflexive turn', *International Journal of Qualitative Studies in Education*, 15(4): 469–90.

Fowler, H.W. (1926) *A Dictionary of Modern English Usage*, Oxford: Clarendon Press.

Fox, K.V. (1996) 'Silent voices: a subversive reading of child sexual abuse', in C. Ellis and A.P. Bochner (eds) *Composing Ethnography: Alternative Forms of Qualitative Writing*, Walnut Creek, CA: Altamira Press.

Friedman, A.L. (2004) 'Strawmanning and labour process analysis', *Sociology*, 38(3): 573–91.

Gannaway, H. (1976) 'Making sense of school', in M. Stubbs and S. Delamont (eds) *Explorations in Classroom Observation*, London: Wiley.

Gargiulo, R., and Jalongo, M.R. (2001) 'Writing for publication in *Early Childhood Education*: survey data from editors and advice to authors', *Early Childhood Education Journal*, 29(1): 17–23.

Geertz, C. (1973) 'Thick description: toward an interpretive theory of culture', in

C. Geertz (ed.) *The Interpretation of Cultures: Selected Essays by Clifford Geertz*, New York: Basic Books.

Germano, W. (2001) *Getting it Published*, Chicago: University of Chicago Press.

Glaser, B.G. and Strauss, A.L. (1967) *The Discovery of Grounded Theory*, London: Weidenfeld & Nicolson.

Glass, G.V. (1999) 'A new day in how scholars communicate', *Current Issues in Education*, http://cie.ed.asu/volume2/number2/index.html.

Goffman, E. (1989) 'On fieldwork', transcribed and edited by Lyn H. Lofland, *Journal of Contemporary Ethnography*, 18: 123–32.

Golden-Biddle, K. and Locke, K.D. (1997) *Composing Qualitative Research*, London: Sage.

Gray, J., Goldstein, H. and Kay, W. (1997) 'Educational research and evidence-based practice: the debate continues', *Research Intelligence*, 59(February): 18–20.

Greenlaw, L. (1996) 'Rhyme with reason', *Times Educational Supplement*: 23.

Hallam, S., Ireson, J. and Davies, J. (2004) 'Grouping practices in the primary school: what influences change?' *British Educational Research Journal*, 30(1): 117–40.

Hamill, P. (1988) 'A romantic in Cuba', *The Age Good Weekend*, August: 42–51.

Hammersley, M. (1992) *What's Wrong with Ethnography? Methodological Explorations*, London: Routledge.

Hammersley, M. (1993) 'The rhetorical turn in ethnography', *Social Science Information*, 32(1): 23–37.

Hammond, R. (1984) *The Writer and the Word Processor: A Guide for Authors, Journalists, Poets and Playwrights*, Sevenoaks: Hodder & Stoughton.

Hannan, A. (1995) The case for school-led primary teacher training, *Journal of Education for Teaching*, 21(1): 25–35.

Hannan, A. (2002) Innovating in UK universities since the late 1990s, *EducatiON-LINE*, http://www.leeds.ac.uk/educol/documents/00002186.htm.

Hannan, A. and Silver, H. (2000) *Innovating in Higher Education: Teaching, Learning and Institutional Cultures*, Buckingham: SRHE/Open University Press.

Hargreaves, A. (1988) Teaching quality: a sociological analysis, *Journal of Curriculum Studies*, 20(3): 211–31.

Hargreaves, A. (1994) *Changing Teachers, Changing Times*, London: Cassell.

Hargreaves, A. (1995) 'Transforming knowledge: blurring the boundaries between research, policy and practice', unpublished paper, Toronto: The Ontario Institute for Studies in Education.

Hargreaves, D.H. (1977) 'The process of typification in the classroom: models and methods', *British Journal of Educational Psychology*, 47: 274–84.

Hargreaves, D.H. (1996) 'Teaching as a research-based profession: possibilities and prospects', The Teacher Training Agency Annual Lecture, London: TTA.

Hewitt, R. (1994) 'Expanding the literary horizon: romantic poets and postmodern sociologists', *The Sociological Quarterly*, 35(2): 195–213.

Hitchcock, G. and Hughes, D. (1995) *Research and the Teacher: A Qualitative Introduction to School-based Research*, 2nd edn, London: Routledge.

Hoadley-Maidment, E. and Mercer, N. (1996) 'English in the academic world', in N. Mercer and J. Swann (eds) *Learning English: Development and Diversity*, London: Routledge.

Hodgson, J. (1972) 'Drama as a social and educational force', in J. Hodgson (ed.) *The Uses of Drama*, London: Eyre Methuen.

Hodkinson, P. (1998) 'Naivete and bias in educational research: The Tooley Report', *Research Intelligence*, 65(August): 16–17.

John, P.D. (2003) 'Conceptions, contentions and connections: how teachers read different genres of educational research', in R. Sutherland, G. Claxton and A. Pollard (eds) *Learning Where World Views Meet*, London: Trentham Books.

Johnson, S. (1757) 'On optimism', reprinted in S. Eliot and B. Stern (eds) (1979) *The Age of Enlightenment: Volume 1*, London: Ward Lock Educational.

Kachru, Y. (1996) 'Culture in rhetorical styles: contrastive rhetoric and world Englishes', in N. Mercer and J. Swann (eds) *Learning English: Development and Diversity*, London: Routledge.

Karl, E.R. and Davies, L. (eds) (1983) *The Collected Letters of Joseph Conrad, Volume One: 1861–1897*, Cambridge: Cambridge University Press.

Kerr, W. (1975) *The Silent Clowns*, New York: Alfred A. Knopf.

Lacey, C. (1976) 'Problems of sociological fieldwork: a review of the methodology of 'Hightown Grammar', in M. Hammersley and P. Woods (eds) *The Process of Schooling*, London: Routledge.

Lacey, C. (1977) *The Socialization of Teachers*, London: Methuen.

Lather, P. (1991) *Getting Smart*, London: Routledge.

Lather, P. (1997) 'Drawing the line at angels: working the ruins of feminist ethnography', *International Journal of Qualitative Studies in Education*, 10(3): 285–304.

Lee, C. and Jackson, R. (1993) *Faking It: A Look Into the Mind of A Creative Learner*, London: Cassell.

Lichtenberg, G.C. (1789) 'Aphorisms and letters', trans. F. Mautner and H. Hatfield (1969), London: Jonathan Cape.

Liggett, A.M., Glesne, C.E., Johnston, A.P., Hasazi, S.B. and Schattman, R.A. (1994) Teaming in qualitative research: lessons learned, *International Journal of Qualitative Studies in Education*, 7(1): 77–88.

Lodge, D. (1996) *The Practice of Writing*, London: Penguin.

Lofland, J. (1971) *Analyzing Social Settings: A Guide to Qualitative Observation and Analysis*, Belmont, CA: Wadsworth.

Lofland, J. (1974) 'Styles of reporting qualitative field research', *American Sociologist*, 9(August): 101–11.

Lucas, F.L. (1974) *Style*, London: Cassell.

MacDiarmid, H. (1969) *Selected Essays of Hugh MacDiarmid*, London: Cape.

Manning, P.K. (1995) 'The challenges of postmodernism', in J. Van Maanen (ed.) *Representation in Ethnography*, London: Sage.

Maines, D.R. (2001) 'Writing the self versus writing the other: comparing autobiographical and life history data', *Symbolic Interaction*, 24(1): 105–11.

Mason, B. and Dicks, B. (2004) 'The digital ethnographer', in *Cybersociology*, 6: *Research Methodology Online*, http://www.wordcircuits.com/htww/dicks1.htm.

McCall, M.M. (2000) 'Performance ethnography: a brief history and some advice', in N. Denzin, and Y. Lincoln (2000) *Handbook of Qualitative Research*, 2nd edn, London: Sage.

McCourt, F. (1996a) *Angela's Ashes*, London: Flamingo.

McCourt, F. (1996b) 'Ashes to ashes', *The Times*, October: 10–16.

Mealyea, R. (1989) Humour as a coping strategy, *British Journal of Sociology of Education*, 10(3): 311–33.

Meighan, R. (1981) *A Sociology of Educating*, London: Holt, Rinehart & Winston.

Mills, C.W. (1959) *The Sociological Imagination*, New York: Oxford University Press.

Moggach, L. (1998) 'How I write', *The Times*: 23.

Morgan, C. (1960) *The Writer and His World*, London: Macmillan.

Mortimer, J. (1983) 'Wig, pen and wisdom', *Radio Times*, 27 August–2 September.

Motion, A. (1993) *Philip Larkin: A Writer's Life*, London: Faber & Faber.

Musgrove, F. (1975) 'Dervishes in Dorsetshire: an English commune', *Youth and Society*, 6(4): 449–80.

Newton, E. (1962) *The Meaning of Beauty*, Harmondsworth: Penguin.

Nias, J. (1991) 'Primary teachers talking: a reflexive account of longitudinal research', in G. Walford (ed.) *Doing Educational Research*, London: Routledge.

Nielson, J. (1990) *Hypertext and Hypermedia*, New York: Academic Press.

Nisbet, R. (1962) 'Sociology as an art form', *Pacific Sociological Review*, Autumn.

Nixon, J. and Wellington, J. (2005) 'A future for academic writing in educational publishing?' *British Journal of Sociology of Education*, 26(1): 91–102.

Olesen, V., Droes, N., Hatton, D., Chico, N. and Schatzman, L. (1994) 'Analyzing together: recollections of a team approach', in A. Bryman and R.G. Burgess (eds) *Analyzing Qualitative Data*, London: Routledge.

Olivero, F., John, P. and Sutherland, R. (2004) 'Seeing is believing: using "videopapers" to transform teachers' professional knowledge and practice', *Cambridge Journal of Education*, 34(2): 179–91.

Osborne, C. (1995) *W.H. Auden: The Life of a Poet*, London: Michael O'Mara Books.

Packwood, A. and Sikes, P. (1996) 'Adopting a postmodern approach to research', *International Journal of Qualitative Studies in Education*, 9(3): 335–45.

Paget, M.A. (1990) 'Performing the text', *Journal of Contemporary Ethnography*, 19(1): 136–55.

Payne, D. (1996) 'Autobiology', in C. Ellis and A.P. Bochner (eds) *Composing Ethnography: Alternative Forms of Qualitative Writing*, Walnut Creek, CA: Altamira Press.

Peterat, L. and Smith, M.G. (1996) 'Metaphoric reflections on collaboration in a teacher education practicum', *Educational Action Research*, 4(1): 15–28.

Pifer, D.A. (1999) 'Small town race: a performance text', *Qualitative Inquiry*, 5(4): 541–62.

Piirto, J. (2002) 'The unreliable narrator, or the difference between writing prose in literature and in social science: a commentary on Tierney's article', *International Journal of Qualitative Studies in Education*, 15(4): 407–15.

Platt, J. (1976) *Realities of Social Research: An Empirical Study of British Sociologists*, London: Chatto & Windus.

Plummer, K. (2002) 'The call of life stories in ethnographic research', in P. Atkinson, A. Coffey, S. Delamont, J. Lofland and L. Lofland (eds) *Handbook of Ethnography*, London: Sage.

Pope, A. (1854) 'An essay on criticism', reproduced in G. Croly (ed.) *Pope's Poetical Works*, London: James Blackwood & Co.

Popper, K. (1968) *Conjectures and Refutations*, New York: Harper.

Read, H. (1931 reissued 1949) *The Meaning of Art*, Harmondsworth: Penguin.

Read, P.P. (1977) *Polonaise*, London: Pan.

Richardson, L. (1985) *The New Other Woman: Contemporary Single Women in Affairs with Married Men*, New York: Free Press.

Richardson, L. (1990) *Writing Strategies: Reaching Diverse Audiences*, London: Sage.

Richardson, L. (1993) 'Poetics, dramatics, and transgressive validity: the case of the skipped line', *The Sociological Quarterly*, 34(4): 695–710.

Richardson, L. (1994a) 'Nine poems: marriage and the family', *Journal of Contemporary Ethnography*, 23(1): 3–13.

Richardson, L. (1994b) 'Writing: a method of inquiry', in N.K. Denzin and Y.S. Lincoln (eds) *Handbook of Qualitative Research*, London: Sage.

Richardson, L. (2000) 'Writing: a method of inquiry' in N.K. Denzin, and Y.S. Lincoln (eds) *Handbook of Qualitative Research*, 2nd edn, London: Sage.

Riseborough, G.F. (1988) 'The great Heddekashun war: a life historical cenotaph for an unknown teacher', *International Journal of Qualitative Studies in Education*, 1(3): 197–223.

Riseborough, G.F. (1992) '"The Cream Team": an ethnography of BTEC national diploma (catering and hotel management) students in a tertiary college', *British Journal of Sociology of Education*, 13(2): 215–45.

Ritter, R.M. (ed.) (2003) *The Oxford Manual of Style*, Oxford: Oxford University Press.

Rizvi, F. (1989) 'Bureaucratic rationality and the promise of democratic schooling', in W. Carr (ed.) *Quality in Teaching; Arguments for a Reflective Profession*, London: Falmer Press.

Robertson, J. (2003) '9/11 and its aftermath: listening to the heartbeat of New York: writings on the wall', *Qualitative Inquiry*, 9(1): 129–52.

Ronai, C. (1995) 'Multiple reflections of child sexual abuse: an argument for a layered account', *Journal of Contemporay Ethnography*, 23(January): 395–426.

Rose, D. (1990) *Living the Ethnographic Life*, London: Sage.

Saxon, D., Garratt, D., Gilroy, P. and Cairns, C. (2003) Collecting data in the information age: exploring web-based survey methods in educational research, *Research in Education*, 69: 51–66.

Schulz, L.Z. (1998) 'Being and becoming a woman teacher: journey through Nepal', *Gender and Education*, 10(2): 163–84.

Schwalbe, M.L. (1995) 'The responsibilities of sociological poets', *Qualitative Sociology*, 18(4): 393–413.

Shaker, P. (1990) 'The metaphorical journey of evaluation theory', *International Journal of Qualitative Studies in Education*, 3(4): 355–63.

Sharples, M. and Pemberton, L. (1992) 'External representations and the writing process', in P.O. Holtand N. Williams (eds) *Computers and Writing: State of the Art*, Boston, MA: Kluwer Academic Publishers.

Sherman, R. (1993) 'Reflections on the editing experience: writing qualitative research', *International Journal of Qualitative Studies in Education*, 6(3): 233–9.

Sikes, P., Measor, L. and Woods, P. (1985) *Teacher Careers: Crises and Continuities*, Lewes: Falmer Press.

Smith, W.N. (2002) 'Ethno-poetry notes', *International Journal of Qualitative Studies in Education*, 15(4): 461–8.

Smulyan, L. (1996) 'Gender and school leadership: using case studies to challenge the frameworks', in R. Chawla-Duggan and C.J. Pole (eds) *Reshaping Education in the 1990s: Perspectives on Primary Schooling*, London: Falmer Press.

Snow, D.A. (2002) 'On the presumed crisis in ethnographic representation: observations from a sociological and interactionist standpoint', *Journal of Contemporary Ethnography*, 31(4): 498–507.

Snow, D.A. and Morrill, C. (1993) 'Reflections on anthropology's ethnographic crisis of faith', *Contemporary Sociology*, 32: 8–11.

Snow, D.A. and Morrill, C. (1995) 'New ethnographies: review symposium: a revolutionary handbook or a handbook for revolution?' *Journal of Contemporary Ethnography*, 24(3): 341–62.

Snyder, I. (1993) 'Writing with word processors: a research overview', *Educational Research*, 35(1): 49–68.

Sparkes, A.C. (1995) 'Writing people: reflections on the dual crisis of representation and legitimation in qualitative inquiry', *Quest*, 47.

Sperber, D. (1979) 'Claude Levi-Strauss', in J. Sturrock (ed.) *Structuralism and Since*, Oxford: Oxford University Press.

Stake, R.E. (1995) *The Art of Case Study Research*, London: Sage.

Standards and Effectiveness Unit (1998) *The National Literacy Strategy: Framework for Teaching*, London: DfEE.

Strauss, A.L. and Corbin, J. (1990) *Basics of Qualitative Research: Grounded Theory Procedures and Techniques*, Newbury Park, CA: Sage.

Thomas, D. (1992) 'Putting nature to the rack: narrative studies as research', Paper presented at the Conference on Teachers' Stories of Life and Work, Liverpool University, Chester College.

Tierney, W.G. (1993) 'The cedar closet', *International Journal of Qualitative Studies in Education*, 6(4): 303–14.

Tierney, W.G. (2002) 'Get real: representing reality', *International Journal of Qualitative Studies in Education*, 15(4): 385–98.

Tillman-Healy, L.M. (2001) *Between Gay and Straight: Understanding Friendship Across Sexual Orientation*, Walnut Creek, CA: Altamira Press.

Tooley, J. (1998) *Educational Research, A Critique: A Survey of Published Educational Research*, report presented to Ofsted, London: Ofsted.

Treble, H.A. and Vallins, G.H. (1936) *ABC of English Usage*, Oxford: Oxford University Press.

Trollope, J. (1994) 'Any questions?' *The Observer Magazine*, 6 March: 46.

Troman, G. (1996) 'No entry signs: educational change and some problems encountered in negotiating entry to educational settings', *British Educational Research Journal*, 22(1): 3–15.

Tyler, S. (1986) 'Post-modern ethnography: from document of the occult to occult document', in J. Clifford and G. Marcus (eds) *Writing Culture*, Berkeley, CA: University of California Press.

Van Maanen, J. (1988) *Tales of The Field*, London: Sage.

Walford, G. (1998) 'Compulsive writing behaviour: getting it published', in G. Walford (ed.) *Doing Research about Education*, London: Falmer Press.

Walford, G. (2004) 'Finding the limits: autoethnography and being an Oxford University Proctor', *Qualitative Research*, 4(3): 403–17.

Wallace, G., Rudduck, J. and Flutter, J. (1998) 'Learning the ropes: accounts of within-school transitions', in G. Walford and A. Massey (eds) *Studies in Educational Ethnography: Volume 1: Children Learning in Context*, London: JAI Press.

Weiner, G. (1998) *Getting Published: An Account of Writing, Refereeing and Editing Practices (1996–8)*, Final report to the ESRC, (Image) Education-line, 26 August.

Weiner, G. (2001) 'The academic journal: has it a future?' *Education Policy Analysis Archives*, 9(9), http://epaa.asu.edu/epaa/v9n9.html.

Wellington, J. (2003) *Getting Published: A Guide for Lecturers and Researchers*, London: Routledge/Falmer.

Willis, P. (1977) *Learning to Labour*, Farnborough: Saxon House.

Willis, P. (1978) *Profane Culture*, London: Routledge & Kegan Paul.

Willis, P. (1982) 'The Triple-X boys', in P. Barker (ed.) *The Other Britain*, London: Routledge.

Wilson, V. (1998) 'The "last blue mountain"? Doing educational research in a contract culture', in G. Walford (ed.) *Doing Research about Education*, London: Falmer Press.

Winter, R. (1988) 'Fictitional-critical writing: an approach to case study research by practitioners and for in-service and pre-service work with teachers', in J. Nias and S. Groundwater-Smith (eds) *The Enquiring Teacher*, London: Falmer Press.

Winter, R. (1989) *Learning from Experience*, Lewes: Falmer Press.

Wolcott, H.F. (2001) *Writing up Qualitative Research*, 2nd edn, Newbury Park, CA: Sage.

Wolcott, H.F. (2002) *Sneaky Kid and its Aftermath: Ethics and Intimacy in Fieldwork*, Walnut Creek, CA: Altamira Press.

Woodfield, R. (2002) *Student Perceptions of the First Year Experience of University, 2000–2001: Results from a Qualitative Email Survey*, Brighton: University of Sussex.

Woods, P. (1979) *The Divided School*, London: Routledge.

Woods, P. (1986) *Inside Schools*, London: Routledge.

Woods, P., Jeffrey, B., Troman, G. and Boyle, M. (1997) *Restructuring Schools, Reconstructing Teachers: Responding to Change in the Primary School*, Buckingham: Open University Press.

Woods, P., Boyle, M. and Hubbard, N. (1999) *Multicultural Children in the Early Years: Creative Teaching, Meaningful Learning*, Clevedon, MA: Multilingual Matters.

Woods, P.J. (1995) 'Teacher biography and educational process', *Topic*, 14: 1–9.

Name index

Subject index